Emotional Intelligence for IT Professionals

The must-have guide for a successful career in IT

Emilia M. Ludovino

BIRMINGHAM - MUMBAI

Emotional Intelligence for IT Professionals

First published: September 2017

Production reference: 1220917

Published by Packt Publishing Ltd.
Livery Place
35 Livery Street
Birmingham
B3 2PB, UK.
ISBN 978-1-78728-579-8

www.packtpub.com

Credits

Author
Emilia M. Ludovino

Reviewer
Robert JHJ Logjes

Commissioning Editor
Amarabha Banerjee

Acquisition Editor
Namrata Patil

Content Development Editor
Eisha Dsouza

Technical Editor
Jovita Alva

Copy Editors
Laxmi Subramanian
Safis Editing

Project Coordinator
Kinjal Bari

Proofreader
Safis Editing

Indexer
Pratik Shirodkar

Graphics
Kirk D'Penha

Production Coordinator
Shantanu Zagade

About the Author

Emilia M. Ludovino is an Amsterdam-based international social and emotional intelligence coach, master practitioner of NLP, reiki master/teacher, lifetime practitioner of mindfulness and meditation, author of six books about emotional intelligence, and founder of the Emotional Intelligence Academy.

Emilia has been an emotional intelligence trainer, and coach at **UNITAR** (United Nations Institute for Training and Research), and an independent trainer, coach, mentor, and consultant worldwide for law firms, law enforcement, private banking, NGOs, hospitals, IT companies, and entrepreneurs.

Emilia puts emotional intelligence into practice by teaching the difference between thoughts, feelings, and actions with passion and humor—and how these three interact and affect us. She helps participants establish an inner foundation and vision for all dimensions of life and find the necessary balance between the challenges of a hectic career and the inner longing for peace and wellbeing.

She helps people find balance in their lives stop feeling overwhelmed, stressed, or anxious; respond not react; feel confident; and develop their communication and leadership skills, and their relationships.

Her aim is to take emotional intelligence to many people as possible, wherever they call her, to support individuals, companies, and communities to flourish and create ripples of awareness, love, compassion, and respect for each other's differences, making a better world.

Acknowledgment

I would like to thank all of the people who helped me deliver this baby in such a few months.

A big thank you to the wonderful Packt Publishing team that had my back throughout this entire process. The first person here being Namrata Patil, who found me and convinced me to write this book, Eisha Dsouza who during the entire process of writing and editing had my back and kept me on track with the changes and deadlines, and dear Jovita Alva who with her insights helped me bring more accuracy to the content.

A very special thanks to my dear friend, Prof. Robert (Rob) Logjes, for taking time out to support me during all this time.

Without the trust, commitment, caring support, and availability of this amazing team of beautiful people, I could not bring to light this book and share the importance of emotional intelligence in the IT world.

About the Reviewer

Robert JHJ Logjes studied education, pedagogy, and psychotherapy at the Radbout University in Nijmegen, the Netherlands.

He is a specialist in motivating and coaching juvenile criminals to change their behavior.

He lives in Maastricht, the Netherlands, and has worked as a coach concerned with multi-problem families as a script supervisor for students at the Zuyd University in Sittard, the Netherlands; as a talent developer, motivator, and coach for criminal youth in multi-problem families to change their interaction and lifestyle, and as a supervisor in cognitive behavior therapy for juveniles placed in preventive detention.

www.Packtpub.com

For support files and downloads related to your book, please visit www.PacktPub.com. Did you know that Packt offers eBook versions of every book published, with PDF and ePub files available? You can upgrade to the eBook version at www.PacktPub.com and as a print book customer, you are entitled to a discount on the eBook copy. Get in touch with us at service@packtpub.com for more details. At www.PacktPub.com, you can also read a collection of free technical articles, sign up for a range of free newsletters and receive exclusive discounts and offers on Packt books and eBooks.

https://www.packtpub.com/mapt

Get the most in-demand software skills with Mapt. Mapt gives you full access to all Packt books and video courses, as well as industry-leading tools to help you plan your personal development and advance your career.

Why subscribe?

- Fully searchable across every book published by Packt
- Copy and paste, print, and bookmark content
- On demand and accessible via a web browser

Customer Feedback

Thanks for purchasing this Packt book. At Packt, quality is at the heart of our editorial process. To help us improve, please leave us an honest review on this book's Amazon page at www.amazon.com/dp/1787285790.

If you'd like to join our team of regular reviewers, you can e-mail us at customerreviews@packtpub.com. We award our regular reviewers with free eBooks and videos in exchange for their valuable feedback. Help us be relentless in improving our products!

Table of Contents

Preface

Do you have that colleague who always looks the organized kind, solves his problems in time, never faces an unbeatable deadline, and still has a smile ? If you ever wanted to become an IT developer/manager/administrator who is not just a perfect employee but also has a brilliant balance and composure of your emotional intelligence, then this book is for you. You will learn to discover your emotional quotient through practices and techniques that are used by the most successful IT people in the world. You will learn to identify the factors that make your behavior consistent not just to other employees, but to your own self. When a deadline lurks, you'll learn the steps to keep yourself calm and composed and can deliver without being affected by the stress of IT industry. These factors and techniques will be explained to you through real-life examples that have been faced by IT employees and you will learn using the choices that they decided to make. This book will give you a detailed analysis of the events and the behavioral pattern of the employees during that time. This will help you improve your own emotional quotient to the extent that you don't just survive, but thrive in a competitive IT industry.

What this book covers

Chapter 1, *What is Emotional Intelligence?*, covers why emotional intelligence is important for IT professionals, Salovey and Mayor's emotional intelligence model, the main difference between emotions and feelings, and the five universal emotions common to all cultures. You will learn that tech companies are already using emotional intelligence skills to build collaborative leadership that creates impact through people, increases global sales, enables managers with a skill set to help managers to connect with people and lead with success, and even develop tools to help social media users be more empathetic in their online communications and combat cyber bullying.

Chapter 2, *The Neuroscience Behind Emotional Intelligence*, covers how the three most important layers of the brain work together to manage your rational and emotional data to help you master the basics of neuroscience. You will learn that the consistent practice of mindfulness meditation helps you enhance your attention, self-awareness, and self-regulation due to the neuroplastic changes in the structure and functioning of brain regions that regulate emotional responses.

Chapter 3, *Core Emotional Intelligence Skills IT Professionals Need*, speaks about core emotional intelligence competencies and the skills you as an IT professional need to master and the strategies to improve each one. You will learn self-awareness, which helps you to be more confident, less stressed, less overwhelmed, accept feedback and stop micromanaging and self-expression which helps you to build quality relationships, improve your employee engagement, decrease turnover, and be liked and appreciated. You will also learn self-regulation, which helps you to cultivate pleasant emotions, prevent conflicts, influence others, and build trustful, successful, and collaborative partnerships. You will also learn social awareness, which helps you to be more empathic, have a greater understanding of the emotional drivers of others, be a motivator and a successful negotiator, and learn social skills, which helps you to be a great leader and inspire and develop others to achieve their best, increase productivity and employee engagement, and build a healthy and happy workplace.

Chapter 4, *How to Build an Emotionally Intelligent IT Organization*, explains that an organization also has emotional intelligence, how to assess the organization's emotional intelligence, and strategies to enhance the level of emotional intelligence, such as how to improve the environment of the office, how to have an office policy of gratitude and kindness, how to raise the levels of emotional intelligence in the customer support team and also in the sales team. Emotional intelligence in an organization needs to be driven by the leaders, whether they are situational leaders or the top-of-the-ladder leaders.

Chapter 5, *How to Be an Emotionally Intelligent IT Manager*, in this chapter, you will learnt how important it is for a IT Manager to have a good level of emotional intelligence that enables him to know himself and to know and manage their people, the emotional intelligence of the five most challenging MBTI personality types—ESTJ, ENTJ, ISTJ, INFJ, INTP, found with more incidence in positions of managers, leaders and high achiever employees in the IT area. The strengths and weakness of these five personality types, how they are seen in the workplace as employees, subordinates and managers, how they can improve their emotional intelligence skills to be easier to work with them. And how to manager extroverts and introverts at work, to have a great workplace environment and increase productivity.

Chapter 6, *How to Be an Emotionally Intelligent IT Leader*, explains that the leader of the future in the IT domain needs to have a global mindset of the business, needs to be technologically savvy, needs to know how to build alliances and partnerships and that a successful and powerful leadership of the future is a shared leadership in this vulnerable, uncertain, complex, and ambiguous world. You will learn that the leadership of the future is developed in a human ecosystem that taps into the intrinsic motivation of people, develops others, and influences them by anticipating and creating change and building a collaborative network to construct the vision of the future.

Chapter 7, *How to Hire Emotionally Intelligent IT Professionals*, covers the best practices to attract the best fit to an open position, the best hiring practices for IT talent, the rules to follow before and during an interview to have the best outcome, preparing the interview and maintaining a legal hire process, and mastering the behavioral and situational interview processes to screen for emotional intelligence in all the candidates, especially in leadership roles, management, sales teams and customer service.

Chapter 8, *Preventing Stressful Situations with Emotional Resilience*, covers the five pillars of emotional resilience: stay calm, cool, and collected (first pillar); calm down when strong emotions arise (second pillar); create positive emotions daily (third pillar); develop self-compassion (fourth pillar); be grateful (fifth pillar) to show how to build emotional resilience and cope with the stress, anxiety, shame, guilt, depression, lack of support from family, friends, employers, the feeling of being overwhelmed, stressed out, depressed and burnedout. Emotional resilience is the skill to adjust to change and move on, from negative or traumatic experiences, in a positive way. To keep a healthy balance between a tough head and a warm heart. As you build your emotional intelligence competencies and skills you are also building your emotional resilience. And that compassion, tolerance, forgiveness and a sense of self-discipline are qualities that help us lead our daily lives with a calm mind.

Who this book is for

This book is for all professionals across the IT domain, who work as developers, administrators, architects, administrators system analysts, and so on who want to create a better working environment around them, by improving their own emotional intelligence.

Reader feedback

Feedback from our readers is always welcome. Let us know what you think about this book-what you liked or disliked. Reader feedback is important for us as it helps us develop titles that you will really get the most out of. To send us general feedback, simply email feedback@packtpub.com, and mention the book's title in the subject of your message. If there is a topic that you have expertise in and you are interested in either writing or contributing to a book, see our author guide at www.packtpub.com/authors.

Customer support

Now that you are the proud owner of a Packt book, we have a number of things to help you to get the most from your purchase.

Downloading the color images of this book

We also provide you with a PDF file that has color images of the screenshots/diagrams used in this book. The color images will help you better understand the changes in the output. You can download this file from
`https://www.packtpub.com/sites/default/files/downloads/EmotionalIntelligencefor ITProfessionals_ColorImages.pdf`.

Errata

Although we have taken every care to ensure the accuracy of our content, mistakes do happen. If you find a mistake in one of our books-maybe a mistake in the text or the code-we would be grateful if you could report this to us. By doing so, you can save other readers from frustration and help us improve subsequent versions of this book. If you find any errata, please report them by visiting `http://www.packtpub.com/submit-errata`, selecting your book, clicking on the **Errata Submission Form** link, and entering the details of your errata. Once your errata are verified, your submission will be accepted and the errata will be uploaded to our website or added to any list of existing errata under the Errata section of that title. To view the previously submitted errata, go to `https://www.packtpub.com/books/content/support` and enter the name of the book in the search field. The required information will appear under the **Errata** section.

Piracy

Piracy of copyrighted material on the internet is an ongoing problem across all media. At Packt, we take the protection of our copyright and licenses very seriously. If you come across any illegal copies of our works in any form on the internet, please provide us with the location address or website name immediately so that we can pursue a remedy. Please contact us at `copyright@packtpub.com` with a link to the suspected pirated material. We appreciate your help in protecting our authors and our ability to bring you valuable content.

Questions

If you have a problem with any aspect of this book, you can contact us at questions@packtpub.com, and we will do our best to address the problem.

1
What is Emotional Intelligence?

In this chapter, we will learn what emotional intelligence is according to Salovey and Mayor's model of emotional intelligence. Why is this intelligence is so important in our personal and professional lives? Why is it important to know the difference between emotions and feelings and what are the five universal emotions? What triggers them, what actions do they enable, and how should we describe the intensity of the basic emotion? Therefore, we will cover:

- The importance of emotional intelligence for IT professionals
- Salovey and Mayor's emotional intelligence model
- The difference between emotions and feelings
- The five universal emotions

The importance of emotional intelligence for IT professionals

The influence of emotional intelligence on popular culture and the academic community has been rapid and widespread. While this has stimulated a great amount of research in domains such as psychology, neuroscience, biology, sociology and management, the swiftness with which the concept of emotional intelligence has caught on, inevitably created a gap between what we know and what we need to know. In March, 2015, in San Francisco, a group of emotional intelligence experts gathered during the fourth vitality emotional intelligence conference to discuss the importance of emotional intelligence in building teams and effective organizations, increasing employee loyalty and retention, and improving overall success.

The novelty of this conference was the amount of representatives from the tech area—Cisco, Google, Facebook, Zappo, Hewlett-Packard, and so on. Though tech companies still hire based on technical and intrapersonal skills in an attempt to find the most tech-savvy employee to come up with the next big thing, they have started to acknowledge that being tech savvy doesn't always mean good people skills. Evidence supports the belief that real success is achieved when people can play and work well with others on top of being smart and creative with technology. Knowing this new reality, these tech companies teamed up with emotional intelligence experts to train and coach their employees, their leaders, and adapt their corporate culture. The takeaway from the gathering of brilliant minds discussing the importance of emotional intelligence in the tech area was that tech companies are already using Emotional Intelligence skills to:

- Build collaborative leaderships that create impact through people (Cisco)
- Increase global sales (Hewlett-Packard)
- Enable a manager with a skill set to help them to connect with people and lead with success (Zappo)
- Develop tools to help social media users be more empathetic in their online communications, and combat cyber-bullying (Facebook)

Despite the good news, the majority of the tech companies around the world dismiss soft skills as a fringe benefit, preferring to hire based on technical skills. Maybe this is one of the reasons that so many tech leaders are increasingly being diagnosed as narcissists and bullies. They are highly valued, very good at what they do, and often highly paid, but the worst nightmare in a leadership position as they lack self-awareness, empathy, self-regulation, social skills, and so on. A workplace is like any other social system - if you don't feel safe, secure, free to voice your view point or your ideas, cared about, or appreciated you will leave to another workplace or burn out. It is time to end the bias that emotions and technical sills cannot work in tandem. You are a human being, therefore, you have emotions and feelings, even if you are not aware of them. Your business is run by emotions—your own emotions, the emotions of your employees, co-workers, stakeholders, shareholders, and customers. The next big thing in the IT area is connected with Artificial Intelligence. And AI is the perfect symbiosis between data and emotions. Don't you think it is time to start learning and enhance the latter, before your smartphone knows more about emotional intelligence than you?

What is emotional intelligence?

Emotional Intelligence is the ability to perceiving, using, understanding, and managing emotions.

Salovey and Mayor, fathers of the concept of emotional intelligence, summarized in this way the ability to recognize and control our own emotions and behaviors—while remaining aware of the effect that these have on others around us. At the same time, you understand the emotional state of other people and use this emotional data to adapt your behavior to achieve the most positive response from them. You are just using emotional data to make sense and navigate the social environment you are in. By viewing emotions as useful sources of information, you are bringing together the wisdom of the limbic system and the rationality of the neocortex. Let's break Salovey and Mayor's definition into four branches: perceive, use, understand, and manage emotions.

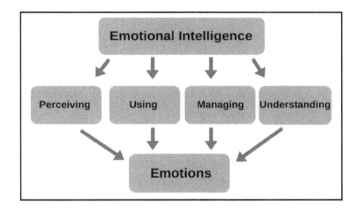

Salovey and Mayor's Model of Emotional Intelligence

Perceiving emotions

Perceiving emotions;is the ability to identify one's own emotions and to detect and decipher emotions in faces, pictures, voices, and cultural artifacts.

Perceiving emotions is the base of the emotional intelligence pyramid. Without the ability to accurately perceive and identify emotions in physical states (including body expressions) and thoughts, none of the other skills can be developed. However, the ability to tell the difference between real and false emotions is considered an especially sophisticated perceiving ability when we are able to identify emotions in stimuli such as artwork and music using *cues* such as sound, appearance, and colors.

How can we begin to develop and improve the ability to perceive emotions? You can always begin by identifying your emotions. To identify your emotions, it is helpful to ask yourself the following questions:

1. Do I know what am I feeling now?
2. Can I label it, correctly?
3. Do I know what am I feeling now?
4. Do I feel this way often?
5. At this time, is it appropriate to feel the way I feel?
6. Did I properly express my feelings to others?

In identifying emotions in others, be aware of the following set of cues:

- Look for facial expressions. Does their smile reflect what is going on with their eyes?
- Be aware of tone, pitch, and pace in their voices. Are their voice and words consistent or inconsistent?
- Look at the body language. Please note, that identifying only one cue can be misleading, that is why we strongly advise to always search for a set of three clues: body language, facial expressions, and tone of voice.

Using emotions

Using emotions is the ability to harness emotions to facilitate thinking such as deductive reasoning, attention to detail, problem solving, and mood adaptation.

What is the big advantage in using your emotions? Emotionally intelligent people can capitalize fully upon their changing moods in order to best fit the task they have at hand. When you understand which mood is the best for a particular type of thinking, then you can get in the right mood to enhance your thinking and influence others' emotions and the environment around you. For instance, would it be better to complete a task at hand to be in a good mood or in a sad mood? It depends on what you need to complete the task at hand. If you need to look for a solution to a problem and think out of the box, a happy positive mood is the best one. But, if you need to be focused on details to spot errors, a sad mood is your best adviser. Moods are long-lasting effects of a first emotion that trigger in us secondary related emotions, repeatedly, without any clear external trigger. A mood is influenced by your environment (weather, lighting, color, or people around you), by your physiology (what you have been eating, how you have been exercising, if you have a cold or not, how well you slept), by your thinking (where you are focusing your attention), and by your current emotions. A mood can last for minutes, hours, or even days and they are more generalized. They are tied to a collection of inputs not to a specific incident. Ready to learn how different moods affect our thinking?

- A happy mood or a positive vibe are very helpful when you need to do the following:
  - **Big picture thinking**: A happy mood expands your thinking and allows you to think outside the box, because it stimulates creative and innovative thinking. This *top-down* method of thinking helps with your inductive reasoning.
  - **Brainstorm**: When brainstorming, you need to be energized so that you can be more creative in developing new ideas, generate new solutions, and make better decisions—which, in turn, motivates you and your team. The downside of thinking when in a positive or happy mood is that we tend to make more mistakes in problem-solving. Use it with care.
- A sad mood is very helpful when you need to do the following:
  - **Stay focused and do detailed thinking**: When we are sad or feeling negative we pay more attention, focus on details, and search for and spot more errors. Being in a slightly sad mood helps people conduct careful, methodical work. This bottom up method of thinking helps with your deductive reasoning.
- A fearful mood is very helpful when you need to do the following:
  - **Be motivated**: Fear is a survival mechanism that motivated our ancestors by signalling danger. When we are evaluating possible problems and considering worst-case scenarios, it helps to be in a bit of a fearful mood rather than in a happy mood.

- An angry mood is very helpful when you need to do the following:
  - **Right a wrong**: Someone lacking any skills in emotional intelligence will be immediately emotionally hijacked when feeling angry. However, for the emotionally intelligent person, anger helps focus on fixing the wrongdoing instead of losing your head.
- A guilty, shameful, or embarrassing mood is very helpful when you need to do the following:
  - **Maintaining appropriate conduct**: Shame and guilt make you apologize when you engage in bad behaviors, which helps you to keep on the right track. Shame and embarrassment help avoid fights since it is more difficult for someone to stay angry with you, if they are feeling shame or embarrassment.

Understanding emotions

Understanding emotions is the ability to comprehend emotional language and to appreciate complicated relationships among emotions.

Understanding emotions encompasses the ability to be sensitive to slight variations in one emotion only, for instance, know the difference between feeling happy and feeling ecstatic. And to recognize and describe how emotions evolve over time, for instance, how shock can turn into grief. The ability to understand emotions is the most cognitive, or thinking-related of the four branches of emotional intelligence and it is based on four underlying principles. The four principles to understand emotions are:

- **Emotions have heir own vocabulary**: For example, feeling *melancholy* is not the same thing as feeling *sad*, or feeling *disappointed* is not the same thing as feeling *angry*. A basic skill in understanding emotions is our ability to accurately label how we are feeling at any given moment as the first step to understand and manage our emotional states. That is why it is so important to enhance your emotional literacy and learn an emotional vocabulary.
- **Emotions have underlying causes**: Salovey and Mayor, the fathers of the concept of emotional intelligence used a mathematical formula to explain that any given emotion has an underlying cause they are not random events: *Event X = Emotion Y*

- **Emotions are complex**: Plutchik built the wheel of emotions with the purpose of helping us understand that the six basic emotions when mixed can create a new myriad of emotions that can be similar, opposite emotions, or combined. We often use the term *bittersweet* to refer to a moment or an event that is simultaneously happy and sad.

- **Emotions change according to set of rules**: You can predict why you or others around you are feeling in a certain way and what will happen next. For example, if a solution architect is feeling content when his development team approved the artifact that he designed to solve a specific problem, it is easy to predict he will feel happy with the results.

Managing emotions

Managing emotions is the ability to regulate emotions in both ourselves and in others, to attain specific goals.

Managing our emotions does not mean we shut down or try to suppress the way we feel. It is exactly the opposite. We stay open to our feelings, even if they are unpleasant. Since emotions contain information, managing our emotions means that we can assimilate our emotional data into our thinking process. An effective emotional management of our emotions is not a question of whether you should strive to control how you feel but rather of understanding how you can, safely, engage and disengage from your emotional states. It is not enough to be aware of what you are feeling. You also need to consider the following:

- The clarity and strength of the feeling
- How the feeling is affecting your thoughts
- How often do you feel this way
- Is this feeling typical or unusual, in you

The difference between emotions and feelings

Emotions and feelings are two entirely different brain processes, though they are often spoken of as being one and the same. Often, but not always, the emotional activation of the brain is over by the time the conscious recognition of the feeling begins. Why is it important that you know the difference between emotions and feelings, anyway?

You should be concerned in learning the difference between the two because the way you behave in this world is the end result of your feelings and emotions. Knowing the difference gives you a better understanding of not only yourself but of the people around you. To control an emotion we need the feeling—we need the conscious awareness of the emotion manifested through the feeling. Unfortunately, due to a lack of emotional education throughout our lives, the majority of our emotional reactions are unconscious for us. How can we control something by reason when we do not even know what is happening? Let's learn the difference between an emotion and a feeling, so that you can start to be more consciously aware of your emotional reactions.

What are emotions?

Emotions are chemicals released in our brain in response to our interpretation of a specific trigger. It takes our brain about 1/4 second to identify the trigger and about another 1/4 second to produce the chemicals. The emotional chemicals are released throughout our bodies, not just in our brain, and they form a kind of feedback loop between our brain and body. They last for about six seconds.

We can say that emotions are lower-level responses occurring in the subcortical regions of the brain—the amygdala and the prefrontal cortices—creating biochemical reactions in your body and altering your physical state. Originally, they helped our species survive by producing quick reactions to threats. Emotional reactions are coded in our genes. In the workplace, an angry tone of voice from your boss represents for you a threat—triggering the fear of being fired. Emotions precede feelings, are physical, and instinctual. Because they are physical, they can be objectively measured by blood flow, brain activity, facial microexpressions, and body language. When you encounter a stranger, you may have a range of sensations such as curiosity or fear. When you give that stranger a name, it becomes a significant symbol of meaning. It is through this process that emotions become attached to every object in the universe. When some object is given a name, it not only becomes a thing, it also becomes something of meaning. Emotions establish our attitude toward reality and provide your drive for all of the life's pleasures. Additionally, these emotions are connected to our biological systems and are designed to alert us of danger, or to draw us to something pleasurable. Intense emotions such as the ones that help us survive a threat, are intense but temporary. They are far too stressful to our body. The constant stress would eventually lead to some very serious physical and mental ailments.

What are feelings?

A feeling is a mental portrayal of what is going on in your body when you have an emotion. It is the by-product of your brain perceiving and assigning meaning to the emotion. Feelings are the next thing that happen after having an emotion. They originate in the neocortical regions of the brain, are mental associations and reactions to emotions, and are subjective, being influenced by personal experience, beliefs, and memories.

Feelings are sparked by emotions and colored by the thoughts, memories, and images that have become subconsciously linked with that particular emotion for you. However, it works the other way around too. For example, just by thinking about something that you feel is threatening to you, an emotional fear response is triggered. While individual emotions are temporary, the feelings they evoke may persist and grow over a lifetime. Because emotions cause subconscious feelings, which in turn initiate emotions and so on, your life can become a never-ending cycle of painful and confusing emotions, which produce negative feelings that cause more negative emotions without you ever really knowing why—if you don't improve your self-awareness. While basic emotions are instinctual and common to us all, the meanings they take on and the feelings they prompt are individually based on our programming, past and present. Feelings are shaped by a person's temperament and experiences and vary greatly from person to person and situation to situation.

Your emotions and feelings play a powerful role in how you experience and interact with the world because they are the driving force behind many behaviors guided by unconscious fear-based perceptions. Living unaware like this almost always leads to problems and unhappiness, in the long run. As the objects in your world induce emotions within you, they are collected in the subconscious and begin to accumulate. This is especially so when similar events are repeatedly experienced. Ultimately, they form a final emotional conclusion about life, how to live it, and more importantly, how to survive physically and mentally in a world of chaos. When this happens, a feeling is born. Once feelings are established, they are often fed back into your emotions to produce the appropriate result to ensure survivability. Feelings are products of emotions. But unlike short-term, intense emotions, feelings are low-key, stable, and sustained over time.

The five universal emotions plus calm

Researchers agree that all humans, no matter where or how we are raised, have in common five universal emotions - anger, disgust, enjoyment, fear, sadness. And I would like to add calm to the five universal emotions. Because, a calm, balanced frame of mind helps us understand our changing emotions. We can reach calmness by developing an awareness of our emotions: what triggers them, how we experience them, and how we can respond constructively. Let's learn the states/intensity, actions, and the most common triggers of the five universal emotions.

States of anger

Anger can be felt mildly, extremely, or somewhere in between. The least intense state of anger is **annoyance** and can progressively escalate to **frustration**, **exasperation**, **argumentativeness**, **bitterness**, **vengefulness**, and **fury**. The following figure shows a graph of each state of anger and its intensity:

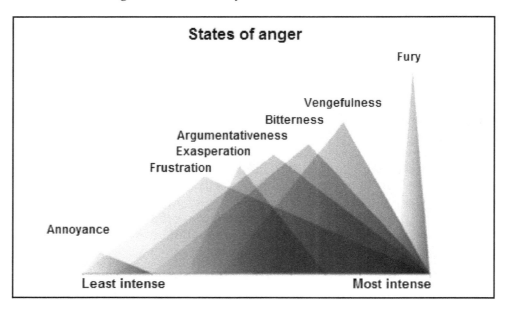

States of Anger

The states of anger are as follows:

- **Annoyance**: This is a very mild anger caused by a nuisance or inconvenience. The possible actions resulting from annoyance are suppression, passive-aggression, simmer/brood. The first action is ambiguous as it could either be a useful response to the emotion or it could cause harm. The last two are destructive as they cause harm.

- **Frustration**: This is a response to repeated failures in overcoming an obstacle. The possible actions resulting from frustration are the three mentioned earlier plus insult, quarrel, scream/yell, undermine. The action of suppressing frustration is an ambiguous action. All the other actions are destructive.

- **Exasperation:** This is anger caused by a repeated or strong nuisance. The possible actions resulting from exasperation are all the ones mentioned earlier plus dispute. Suppressing exasperation is an ambiguous action. All the other ones are destructive actions.

- **Argumentativeness**: This is a tendency to engage in disagreements. The possible actions resulting from argumentativeness are suppress, insult, quarrel, simmer/brood, undermine. Suppressing an argument is an ambiguous action; it could be useful or cause harm. All the other actions are destructive.

- **Bitterness**: This is anger after unfair treatment. The possible actions resulting from bitterness are suppress, passive-aggressive, dispute, insult, scream/yell, simmer/brood, undermine. Suppressing bitterness is an ambiguous action; it could be useful or cause harm. All the other actions are destructive.

- **Vengefulness**: The desire to retaliate after one is hurt. The possible actions resulting from vengefulness are dispute, insult, quarrel, scream/yell, simmer/brood, suppress, undermine, or using physical force; all the actions are destructive.

- **Fury:** This is uncontrolled and often violent anger. The possible actions resulting from fury are insult, quarrel, scream/yell, simmer/brood, suppress, undermine, or use physical force; all the actions are destructive.

Actions of anger

The possible actions resulting from any of the states/intensity of anger as mentioned previously are shown in the following figure:

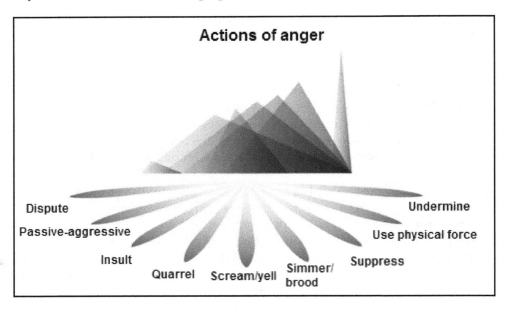

Actions of Anger

We will now see what they represent:

- **Dispute**: This means disagreeing in a manner that may escalate the conflict
- **Passive-aggressive**: This means taking indirect actions that have an angry undercurrent
- **Insult**: This involves belittling an other person in an offensive or hurtful way that is likely to escalate the conflict rather than resolve it
- **Quarrel**: This involves verbally opposing in a manner intended to escalate the disagreement
- **Scream/Yell**: This involves losing control of one's speech, speaking loudly, and possibly at a higher pitch
- **Simmer/Brood**: This involves expressing your anger by sulking
- **Suppress**: This involves trying to avoid feelings or acting upon the emotion that is being experienced

- **Use physical force**: This involves harming or trapping someone
- **Undermine**: This is when we take action to make someone or something weaker or less effective, usually in a secret or gradual way

Triggers of anger

The most common universal triggers of anger are as follows:

- Interference with locomotion
- Interference with action
- Rejection by a loved one

Everyone has the same universal triggers as we are born with them. They affect us more intensely than learned triggers. The following figure shows the different triggers of anger:

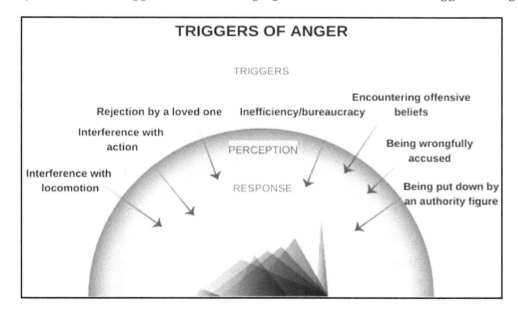

Triggers of Anger

The most common learned triggers in anger are as follows:

- Being wrongfully accused
- Being put down by an authoritative figure
- Encountering offensive beliefs
- Inefficiency or bureaucracy

Learned triggers can be part of your culture or highly personal and created by your individual experiences.

States of enjoyment

Enjoyment can be felt mildly, extremely, or somewhere in between. The least intense state of enjoyment is sensory pleasure that can progressively, escalate to rejoicing, compassion/joy, amusement, schadenfreude, relief, peace, pride, fiero, naches, wonder, excitement, and ecstasy. The following figure shows a graph of each state of enjoyment and its intensity:

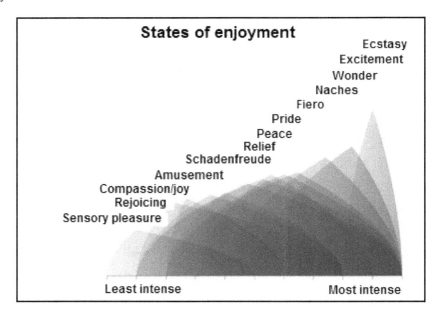

States of Enjoyment

Now we will see what each of them represent:

- **Sensory pleasure**: This refers to enjoyment derived through one of the five physical senses: sight, sound, touch, taste, and smell. The possible actions resulting from this state are savor and seek more—both actions are constructive actions as they are useful responses to the emotion felt.
- **Rejoicing**: This refers to a warm, uplifting feeling that people experience when they see acts of human goodness, kindness, and compassion. It is also called elevation. The possible actions resulting from this state are savor, seek more, exclaim, engage/connect, and indulge. The first four actions are **constructive** actions as they are useful responses to the emotion felt. Indulge in rejoicing is ambiguous as it could either be a useful response to the emotion or it could cause harm.
- **Compassion/joy**: This refers to the enjoyment of helping to relieve another person's suffering. The possible actions resulting from this state are engage/connect, savor, seek more, and exclaim. All four actions are constructive actions as they are useful responses to the emotion felt.
- **Amusement**: This involves light, playful feelings of enjoyment and good humor. The possible actions resulting from this state are engage/connect, exclaim, maintain, seek more, and indulge. The first four actions are constructive actions as they are useful responses to the emotion felt. Indulge in amusement is ambiguous as it could either be a useful response to the emotion or it could cause harm.
- **Schadenfreude**: (a German word) This involves enjoyment of the misfortunes of another person, usually a rival. The possible actions resulting from this state are engage/connect, exclaim, gloat, maintain and seek more. All the five actions are destructive actions as they could cause harm.
- **Relief**: This is when something is expected to be unpleasant, especially the threat of harm, but is avoided or comes to an end. The possible action resulting from this state is exclaim, which is a constructive action.
- **Peace**: This is an experience of ease and contentment. The possible actions resulting from this state are engage/connect and maintain—both constructive actions.

- **Pride:** This involves deep pleasure and satisfaction derived from one's own achievements or the achievements of an associate. The possible actions resulting from this state are seek more, engage/connect, exclaim, indulge and savor—the action of seeking more pride is a constructive action, though, all the remaining actions are ambiguous.
- **Fiero:** (an Italian word) This is an enjoyment of meeting a difficult challenge. The possible actions resulting from this state are maintain, seek more, engage/connect, indulge, savor, and gloat—the action of maintaining fiero is a constructive action, though gloat fiero is a destructive action as it could cause harm and the other actions are ambiguous.
- **Naches:** (a Yiddish word) This involves joyful pride in the accomplishments of one's children or mentees. The possible actions resulting from this state are engage/connect, exclaim, savor and gloat; the first three actions are ambiguous and gloat is a destructive action.
- **Wonder:** This is an experience of something that is very surprising, beautiful, amazing, or hard to believe. The possible actions resulting from this state are engage/connect, exclaim, savor, seek more, and indulge; the first four actions are constructive actions. Indulge in wonder is an ambiguous action.
- **Excitement:** This is a powerful enthusiasm. The possible actions resulting from this state are engage/connect, exclaim, maintain, seek more, and indulge; the first four actions are constructive actions. Indulge in excitement is an ambiguous action.
- **Ecstasy:** This is rapturous delight. A state of very great happiness, nearly overwhelming. The possible actions resulting from this state are maintain, savor, and indulge; the first two actions are constructive actions. Indulge in ecstasy is an ambiguous action.

Actions of enjoyment

The possible actions resulting from any of the states/intensity of enjoyment are shown in the following figure:

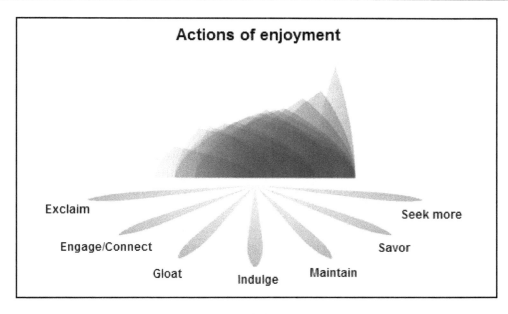

Actions of Enjoyment

We will now see what they represent:

- **Exclaim**: This is when you vocally express enjoyment to others
- **Engage/Connect**: This is when you share your feelings of enjoyment with others without a desire to cause jealousy
- **Gloat**: This is when you enjoy other people's envy of your state of enjoyment
- **Indulge**: This is when you allow yourself to fully experience the pleasure of good feelings
- **Maintain**: This is when you continue to do what is necessary in order to continue the enjoyable feelings
- **Savor**: This is when you appreciate the good feelings around an experience completely, especially by dwelling on them
- **Seek more**: This is when you attempt to increase the enjoyable feelings

Triggers of enjoyment

The most common **universal triggers** of enjoyment are as follows:

- Spending time with family
- The taste of chocolate cake
- Places associated with enjoyable memories
- Playing a sport

Everyone has the same universal triggers as we are born with them. They affect us more intensely than learned triggers. The following figure shows the different triggers of enjoyment:

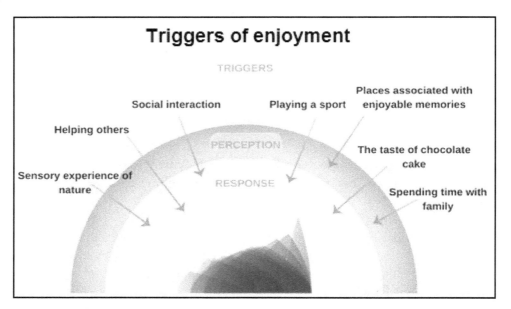

Triggers of Enjoyment

The most common **learned triggers** in enjoyment are as follows:

- Social interaction
- Helping others
- Sensory experience of nature

Learned triggers can be part of your culture or highly personal and created by your individual experiences.

States of fear

Fear can be felt mildly, extremely, or somewhere in between. The least intense state of fear is trepidation; this can progressively escalate to **nervousness**, **anxiety**, **dread**, **desperation**, **panic**, **horror**, and **terror**. The following figure shows a graph of each state of fear and its intensity:

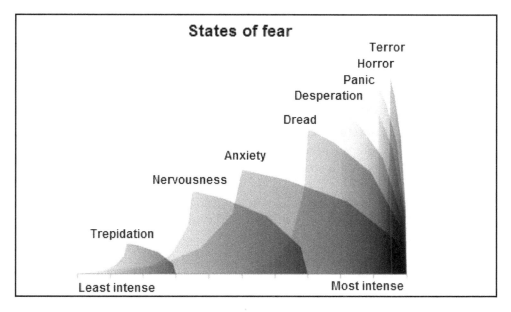

States of Fear

We will now see what each of them represents:

- **Trepidation**: This involves the anticipation of the possibility of danger. The possible actions resulting from this state are hesitate, ruminate, and worry; the first action is a constructive action, though the last two are destructive actions.
- **Nervousness:** This involves an uncertainty as to whether there is a danger. The possible actions resulting from this state are hesitate, ruminate, and worry; the first action is a constructive action, though the last two are destructive actions.
- **Anxiety**: This is a fear of an anticipated or actual threat and uncertainty about one's ability to cope with it. The possible actions resulting from this state are hesitate, freeze, withdraw, ruminate, and worry; the first action is a constructive action. Freeze and withdraw are ambiguous actions and the last two are destructive.
- **Dread:** This involves an anticipation of severe danger. The possible actions resulting from this state are freeze, withdraw, ruminate, scream/yell, and worry. Freeze, withdraw, and scream are ambiguous actions. Ruminate and worry are destructive
- **Desperation:** This is a response to the inability to reduce danger. The possible actions resulting from this state are avoid, freeze, hesitate, ruminate, and scream/yell. Ruminate is a destructive action when we feel desperate. All the other actions are ambiguous.
- **Panic**: This involves sudden uncontrollable fear. The possible actions resulting from this state are freeze, scream/yell, withdraw, ruminate, and worry. The last two actions are destructive. All the others are ambiguous.
- **Horror:** This involves a mixture of fear, disgust, and shock. The possible actions resulting from this state are: freeze, scream/yell, withdraw - all the actions are ambiguous.
- **Terror:** This involves an intense overpowering fear. The possible actions resulting from this state are freeze, scream/yell, and withdraw.

Actions of fear

The possible actions resulting from any of the aforementioned states/intensity of fear are shown in the following figure:

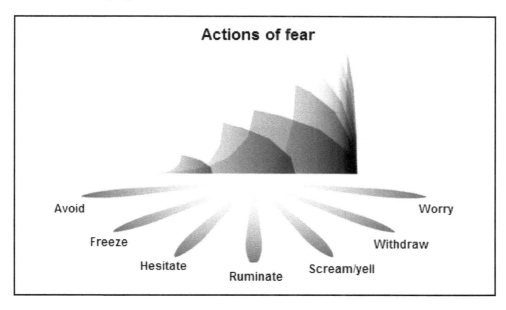

Actions of Fear

We will see what each of these represents:

- **Avoid:** This involves either physically staying away from the threat or keeping yourself from thinking about it
- **Freeze:** This is when you become incapable of acting or speaking
- **Hesitate:** This is when you hold back in doubt or indecision, often momentarily
- **Ruminate:** This is when you obsessively think about a past emotional experience
- **Scream/yell:** This is when you lose control of your speech and cry out in a loud and high voice
- **Withdraw:** This is when you physically or mentally leave the scene of the threat.
- **Worry:** This is when you anticipate the possibility of harm

Triggers of fear

The most common **universal triggers** of fear are as follows:

- Public speaking
- Thunder
- Threat of losing a job

Everyone has the same universal triggers as we are born with them. They affect us more intensely than learned triggers. The following figure shows the different triggers of fear:

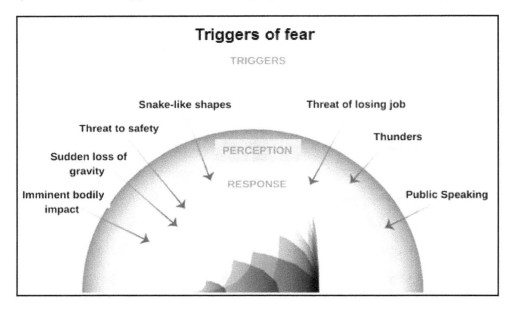

Triggers of Fear

The most common **learned triggers** in fear are as follows:

- Snake-like shapes
- Threat to safety
- Sudden loss of gravity
- Imminent bodily impact

Learned triggers can be part of your culture, or highly personal and created by your individual experiences.

States of sadness

Sadness can be felt mildly, extremely, or somewhere in between. The least intense state of sadness is disappointment; this can progressively escalate to **discouragement, distraughtness, resignation, helplessness, hopelessness, misery, despair, grief, sorrow,** and **anguish**. The following figure shows a graph of each state of sadness and its intensity:

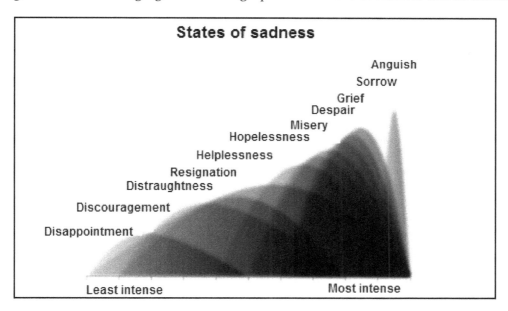

States of Sadness

We will see what each of these represent:

- **Disappointment**: This is the feeling that expectations are not being met. The possible actions resulting from this state are seek comfort, mourn, feel ashamed, ruminate, withdraw. Seek comfort is a constructive action. Mourn is ambiguous and all the other actions are destructive.

- **Discouragement**: This is a response to repeated failures to accomplish something—the belief that it can't be done. The possible actions resulting from this state are protest, seek comfort, mourn, ruminate, withdraw. Protest and seek comfort are **constructive** actions. Mourn is ambiguous and all the other actions are destructive.

- **Distraughtness**: This involves sadness and makes it hard to think clearly. The possible actions resulting from this state are seek comfort, protest, feel ashamed, withdraw. Seek comfort is constructive. Protest is ambiguous and all the other actions are destructive.

- **Resignation**: This is the belief that nothing can be done. The possible actions resulting from this state are seek comfort, protest, withdraw, feel ashamed, mourn, ruminate. Seek comfort is constructive. Protest is ambiguous and all the other actions are destructive.

- **Helplessness**: This is the realization that one cannot make a situation better or easier. The possible actions resulting from this state are seek comfort, protest, withdraw, feel ashamed, ruminate, withdraw. Seek comfort is constructive. Protest is ambiguous and all the other actions are destructive.

- **Hopelessness**: This is the belief that nothing good will happen. The possible actions resulting from this state are: seek comfort, mourn, feel ashamed, ruminate, withdraw. Seek comfort is constructive. Mourn is ambiguous and all the other actions are destructive.

- **Misery**: This is a strong feeling of suffering or unhappiness. The possible actions resulting from this state are seek comfort, mourn, protest, ruminate, withdraw. Seek comfort is constructive. Mourn and protest are ambiguous and the last two actions are destructive.

- **Despair**: This involves the loss of hope that a bad situation will improve or change. The possible actions resulting from this state are seek comfort, mourn, ruminate, withdraw. Seek comfort is constructive. Mourn is ambiguous and the last two actions are destructive.

- **Grief**: This involves sadness over a deep loss. The possible actions resulting from this state are seek comfort, mourn, protest, feel ashamed, ruminate, withdraw. Seek comfort is constructive. Mourn and protest are ambiguous and all the other actions are destructive.

- **Sorrow:** This involves a feeling of distress and sadness, often caused by a loss. The possible actions resulting from this state are seek comfort, mourn, feel ashamed, ruminate, withdraw. Seek comfort is constructive. Mourn is ambiguous and all the other actions are destructive.
- **Anguish**: This involves intense sadness or suffering. The possible actions resulting from this state are seek comfort, mourn, protest, ruminate, withdraw. Seek comfort is constructive. Mourn and protest are ambiguous and the last two actions are destructive.

Actions of sadness

The possible actions resulting from any of the states/intensity of sadness mentioned earlier are shown in the following figure:

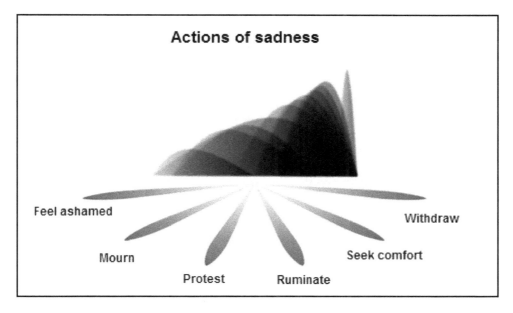

Actions of Sadness

We will now see what they represent:

- **Feel ashamed**: This is when you feel embarrassed about the loss
- **Mourn**: This is when you express grief for your loss through actions, dress, and speech
- **Protest**: This is when you object to the loss

- **Ruminate**: This is when you obsessively think about the emotional experience
- **Seek comfort**: This is when you seek help or support from others
- **Withdraw**: This is when you either physically stay away from what is triggering the sadness or keep yourself from thinking about it

Triggers of sadness

The most common universal triggers of sadness are:

- Losing a loved one
- Being rejected by someone important

Everyone has the same universal triggers as we are born with them. They affect us more intensely than learned triggers. The following figure shows the different triggers of sadness:

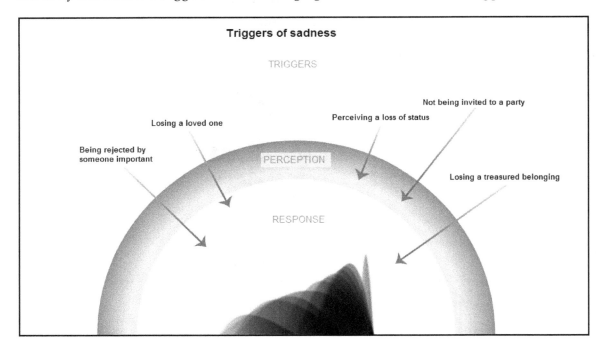

Triggers of Sadness

The most common learned triggers in sadness are:

- Perceiving a loss of status
- Not being invited to a party
- Losing a treasured belonging

Learned triggers can be part of your culture, or highly personal and created by your individual experiences.

States of disgust

Disgust can be felt mildly, extremely, or somewhere in between. The least intense state of disgust is dislike that can progressively, escalate to aversion, distaste, repugnance, revulsion, abhorrence, loathing. The following figure shows a graph of each state of disgust and its intensity:

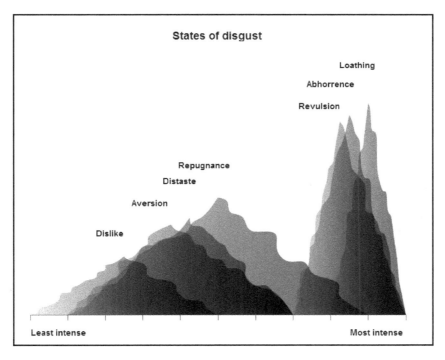

States of Disgust

We will now see what they represent:

- **Dislike**: This involves a preference against something. The possible actions resulting from this state are withdraw, avoid, and dehumanize. The first two actions are ambiguous. The last one is destructive.
- **Aversion**: This involves an impulse to avoid something disgusting. The possible actions resulting from this state are avoid, withdraw, and dehumanize. Avoid is constructive. Withdraw is ambiguous. Dehumanize is destructive.
- **Distaste**: This involves a reaction to a bad taste, smell, thing, or idea. It can be literal or metaphorical. The possible actions resulting from this state are avoid, vomit, and withdraw. Avoid and vomit are constructive. Withdraw is ambiguous.
- **Repugnance**: This involves a strong distaste for something, often a concept or idea. The possible actions resulting from this state are withdraw, avoid, and dehumanize. Withdraw and avoid are ambiguous. Dehumanize is destructive.
- **Revulsion**: This involves a mixture of disgust and loathing. The possible actions resulting from this state are avoid, vomit, withdraw, and dehumanize. Avoid and vomit are constructive. The last two are destructive.
- **Abhorrence**: This involves a mixture of intense disgust and hatred. The possible actions resulting from this state are avoid, withdraw, and dehumanize. Avoid is constructive. The last two are destructive.
- **Loathing**: This involves intense disgust focused on a person. Intense disgust focused on oneself is called self-loathing. The possible actions resulting from this state are withdraw, avoid, and dehumanize. All of them are destructive.

Actions of disgust

The possible actions resulting from any of the states/intensity of disgust mentioned earlier are shown in the following figure:

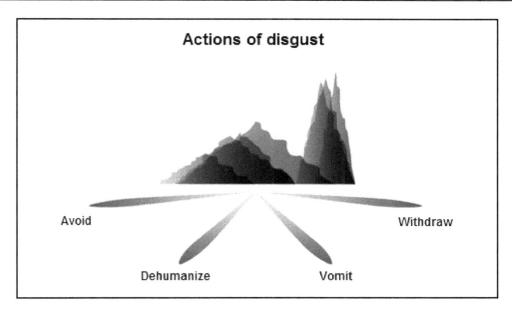

Actions of Disgust

We shall now see what they represent:

- **Avoid**: This is when you either physically stay away from whatever is triggering the disgust or keep yourself from thinking about it
- **Dehumanize**: This is when you treat someone as though he or she is not a human being—you deprive someone of human qualities, personality or spirit
- **Vomit**: This is when you respond to feelings of disgust by throwing up
- **Withdraw**: This is when you physically or mentally leave the scene of what is triggering the disgust

Triggers of disgust

The most common universal triggers of disgust are as follows:

- Rotting or decay
- Anything coming out of the body

Everyone has the same universal triggers as we are born with them. They affect us more intensely than learned triggers. The following figure shows the different triggers of disgust:

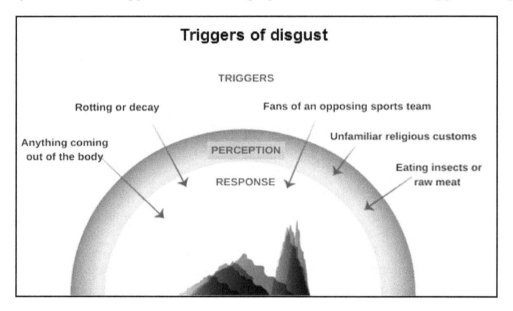

Triggers of Disgust

The most common learned triggers in disgust are as follows:

- Eating insects or raw meat
- Unfamiliar religious customs
- Fans of an opposing sports team

Learned triggers can be part of your culture, or highly personal and created by your individual experiences.

Though, the five emotions we just learned are the ones that the scientific community accepts as being universal—independently of the culture—two of the pioneer researchers in the field of emotions, the psychologists Paul Ekman and Robert Plutchik, after more than four years of field research across cultures worldwide decided to add more emotions to the five universal emotions that we have covered. Paul Ekman identifies six basic emotions and Robert Plutchik eight basic emotions. Both of them use the five universal emotions as a basis for their work.

Paul Ekman understands that the core of human emotions are: joy (happiness), surprise, sadness, anger, disgust, and fear. All the other emotions radiate from these basic core universal emotions as we can see in the following figure:

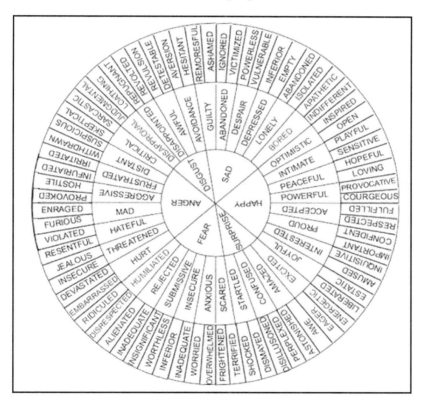

Paul Ekman's Six Core Universal Emotions

Robert Plutchik's wheel of emotions is based in eight primary emotions—joy, trust, fear, surprise, sadness, disgust, anger and anticipation—and uses a color wheel to help visualize the spectrum of emotions and how emotions relate to each other from the viewpoint of intensity, complementary emotions and contrasting emotions, as we can see in the following figure. If your figure is in greyscale and you cannot see the colors you can color the image—coloring is a very relaxing way to meditate. Choose your eight basic colors and imagine an explosion of colors going from the strong brightness in the core center and dissipating its intensity in softer tones towards the edges. It is the same with the emotions, the strong emotion at the core, dissipating intensity towards the edge.

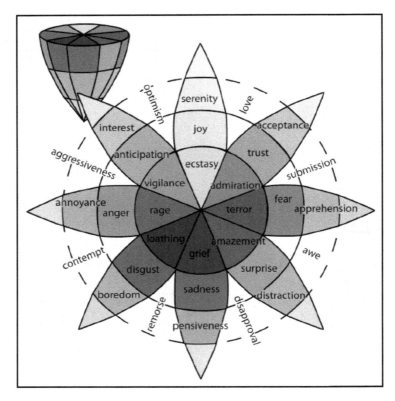

Plutchik's Wheel of Emotions

Summary

In this chapter, we covered why emotional intelligence is important for IT professionals, Salovey and Mayor's emotional intelligence model, the main difference between emotions and feelings, the five universal emotions common to all cultures. Therefore, you have learned that tech companies are already using EI skills to build collaborative leaderships that create impact through people, increase global sales, providing managers with a skill set to help them connect to people and lead with success and even develop tools to help social media users be more empathetic in their online communications, and thus combat cyber bullying.

You have learned that according to the Salovey and Mayor's model, emotional intelligence is the ability to perceive, use, understand, and manage emotions. You learned that these four branches of emotional intelligence work together, what they are and how to enhance them.

You learned what emotions and feelings are and the difference between them. Emotions and feelings are two entirely different brain processes, but we need feelings to control emotion.

You have learned that all humans, no matter where or how they are raised, have in common five universal emotions—anger, disgust, enjoyment, fear, and sadness.

You have learned that each of the five universal emotions has several states depending on the intensity of the emotion and that each state of the emotion is correlated with specific actions that can have a constructive or destructive outcome on your life. You now understand the most common emotional triggers of each emotion and whether they are universal triggers or learned triggers and also learned how secondary and tertiary emotions radiate from the core emotions according to Paul Ekman and Robert Plutchik.

In the next chapter, you will learn the basics of neuroscience behind the most important competencies of emotional intelligence. You will know how the brain processes our emotional data, understands the role of emotions in self-awareness, self-control, change in behavior and defeating thoughts, manages stress, improves decision-making, builds strong and meaningful relationships. You cannot master the emotional intelligence competencies without mastering the basic knowledge behind it.

2
The Neuroscience Behind Emotional Intelligence

In this chapter, we will learn the basics of neuroscience behind the most important competencies of emotional intelligence. You cannot master the EI competencies without mastering the basic knowledge behind them. To know how the brain processes our emotional data it is important to understand the role of emotions in self-awareness, self-control, changing behavior and defeating thoughts, managing stress, improving decision-making, and building strong and meaningful relationships. We will cover:

- The three functional brains
- Emotions and the emotional brain:
    - Neuroscience behind decision making
    - Neuroscience behind mindfulness
    - Neuroscience behind gratitude
    - Neuroscience behind empathy

Emotions are not just a matter of the heart, they are also a result of brain biochemistry--this is the conclusion from neuroscience, medicine, psychology, and management. Neuroscientists believe that the control center of emotions in the brain is the limbic system, as it stores every experience we have from the first moments of life. The limbic system is like a chain of warehouses where our personal impressions are stored since before we acquired the verbal or higher thinking abilities to put them into words. It is this vast warehouse of feelings and impressions that provides a context and meaning for our memories. Without memories we can hardly make decisions.

Messages are transmitted to the brain by neurons, traveling through an electrical transmission system. However, in the 70s, scientists discovered that our bodies also contain a chemical system for transmitting messages. This system is based on chemicals called peptides, which have receptors in every cell of our bodies. These highly sensitive information substances are thought to be the chemical substrates of emotion, triggering impression memories throughout our lives. Our brains are linked to all our body systems-- the gut, the heart, the head, the neck, and so on. These sensations are important signals and if we learn to read them, they will help us make decisions and initiate action.

Do you ever experience that situation where you know you should change your behavior and you know how to do it but never put it into practice? Let's say you want to be more fit, therefore, you need to go to the gym and have a regular practice. Let's say you are a bit of a procrastinator and you know what you need to do to stop that behavior but you do nothing. Or, the example of the Junior Software Engineer whose career is stymied because he is staunchly introverted, and totally absorbed in the technical aspects of his job. Through cognitive learning, he might come to understand that it would be better for him to consult other people more, make connections, and build relationships. But just knowing he should do these things would not enable him to do them. The ability to do these things depends on emotional competence, which requires emotional learning as well as cognitive learning. Neuroscience helped us to understand that knowing something operates in the neocortex and doing something operates in the limbic region of the brain, also known as the emotional brain. And the limbic system learns by experiment, by doing--it's a hands-on brain. Thus, in order to turn intentions into habits, an individual needs to put them into practice through rehearsal and physical experience.

Neuroscience contradicted the early models of human behavior psychology that described the human behavior in terms of a stimulus and response. Neuroscience showed that between stimulus and response our brain has some layers of filters and we will learn some of them now:

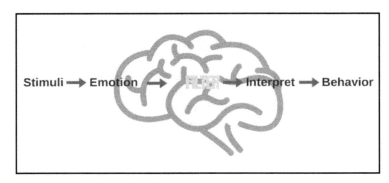

Filter brain

The three functional brains

Understanding the basic neuroscience of how our brain works helps to faster understand and develop the skills of emotional intelligence. For this reason, we are going to look to the brain model formulated in 1966, by the neuroscientist Paul D. MacLean - the triune brain. Although, this model is a highly simplified explanation of brain activity and organization, it provides an easy-to-understand approximation of the hierarchy of the brain functions.

In 1990, in his book *The Triune Brain in Evolution*--MacLean look to the evolutionary theory to describe the brain in terms of three distinct structures that emerged during the evolution of the human body. The **primitive brain** was the first brain layer to emerge, followed by the **emotional brain** (limbic system) and the **rational brain** (cerebrum). The following figure shows us the structure of the triune brain:

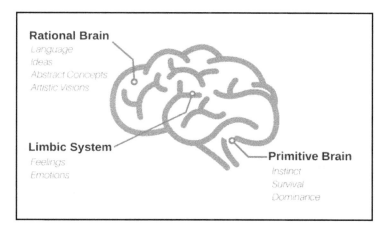

The triune brain

The primitive brain

The primitive brain, also known as the **reptilian brain** was the first one to emerge in the evolutionary theory of human beings. It is the oldest part of the brain structure and is responsible for the basic survival functions, such as breathing, heart rate, body temperature, and spatial orientation. It is also known as the reptilian brain because it is similar in architecture to the brainstem of reptiles. Its goal is to make sure we stay alive and reproduce. Because it regulates the survival mode of the human species it cannot be reprogrammed and its survival functions will always take precedence over other brain activity. For instance, when you hold your breath (a prefrontal cortex activity), the primitive brain will take over to make you breathe again.

Through specific training we are able to increase our resistance to breathe, but inevitably we give in and take a breath. Such threats to our survival are first addressed by the primitive brain and take precedence over other brain functions:

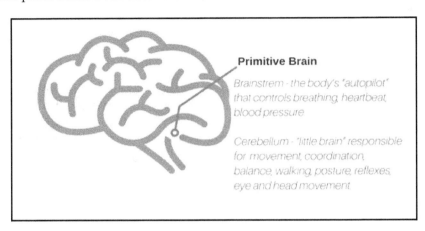

Primitive brain

The primitive brain consists of:

- **Brain stem**: The brain stem sits above the spinal cord and has many connections between them. The brain stem, the most primitive part of the brain, is made up of the medulla, pons, cerebellum, midbrain, hypothalamus, and thalamus. It is the body's *autopilot* that carries out vital functions of the body for maintenance and survival such as breathing, the heartbeat, and blood pressure. It also controls vomiting, coughing, sneezing, and swallowing.
- **Cerebellum:** The cerebellum, or *little brain*, is the second largest region of the brain and it is located behind and below the cerebrum and at the back of the brain stem, attached to the midbrain. The cerebellum is responsible for movement and coordination, walking, posture, reflexes, and eye and head movement. It coordinates subconscious movements such as balance and coordinated movement and is constantly receiving updates about the body's position and movement. It also sends instructions to our muscles that adjust our posture and keeps our body moving smoothly.

The primitive brain is the seat of the autonomic response, as well as the seat of habits. It connects us to our external world through our skin, our pores, and our nerves. It controls what impulses get recognized and passed along to the two higher levels. This brain learns through imitation, avoidance, and repetition until something becomes habitual. Information usually enters at this point without our conscious awareness. We can make much of this information conscious and use it to our benefit, as biofeedback and hypnosis have shown us.

The limbic system

The limbic system, also known as the **emotional brain,** is thought to have developed out of the first brain, in the expression of intimate behaviors and emotions, hunger, and aggression. The limbic system in humans is located in the approximate center of the brain. When information enters the limbic system, we experience bodily sensations, transmitted by chemical information substances in the form of a reaction to the stimulus with much more awareness of what is happening than at the level of the first brain. The limbic system stores every experience we have from the first moments of life--impressions are stored in these areas long before we acquire the verbal or higher thinking abilities to put them into words. It is this vast warehouse of feelings and impressions that provides a context or meaning for those memories, which helps us to learn from past experiences. The following figure shows the limbic system:

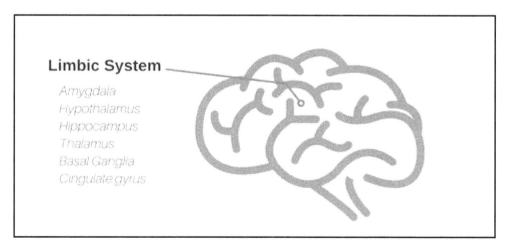

Limbic system

The limbic system consists of the following parts:

- **Amygdala**: The "security guard"--the amygdala is like warning system, with the motto "safety first". When facing a threat to your survival the amygdala makes very fast evaluations (though, not always accurate ones as she doesn't consult the executive brain- the neocortex) and has a fast track from the thalamus (incoming information) through to the hypothalamus that can initiate a stress response to the threat. To your amygdala--you facing a lion in the wilderness or facing your boss with that look that they're going to fire you--is the same stimulus, it's always a threat.

- **Hypothalamus**: The "management representative"--the hypothalamus affects body temperature, appetite, water balance, pituitary secretions, emotions, and autonomic functions including cycles of waking and sleeping.

- **Hippocampus**: The memory--the hippocampus plays the role of encoding events in time and space and consolidating them from the short-term to long-term memory.

- **Thalamus**: The "entrance way"--the thalamus is involved with sensory signals sent to the forebrain, in particular the cerebral cortex. And, it also participates in motor control and regulating cortex excitement.

- **Basal ganglia**: The "habits"--the basal ganglia consist of structures involved in motor processes. The basal ganglia works along with the motor areas of the cortex and cerebellum for planning and coordinating certain voluntary movements.

- **Cingulate gyrus**: The "secretary"--the cingulate gyrus helps regulate emotions and pain. The cingulate gyrus directly drives the body's conscious response to unpleasant experiences. In addition, it is involved in fear and the prediction and avoidance of negative consequences and can help orient the body away from negative stimuli.

The limbic system or emotional brain helps us know what to approach and what to avoid by guiding our preferences. As we move through life and have more experiences, we have stronger intuitions, hunches, and gut reactions because more things are stored in the limbic warehouse. Intuition is emotional learning gained over many years--as we mature, we accumulate more reliable emotional data that can offer us valuable clues and guide our behavior, providing we become aware of its existence and learn how to interpret it. Unfortunately, many adults have been taught to ignore this type of information.

Learning to avoid negative consequences is an important feature of memory. Of particular interest is the case where the limbic system gets the cues wrong--where there is no actual danger, but the body is thrown into the stress response anyway. From chronic low-grade stress to full-blown panic attacks, a maladaptive limbic system may be the key to what is troubling you.

The cerebrum

The cerebrum, also known as the neocortex (executive brain), came out of the limbic system--it is the part of the brain that developed most recently in evolutionary terms. The cortex enables us to comprehend sensory information and plan accordingly. The neocortex is responsible for higher order thinking and symbolic communication, art and ideas, and long-term planning. The billions of connections between the limbic system and the cerebrum allow for the free-flow of information between these layers. The cerebrum is proportionately larger in animals that are able to take in sensory information and analyze it in some way. But only in humans is it so massive and complex. It is made up of right and left cerebral hemispheres, with a large groove called the cerebral fissure separating the two sides. Deep inside the brain, in the middle, is the corpus callosum, a bundle of nerve fibers connecting the halves of the brain, allowing information to move back and forth between the two sides. It is estimated that if the cortex were unfolded, its area would be three times larger than the surface of the brain. This folding accomplishes an important conservation of space, which means many more nerve cells are concentrated in each unit of volume. The following figure shows the cerebrum:

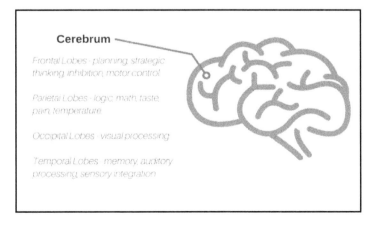

Cerebrum

The cerebrum consists of the following parts:

- **Frontal lobes**: Planning, strategic thinking, inhibition, motor control--the frontal lobes are involved with intellect and the ability to fit into a social group, helping us plan and prioritize, concentrate and recall, and exert control over our behavior. Damage to the most forward section of the frontal lobes can cause offensive social behaviors. Toward the back of the frontal lobe is the motor area, a strip of brain with distinct sections controlling motor activity such as swallowing, chewing, talking, and movement of the hands, legs, toes, and so on. Doctors often need to map this area of the brain by using cortical stimulation before surgery to make sure they know exactly where the functions are otherwise, they might disturb or remove tissue that would affect those functions.

- **Parietal lobes:** Logic, math, taste, pain, sensations of pressure, pain, and temperature. The parietal lobes have a sensory area concerned with sensations coming in from the eyes, ears, nose, tongue, and other organs, and a motor area that controls movement.

- **Occipital lobes**: Visual processing--the occipital lobes are the visual center of the brain. Making sense of information coming into the brain from the eyes. The left occipital lobe receives input from the right field of vision, and the right occipital lobe receives input from the left field of vision.

- **Temporal lobes**: Memory, auditory processing, sensory integration--the temporal lobes are involved with speech and language, hearing, and memory. The temporal lobes have additional complex features.

The rational brain (neocortex) assists us with functions related to thinking and language: planning, questioning, making decisions, solving problems, and generating new ideas. This layer is connected to the emotional brain with millions of connections, allowing the emotional and the thinking brains to influence one another in a myriad of ways and providing rich data on which to draw conclusions and initiate action. But, significantly, the prefrontal cortex can be hijacked by the limbic system in the event of a perceived threat (whether imagined or real). Our prefrontal brain can go offline as blood flow is directed to the deeper limbic system--the first responder on a priority mission--to keep us safe.

Emotions and the emotional brain

Why call it the emotional brain? Because neuroscientists have shown that emotions are not just a matter of the heart they are also a result of brain biochemistry, thus they named the limbic system the emotional brain. The emotional brain/limbic system stores every emotional experience we have from the first moments of life, long before we acquire the verbal or higher thinking abilities to put them into words. It is like this big warehouse of feelings and impressions that provides a context or meaning for those memories. Traditionally, neuroscientists defended that messages were transmitted to the brain by neurons, traveling through an electrical transmission system. However, in the 70s scientists discovered that our bodies also contain a chemical system for transmitting messages. This system is based on chemicals called peptides, which have receptors in every cell of our bodies. These highly sensitive information substances are thought to be the chemical substrates of emotions, triggering impression memories throughout our lives. Our brains are linked to all our body systems, and it is these peptides that are responsible for the emotions we feel in various parts of our bodies. Though the most curious thing is that this chemical transmission system is in evolutionary history, far older than the electrical brain. When external stimuli are received through one of our five senses, the signal is then sent to the thalamus and translated into the brain's language of chemical signals. The majority of the signal is then sent to the area of the brain that is responsible for the rational thoughts-- the neocortex:

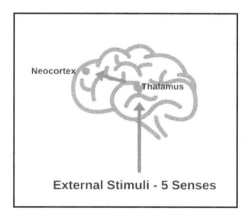

Normal brain pathway

Though, if the correct response involves an emotion, the signal is sent on to the amygdala, the brain's emotional center. At the same time that most of the signal is sent to the rational area of the brain for processing, a portion of it is sent straight to the amygdala, before the brain has had the chance to cognitively process the signal. In other words, a strong enough signal from our senses will trigger an immediate emotional response before we have been able to rationalize how we should respond--what Daniel Goleman called an *amygdala hijack*:

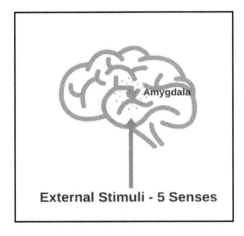

External Stimuli - 5 Senses

Amygdala hijack

The relationship between the rational and emotional parts of the brain, develops from infancy, as children learn through the emotional relationships they have with their caregivers at the same time that the rational part of the brain is developing. Hence, we can say that emotional incompetence often results from habits deeply learned early in life. These automatic habits are set in place as a normal part of living, as experience shapes the brain. As people acquire their habitual repertoire of thoughts, feelings, and actions, the neural connections that support these are strengthened, becoming dominant pathways for nerve impulses. Connections that are unused become weakened while those that people use over and over grow increasingly strong. When these habits have been so heavily learned, the underlying neural circuitry becomes the brain's default option--what a person does automatically and spontaneously, often with little awareness of choosing to do so. Thus, for the shy person, diffidence is a habit that must be overcome and replaced with a new habit, self-confidence.

Emotional capacities, such as empathy or flexibility, differ from cognitive abilities because they draw on different brain areas. Purely cognitive abilities are based in the neocortex. Yet, with social and emotional competencies, additional brain areas are involved, mainly, the circuitry that runs from the emotional centers--particularly the amygdala--deep in the center of the brain, up to the prefrontal lobes--the brain's executive center. Effective learning for emotional competence has to retune these circuits.

Cognitive learning involves fitting new data and insights into existing frameworks of association and understanding, extending and enriching the corresponding neural circuitry. Although, emotional learning involves that, and more - it requires that we also engage the neural circuitry where our social and emotional habits' repertoire is stored.

Changing habits such as learning to approach people positively, instead of avoiding them, to practice active listening, or to give feedback skillfull, is a more challenging task than simply adding new information to old. What this means for social and emotional learning is that one must first unlearn old habits and then develop new ones. For the learner, this usually means a long and sometimes difficult process involving much daily practice.

The moment you begin to feel the way you think - you begin to think the way you feel. This is because the brain is in constant communication with your body, which makes more chemicals for you to feel the way you think, and then you think the way you feel and so on:

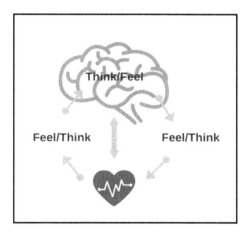

Think-Feel Pathway

Neuroscience behind decision making

The world famous neuroscientist, Antonio Damasio, was the first scientist to state that without emotions there is no good decision making. Damasio came to this conclusion after a thorough study of his patient, Elliot. Elliot is one of the most well-known cases of Damasio and he was profiled by him in his book, *Descartes' Error*: *Emotion, Reason and the Human Brain*, first published in 1994. Elliot was a successful businessman, in the 97th percentile for IQ, a caring and lovely father and husband that suffered from a brain tumor, located in the frontal lobe. Elliot was submitted to a brain surgery to remove the tumor. After the surgery Elliot's life started to fall apart--his marriage and new business collapsed. He lacked any motivation, frustration, impatience, or sadness. He was like an uninvolved spectator of his own life. It was clear to Damasio that as a result of his surgery, Elliot was incapable of making decisions. Elliott was still a man with a normal intellect but was unable to make proper decision about personal or social matters. Elliot's lack of emotions paralyzed his decision-making process to the point that even to choose the color of a pen to fill out a form was fraught with endless deliberation.

Although neuroscience has built a strong body of evidence over the past 25 years to show the link between reason, emotion and decision-making, most mainstream cultures still warn that emotions have no place in decision-making. Many businesses still follow the old saying: *Emotions have no business in the office*--despite that neuroscience has already thoroughly proved that emotions assist in the reasoning process. We are brainwashed to regard emotions as irrational impulses which need to be overcontrolled and put aside. The mainstream thinking about reason over emotions is based on three assumptions:

- We can choose whether to feel or not
- Emotional suppression works in the long-term
- Thought-stopping works as a regulation strategy

The flaw of these three assumptions is that when you consciously stop trying to distract yourself, the unconscious mind carries on looking out for the thing you are trying to suppress. If you consciously don't change your emotional triggers, your thought pattern will never change, therefore, what you are desperately trying to forget will come to torture you. No, you are not mentally disturbed--this is only the brain doing its work at pattern detection, firing and rewiring neurons in the process.

Over thinking a problem or a decision is the root cause of overwhelming the rational prefrontal cortex. Short-term memory capacity varies from being able to hold between 4 and 9 bits of information at one time. When faced with too many variables, the brain simply makes the wrong decision because its resources are overburdened, adding to our body's allostatic load and resulting in a chronic response to stress. The prudent use of our thinking process to measure or understand any problem is essential to prevent overloading the system, especially, in an era when external distractions are permanently challenging the brain's energy reservoir to stay alert and focused amidst a constant flow of information. Though, we can learn how to approach the decision-making process in a more balanced way. Like in everything you want to be brilliant at, you need to practice everyday and as the Portuguese saying goes, about the things we don't know *First we strange it. Then, it becomes part of us.* Just practicing for five minutes before an important and challenging decision that needs to be made is not going to work--it is only going to overload your pre-frontal cortex. To achieve the balance between "what we think " and "how we feel and act" you need to practice the four following steps:

1. Observe the patterns of your thinking process by bringing conscious awareness to your thought process. How? By noticing the content of your thoughts. The language you use to talk to yourself--is it kind or harsh? Does that vary? If so, when? What's your decision-making style? Do you tend to overanalyze, generalize or cut, perhaps prematurely to the chase of a problem? Understanding what you think and how you think under different circumstances is critical to this process.

2. Identify the beliefs you hold--as they influence our decision-making process. One of the main reason we resist making decisions is because, often, to decide implies going against our beliefs. And that is putting ourselves outside of our comfort zone and our comfort zone is the realm of our feelings. The first step in uncovering beliefs that may limit your decisiveness is to understand what you believe about rationality versus emotionality.

3. Increase your emotional self-awareness--if you don't want to be ruled by feeling, you must allow your emotions to experience the light of day and give them some breathing room. According to the neuroscientist Antonio Damasio, no single center of the brain dominates decision-making--"the lower levels in the neural edifice of reason are the same ones that regulate the processing of emotions. In turn, these lower levels maintain direct and mutual relationships with virtually every bodily organ thus placing the body directly within the chain of operations that generate the highest reaches of reasoning and decision-making". In other words, if you are rationalizing what is a bodily experience, (not a mental one) by ignoring, devaluing, or burying emotions, you are just draining your cortical batteries, steeping up your stress levels and on the right path to "burn-out".

4. Limit the amount of information you need to make a decision--a great quantity of research already showed that too much information hinders decision-making. Long before your reasoning mind kicks in, your emotional brain senses the way to go, thus make sure the information you consider takes into account your intuitive sense of the right direction to take. Your feeling brain is listening through your body, so the information that you receive is sometimes subtle and somatically based.

To optimize your decision-making process, you have to build capacity and resilience in the rational and emotional brains as they are interwoven to maximize the understanding of your inner and outer worlds.

Neuroscience behind mindfulness

Mindfulness meditation caught the interest of the neuroscientist community, not only because of is increasing popularity, but also because of the mounting evidence of benefits in mental health, enhanced self-awareness, relaxation, more focused attention, positive shifts in mood and improved well-being. Neuroscientists are also interested in understanding the biological mechanisms that cause neuroplasticity changes in the structure and function of brain regions involved in the regulation of attention, emotion, and self-awareness.

During the past decade, numerous neuroimaging studies have investigated changes in brain morphology related to the practice of mindfulness. In an attempt to consolidate the findings, one meta-analysis pooled data from 21 neuroimaging studies examining the brains of about 300 experienced meditation practitioners. The study found that eight brain regions of these experienced mindfulness practitioners were consistently altered. The consistent brain alterations occurred in the prefrontal cortex--associated with introspection, processing of complex abstract information and meta-awareness (awareness of how you think). The insular cortex--associated with the processing of sensory information such as touch, pain and body awareness. The hippocampus involved in memory formation and facilitating emotional responses. The anterior cingulate cortex--involved in attention, emotional regulation, self-regulation and self-control. And the corpus callosum--involved in communicating within and between brain hemispheres. People participating in mindfulness meditation programs experienced less anxiety, depression, and pain, and reduced negative emotions and neuroticism. A number of brain-imaging studies support the hypothesis that mindfulness meditation:

- Strengthens prefrontal higher order cognitive (thinking) processes which in turn modulate activity in brain regions relevant to emotion processing, such as the amygdala.

- Strongly activates the insular cortex, representing amplified awareness of the now moment, more positive self-representation and higher self-esteem. This shift in self-awareness is one of the major beneficial effects of mindfulness meditation.

In a research study named "Mindfulness meditation reveals distinct neural modes of self-reference", the neuroscientist Norman Farb, from the University of Toronto, in 2007, broke new ground in our understanding of mindfulness from a neuroscience perspective. Farb and his colleagues studied how human beings experience their own moment-to-moment experience. With their study they discovered that people interact with the world using two different networks: the default network and the direct experience network.

The **default network** includes regions of the medial prefrontal cortex, along with memory regions such as the hippocampus. This network is called default because it becomes active when nothing very important is happening and you become distracted thinking about yourself. For instance, when you are enjoying your vacation on a beautiful sunny beach, watching the sunset, instead of enjoying the now moment where you find yourself thinking about what restaurant to choose for dinner, and if they have your favorite wine and the oysters that your partner loves. This is your default network in action. It is the network involved in planning, daydreaming, and ruminating. In the Farb study they like to call the default network the *narrative* circuitry, because the default network also becomes active when you think about yourself or other people--you are mulling about your history and your future and all the people you know, including yourself, and how this giant network of information weaves together. When you experience the world using this narrative network, you take in information from the outside world, process it through a filter of what everything means, and add your interpretations. Sitting on the beach with your narrative circuit active, the sunset is not a sunset, but a sign that your day will be over soon, which puts you thinking about where to go for dinner, and whether the restaurant has your favorite wine and the oyster for your partner. The default network is active for most of your waking moments and doesn't take much effort to operate. There's nothing wrong with this network--the point here is you don't want to limit yourself to only experiencing the world through this network.

The **direct experience** network includes the insular cortex, a region that relates to perceiving bodily sensations and the anterior cingulate cortex is also activated, which is a region central to switching your attention. When this direct experience network is activated, you are not thinking intently about the past or future, other people, or yourself, or considering much at all. Rather, you are living in the now, experiencing information coming into your senses in real time. Sitting on the beach, your attention is on the warmth of the sun on your skin, the cool breeze in your hair, your partner's scent and the beauty of the sunset. When the direct experience network is active, several different brain regions become more active.

These two circuits, narrative and direct experience, are inversely correlated. In other words, if you think about an upcoming meeting while you drive your car, you are more likely to overlook a person crossing on the "zebra"--the brain map involved in visual perception is less active when the narrative map is activated. You don't see, hear, feel or sense anything as much when you are lost in thought. Even your favorite wine doesn't taste as good, in this state. Luckily, this scenario works both ways. When you focus your attention on incoming data, such as the feeling of the cold wind on your face while you drive, it reduces activation of the narrative circuitry. This explains why, for example, if your narrative circuitry is going crazy worrying about an upcoming stressful event, it helps to take a deep breath and focus on the present moment.

The direct experience network allows you to get closer to reality. You perceive more information about events occurring around you, and more accurate information about these events. Noticing more real-time information makes you more flexible in how you respond to the world. You also become less trapped in the past, old habits, expectations or assumptions, and are more able to respond to events as they unfold. In the Farb experiment, regular mindfulness meditators, had stronger differentiation between the two paths. They knew which path they were on at any time, and could switch between them more easily. Whereas people who had not practiced noticing these paths were more likely to automatically take the narrative path.

Long-term mindfulness meditators are more aware of their unconscious processes. Thus, they have more cognitive control, and a greater ability to shape what they do and what they say, compared to short-term or non-meditators. If you are on the sunny beach and you are a mindfulness practitioner, you are able to notice that you are missing a lovely day worrying about tonight's dinner, and focus your attention onto the warm sun instead. When you make this change in your attention, you change the functioning of your brain, and this can have a long-term impact on how your brain works too. Though, we need to keep being reminded about being mindful. Why? According to the leading mindfulness researcher John Teasdale:

> *Mindfulness is a habit, it's something the more one does, the more likely one is to be in that mode with less and less effort... it's a skill that can be learned. It's accessing something we already have. Mindfulness isn't difficult. What's difficult is to remember to be mindful.*

Practicing mindfulness is important and easy. You can practice mindfulness while you are eating, walking, talking, or any daily activity just focusing your attention into the details of what you are doing, for instance, if walking--hold your attention to the feeling of your foot on the floor and practice a deep, smooth, and rhythmic breathing. Building a mindfulness practice does not mean you have to sit still. You can find a way that suits your lifestyle. Though, whatever practice you do develop, practice it. The more mindful you become, the better decisions you will make.

Neuroscience behind gratitude

Gratitude is defined as the quality of being thankful and readiness to show appreciation for and to return kindness. Seneca, the ancient Roman philosopher, in his time spoke of gratitude as being a fundamental motivational drive - critical for building interpersonal relationships. And Cicero proclaimed that gratitude was the *mother of all virtues*.

Recent psychological and neurobiological studies have shown that generosity and gratitude go hand in hand. They are symbiotic. Fortunately, each of us has the free will to initiate the neurobiological feedback loop that is triggered by small acts of generosity and gratitude each and every day of our lives.

In 2015, the neuroscientist and director of the Brain and Creativity Institute, from the **University of Southern California** (**USC**), Antonio Damasio and his team conducted a study named *Neural Correlates of Gratitude.* With the objective was to examine a wide range of gratitude experiences in the context of gift-giving to identify neural correlates of gratitude at the whole brain level, because emotions play a central role in our social cognition and decision-making, according to Damasio. Feelings of gratitude nurture our individual mental health and fortify our bonds with other people. The personal and interpersonal benefits of gratitude occur at both a psychological and neurobiological level.

Another study on gratitude, lead by scientist researcher Glenn R. Fox, also from the Brain and Creativity Institute at USC revealed that ratings of gratitude correlated with brain activity in the anterior cingulate cortex and medial prefrontal cortex "The results provide a window into the brain circuitry for moral cognition and positive emotion that accompanies the experience of benefitting from the goodwill of others." said Fox. The stimuli used to elicit gratitude were drawn from stories of survivors of the Holocaust, as many survivors' report being sheltered by strangers or receiving lifesaving food and clothing, and having strong feelings of gratitude for such gifts. The participants were asked to place themselves in the context of the Holocaust and imagine what their own experience would feel like if they received such gifts.

For each gift, they rated how grateful they felt. Fox said, that he and his colleagues found that "when the brain feels gratitude, it activates areas responsible for feelings of reward, moral cognition, subjective value judgments, fairness, economic decision-making and self-reference. These areas include the ventral and dorsal medial prefrontal cortex, as well as the anterior cingulate cortex." The small acts of generosity that the survivors received helped them hold on to their humanity. After this research *Neural Correlates of Gratitude*, Damasio concluded, that "Gratitude rewards generosity and maintains the cycle of healthy social behaviour." Generosity and gratitude work in tandem in ways that benefit both the giver and receiver. Hopefully, this research will inspire each of us to infuse small acts of generosity into our daily interactions with others and to reciprocate this goodwill with gratitude.

Now, that even neuroscientists proved that gratitude can nurture our individual mental health and fortify our bonds with other people, why don't we use it more often in the workplace? Why is so difficult to say thank you to your coworkers? To be grateful for the benefits your job brings to you?

In 2013, the John Templeton Foundation released the results of a survey they did about gratitude in the workplace and the results were surprising--93% agreed that grateful bosses are more likely to succeed, and only 18% thought that gratitude made bosses weak. Almost all respondents reported that saying thank you to colleagues makes them feel happier and more fulfilled, but only 10% acted on that impulse. A stunning 60% said they either never express gratitude at work or do so perhaps once a year.

In short, people actively suppress gratitude in the workplace, even to the point of robbing themselves of happiness. Why? Templeton's survey hints at one of the factors that undermines gratitude at work--power and pay imbalances. People with power tended to believe others thanked them mainly because it was part of their duties, not out of authentic feeling as a result of this cynicism, supervisors are less likely to express gratitude. And this becomes in a vicious, culturally, ingrained circle of ingratitude, which have a terrible effect on workplace morale and cohesion. The need for a paycheck is only one of the motivations people bring to work. But it is not the only reason workers also work for respect, for a sense of accomplishment, for a feeling of purpose. Our work influences our emotional states and well-being. The benefits of gratitude go beyond a sense of self-worth, self-efficacy, and trust between employees. People who have a daily attitude of gratitude towards their co-workers showed significantly increased happiness, greater satisfaction with life, and higher resilience to stress, and fewer headaches and illnesses. The expression of gratitude has a spillover effect--individuals become more trusting with each other and more likely to help each other out.

Though the major take away from this survey is that--*Employees need to hear thank you from the boss first. That's because expressing gratitude can make some people feel unsafe, particularly in a workplace with a history of ingratitude. It's up to the people with power to clearly, consistently, and authentically say thank you in both public and private settings.*

Neuroscience behind empathy

In a study published in the Journal of Neuroscience in October 2013, Max Planck researchers identified that the tendency to be egocentric is innate for human beings, but part of our brain recognizes a lack of empathy and autocorrects. This specific part of our brain is called the right supramarginal gyrus. When this brain region doesn't function properly or, when we have to make particularly quick decisions, the ability for empathy is dramatically reduced. This area of the brain helps us to distinguish our own emotional state from that of other people and is responsible for empathy and compassion. The supramarginal gyrus is a part of the cerebral cortex and is approximately located at the junction of the parietal, temporal, and frontal lobe. The same neural systems get activated in a part of the cortex called the insula, which is part of the mirror neuron system, and in the emotional brain areas associated with the observed emotion. However, the amount of activation is slightly smaller for the mirrored experience than when the same emotion is experienced directly. Iacoboni says, these results indicate that a healthy mirror neuron system is crucial for normal social development. If you have broken mirrors, or deficits in mirror neurons, you likely end up having social problems as patients with autism do and sociopaths.

What are mirror neurons? Mirror neurons were first discovered in the early 1990s by Italian scientists who noticed that the cells in the observer's brain mirrored the activity in the performer's brain. A similar phenomenon takes place when we watch someone experience an emotion and feel the same emotion in response, says Marco Iacoboni, a neuroscientist at the University of California. Mirror neurons are smart cells in our brains that allow us to understand others' actions, intentions, and feelings. The mirror neurons are in many areas of our brain, and they fire when we perform an action or when we see others performing the action. As it turns out, our mirror neurons fire when we experience an emotion and similarly when we see others experiencing an emotion, such as happiness, fear, anger, or sadness. When we see someone feeling sad, for example, our mirror neurons fire and that allows us to experience the same sadness and to feel empathy. We don't need to think about the other person being sad, we actually experience it firsthand.

When assessing the world around us and our fellow humans, we tend to project our own emotional state onto others, when our mirror neurons are working properly. It is assumed that our own emotional state can distort our understanding of other people's emotions, in particular if these are completely different to our own. But this emotional egocentricity had not been measured before now. When you are in a nice, beautiful, agreeable and comfortable situation it is more difficult to empathize with another person's suffering. Without a properly functioning supramarginal gyrus, your brain has a tough time putting itself in someone else's shoes. To test this in the laboratory the Max Planck researchers used a perception experiment in which participants, who worked in teams of two, were exposed to either pleasant or unpleasant simultaneous visual and tactile stimuli. Major differences arose during the test when one partner was confronted with pleasant stimuli and the other with unpleasant ones. In this scenario a person's capacity for empathy plummeted. The participants' own emotions distorted their assessment of the other person's feelings. The participants who were feeling good themselves assessed their partner's negative experiences as less severe than they actually were. In contrast, those who had just had an unpleasant experience assessed their partner's good experiences less positively.

Until now, social neuroscience has assumed that people simply rely on their own emotions as a reference for empathy. However, this only works if we are in a neutral state or the same state as our counterpart. Otherwise, the brain must use the right supramarginal gyrus to counteract and correct a tendency for self-centered perceptions of another's pain, suffering or discomfort. When psychopaths imagine others in pain, the brain areas responsible for feeling empathy and concern for others fail to become active and connect to the brain regions involved in affective processing and compassionate decision-making. Because our brain's neural circuitry is malleable and can be rewired through neuroplasticity one's tendency for empathy and compassion can always be improved. We all need to practice putting ourselves in someone else's shoes to reinforce the neural networks that allow us to care more for our family, friends, co-worker, organization, community, and humankind at large. But please, when practicing your empathy daily, don't follow the flawed old sayings: "Love thy neighbor as thyself" and "Do unto others as you would have them do unto you"-- if you don't love yourself, you don't love your neighbor and what makes you happy doesn't necessarily make others happy. Love thy neighbor with an open-heart, no-judgment, acceptance and compassion. Do unto others what makes them happy.

Neuroscience allows us to see inside the human brain and better understand our minds. With this knowledge we can begin to make daily choices of mindset and behavior that not only reshape our neural circuitry, but can alter the way human beings interact with one another. Mindfulness meditation that includes loving-kindness meditation (**LKM**) can rewire your brain. Practicing LKM is easy. All you have to do is take a few minutes everyday to sit quietly and systematically send loving and compassionate thoughts to:

- Family and friends
- Someone with whom you have a tension or a conflict
- Strangers around the world who are suffering
- Self-compassion, forgiveness and self-love to yourself

Doing this simple four step LKM practice, literally, rewires your brain by engaging neural connections linked to empathy. Volunteerism also reinforces the empathetic wiring of your brain while making a contribution to reduce the suffering of someone less fortunate. Are you or your organization a part of a volunteerism association or group? These are all small steps, but taken together they can fortify empathy and altruism at a neurobiological level for each individual. Collectively, these small steps can help make the world a better place.

Summary

In this chapter, we covered how the three most important layers of the brain work together in managing our rational and emotional data to help you master the basics of neuroscience.

You have learned the triune brain model to understand the hierarchy of the brain functions, such as the primitive brain, a.k.a reptilian brain--it is the guardian of our survival its goal is to make sure we stay alive and reproduce. Also the limbic system a.k.a emotional brain is the chain of warehouses where our emotional memories are stored, which helps us to learn from our past experiences. And finally the cerebrum a.k.a neocortex is our executive brain with functions related to thinking and language: planning, questioning, making decisions, solving problems, and generating new ideas.

You have learned that all your memories, since you were born are stored in the limbic system to help you make decisions throughout your whole life and providing you with the context and meaning for your emotional triggers, behaviors, and decision-making process.

You learned that the mainstream thinking about reason over emotions is based on three flawed assumptions:

- We can choose whether to feel or not
- Emotional suppression works in the long-term
- Thought stopping works as a regulation strategy

And the four steps you need to practice to achieve the balance between what you think and how you feel and act, and stop the over-thinking default mode.

You have learned that the consistent practice of mindfulness meditation help you enhance your attention, self-awareness, and self-regulation due to the neuroplastic changes in the structure and functioning of brain regions that regulate emotional responses.

You have learned that feelings of gratitude nurture our individual mental health and fortify our bonds with other people and that gratitude rewards generosity and maintains the cycle of healthy social behavior, which can improve your social skills, leadership style, and corporate culture.

You have learned that a healthy empathy system is crucial for normal social development. And if you don't have empathy or doesn't cultivate it in yourself you likely end up having social problems as patients with autism do and sociopaths.

In the next chapter, we will learn the five core emotional intelligence competencies and their skills that a IT professional, from all the different areas, needs to master. The five core competencies are: self-awareness, ;self-expression, social awareness, and social skills.

3
Core Emotional Intelligence Skills IT Professionals Need

In this chapter, we will cover the five core emotional intelligence competencies and their skills that a great IT professional, in any field, needs to master. The five core competencies are listed as:

- Self-awareness
- Self-expression
- Self-regulation
- Social awareness
- Social skills

Self-awareness

Self-awareness is the ultimate human super-power that is directly connected with our survival mechanism as human beings. Without this super-power, the human species and you as an individual would not exist. Why? Because self-awareness (even if you are not aware of it) is the support mechanism that enables us to learn from our experiences. This process of self-reflection allows us to observe how we think, speak, and act. And that observation provides clues about where we can create gains in life by understanding our motives and emotional triggers, reviewing our beliefs, and changing our thoughts and our behaviors, to thrive.

What is self-awareness?

Self-awareness is the ability to, effectively, perceive and understand one's own emotions - as they happen.

Self-awareness is about understanding ourselves. It is about the realization that we are the source of our own success based on how we think and react to the emotional triggers in our daily lives. Knowing our tendencies, actions, and reactions is important, since they hold the key to our outcomes. How we think leads to how we speak, and to how we act and react when triggered by a situation. Therefore, it is so important to learn how to develop this super-power that can turn us into a peak performance professional. To master the emotional intelligence competence of self-awareness, you need to work and develop the three core skills of this power. Let's learn what these three core skills are and how to develop them.

The core skills of self-awareness

The three core skills of emotional self-awareness are built upon each other pyramid-like:

- **Accurate self-awareness**: This is the base of the pyramid because, first off, you need to be aware of your emotional triggers, patterns of thoughts, behaviors, inner strengths, and weaknesses.
- **Accurate self-assessment**: Secondly, you need to be able to accurately assess how your emotions are affecting your performance, your behaviors, and relationships.
- **Self-confidence**: This is the top of the pyramid because only when you are consciously aware of your emotional triggers and understand how they manifest, are you in control. And being in control of your emotional triggers boosts your self-confidence.

Accurate self-awareness

Accurate self-awareness is the ability to, clearly, see your own inner strengths and weaknesses.

Professionals with an accurate self-awareness are able to know which emotions they are feeling, at any time, and why they are feeling them, without judgment. They can connect the dots and build the links between their feelings and what they think, do, and say. Therefore, they can easily recognize how their emotions and feelings are affecting their performance and the teamwork or the environment--as emotions are a contagious virus.

Professionals who lack emotional self-awareness often feel stressed and overwhelmed, because they don't know how to establish priorities--health, family, and a balanced work life. Therefore, they easily get irritated, frustrated, or angry, and even treat others in an abrasive manner. Emotions are a virus and only one person can badly infect the whole workplace. I know that you have someone with these traits in your workplace.

Now, let's see how to improve self-awareness:

- **Check in your emotions**: Schedule a time to practice checking in your emotions regularly, in order to get in to the habit of flexing your *identifying* muscles. Bedtime would be a good time to start. It's just like going to the gym, flexing your muscles. At the beginning it's difficult and frustrating but with consistent daily practice the results will show up. Sit quietly, close your eyes, and take a deep breath. Ask yourself the following questions and be sure to answer them honestly. There is no right or wrong answer. Just listen to your responses. Use a self-awareness journal to write the answers down:

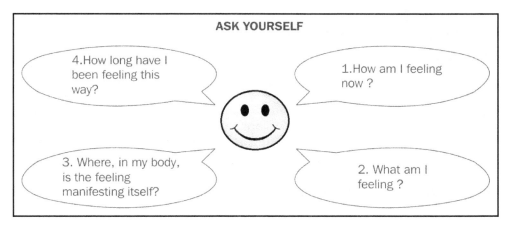

- As a consequence of increasing the awareness of your own feelings and emotions you increase your ability to self-reflect, and to understand the emotional drivers of your behavior. Self-reflection is a typical activity of people with high emotional intelligence.

- **Label your emotions**: Once you are able to tell how you are feeling, you will be able to identify what triggered your feelings. Remember that not all emotions are negative--practice recognizing and labeling the positive ones too. Some suggestions for labels might be single words such as anger, joy, fear, or sadness. Or you can give shades of meaning to your labels by using phrases such as *fed up, tired, and worn out,* or whatever rings truest for you. The next questions help you to identify your triggers:

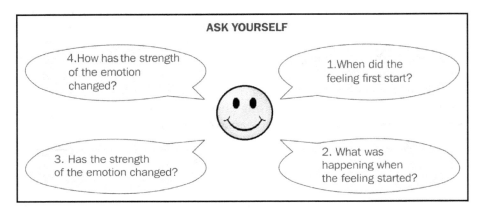

- **Be in the moment**: Try to *hear* your emotions as they happen. What are they telling you? For example, if you have to take on a challenging new project at work but you, suddenly, feel angry or irritated - what does that tell you? You might really be feeling that you are taking on more than your share of work and you need to revisit the decision to accept the project. Try to verbalize the emotion--"OK, I am feeling really angry right now. I can feel it in my stomach and my back. What's the anger trying to tell me?". Acknowledging your emotions as they occur gives you more opportunities to learn about yourself by connecting emotions to their causes.
- **Explore the root of the emotion**: First you identified your emotion with a label now you are exploring what the emotion is telling you, though you need to make sure that you are dealing with the full emotional story. Often, we feel an emotion that is only the tip of everything that we are feeling. For instance, if you are feeling angry:

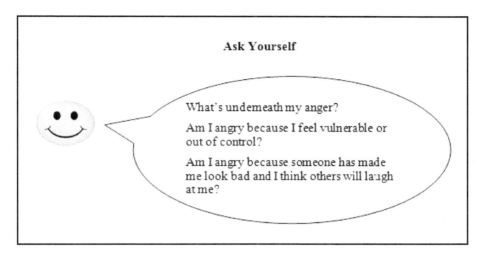

All of these roots of your anger are different, but the resulting emotion is the same. So you need to be willing to look beyond the initial emotion and explore what else you might be feeling, in order to be able to manage your emotions. Otherwise, you are just addressing a symptom, not the root cause.

Accurate self-assessment

Accurate self-assessment is the ability to, accurately, assess how your emotions are affecting your performance, your behaviour, and your relationships.

Professionals with a good and accurate self-assessment see their failures and weaknesses as opportunities for self-improvement and development because they are life-learners who are open to new perspectives. Their passion for learning and growth keeps them always looking for areas to change and improve. They learn from experiences by reflecting on the situations, hence they know very well what they can and cannot do. They are open to and even proactively seek out feedback from others because they want to know that they have gotten all the information possible for their self-assessment. They are able to laugh at themselves and accept their weaknesses as their current state, not their inevitable reality.

Professionals who lack self-assessment are easy to identify in your workplace and life. Usually, they cannot admit mistakes, take criticism, or even candid feedback. They cannot delegate and always micromanage others, don't ask for help, and are competitive instead of collaborative. They always want to be *right*, blaming others for their mistakes, and exaggerating their own value and contribution to the teamwork.

How to improve self-assessment:

- **Ask for feedback**: Simply ask your co-workers, manager, and stakeholders for feedback about your strengths and weaknesses. We all have blind spots in our thinking patterns and behaviors.

Asking for regular constructive feedback cuts through any self-deceit or one-dimensional views you might hold. When receiving feedback:

- Just listen. Avoid interjecting, interrupting, defending yourself or justifying your actions. You can ask clarifying questions. You don't defend, explain, or rebut what is said to you. Keep an open mind and listen to the other person with the understanding that what they are saying is how you appeared to them in your interchanges. This is a chance for you to learn about yourself, not an opportunity to justify past behavior.
- Don't hold anything against the person giving you feedback, even if you don't like what you hear. You need to be able to hear the good and the bad and to appreciate the other person's candor. You should appreciate that they feel comfortable enough to tell you what might be difficult to hear. And, if you find out you have something to apologize for, do it! Take the chance of cleaning up your relationship.

Self-confidence

Self-confidence is knowing that you control your destiny and you have the personal power to overcome life's challenges and live the life you want.

Professionals who have a great self-confidence believe that they are the master of their destiny therefore, they know that they are the only ones accountable to set the direction for their life. They have an inner conviction about who they are and what they want which makes them go and get the things they want and need in their life. Though they understand what they can control in their life and accept the things that they cannot control. They know their own value and capabilities, don't mind expressing an unpopular opinion if it is what they truly believe, and they are able to make quick decisions even in uncertain circumstances.

On the other hand, professionals who lack self-confidence lack confidence in their own judgement, and therefore have difficulty defending their ideas. They avoid challenges and confrontations with people at all costs, even if it will solve a problem, such as speaking the truth to a powerful authority. They don't know how to set personal boundaries and demand to be treated with respect from others.

How to be self-confident:

- **Make a strengths list:** Start a journal where you make a list of your significant achievements. You know the areas where you excel already and you can get additional areas of strengths from your feedback sessions. You can refer to this list, when you need to remind yourself of all the things you are good at. Just be sure to keep it updated.

- **Make a weaknesses list:** Use this list not to chastise yourself, but to track your progress in the areas you need to improve. Eventually, you can move some of these weaknesses over to your strengths list. Seeing that you have achieved something you set your mind to boosts your confidence. After finishing your honest listing of strengths and weaknesses, you are now aware of some of your emotional triggers. YES! Some of our strengths can be emotional triggers.

- **Say no:** How many times have you been asked to agree to something, and said "Yes" when you really wanted to say "No?" In order to stand up for yourself, to stay healthy and gain respect, you need to be able to use the right emotional intelligence techniques to say "Thank you! No."

- **Be respectful:** Saying "No" is not about being rude, uncaring, or aggressive; start saying "No" by first saying, "Thank you!" The ability to say "No" is a skill that can help you to look after yourself, to stop becoming overwhelmed by taking on too much, and to gain the respect of other people.

- **Don't justify:** When you justify your answers people pursue your reasons and wear you down on those rather than the "No." When you give reasons, people usually keep on at you for longer. Instead of saying "I'm sorry I can't, I'm busy."-- you drop off the reasoning and politely say, "Thank you, no. I won't be joining you." Sometimes reasons may be needed, though you need to be able to have the choice as to when you give them and not just give them automatically.

- **Use a pleasant voice:** Even if you are saying "Thank you! No," keep a pleasant, warm voice tone throughout. It is easy to sound sarcastic but sarcasm can sour relationships.

- **Stick to what you say:** Stick to what you say and repeat it. For instance, if you say "That's confidential." Say the same thing, "That's confidential," the second time, and "That's confidential," the third time. This is better than arguing points. Usually, after about three times people stop attempting to persuade you otherwise.

Benefits of having high self-awareness

With mastery of the three core skills of the emotional intelligence competence, self-awareness gives you a greater control over the decisions you make. Therefore:

- You can identify and understand the impact that your own feelings are having on your thoughts, memory, and creativity. For instance: you know you are excited by the chance of getting promoted to a new executive role, yet you feel vulnerable--in case you cannot meet all the criteria and feel silly in case people think you are arrogant. By identifying all three emotions (excitement, vulnerability, and silliness), you can work through them and apply confidently for the role. If you are not aware of your emotional triggers, you are more likely to feel stuck, procrastinate, and miss the opportunity.

- You are able to protect yourself from harm. Emotions can give you important warnings that you are not safe, or that you are about to make an error, that you are not well and need help. By knowing how you feel you have the opportunity to heed these warnings early. This could save you from embarrassing yourself, your team, or your organization.

- You can recognize the fluctuations in your emotions and accurately identify which emotion you have and whether you have a simple emotion or a complex of emotions--as emotions often occur together. For example, you might feel excited and fearful at the same time, or hurt may be underlying your anger, thus you are aware of the emotions behind what you are saying.

- You are able to recognize the patterns and habits in your emotional responses and reactions and understand what triggers particular emotions in you--the reasons behind some of your emotions. (Some emotions arise because of our history and not always because of our immediate situation.) Therefore, you may feel more in control of your life and know what you want. Hence, you are less likely to get stuck with decision-making and problem-solving when there are conflicting emotions at play.

- You will be more able to develop trust between yourself and the people with whom you work--whether stakeholders, executives, or clients. Self-awareness can be enormously beneficial for the development of productive and engaging relationships.

Consequences of having low self-awareness

In psychology we use the term *blind spots* when referring to a lack of, or very low emotional self-awareness. At this moment, you already understand how important it is to have and improve this competence. However, it is important to learn some of the worst consequences of having a very low emotional self-awareness, so you can be more motivated to improve yours. For instance:

- You don't know what your passions in life are, thus you feel bad and lost in life.
- You blame others or external factors for your bad luck and failures, whether in the workplace or in your life.
- You sound sarcastic and snide when congratulating your teammate for his new position as Team Manager, instead of sounding happy and proud. Deep inside you are envious of your colleague--but you are not aware of it. It's difficult to build trust and bonds when we sound sarcastic and snide. Remember, it's a blind spot because you cannot see it but others can. You may not understand how people are perceiving you but others may perceive changes in your emotions, even if you don't. And they will react to you accordingly.
- Your lack of social skills and empathy make you hurt your colleagues, behave in a negative way in meetings, and undermine or disagree with every one without you realizing it, and this annihilates your chances of getting promoted or winning that new project you dream about. Thus, you are not bringing value to the company and you damage teamwork, partnerships, and stakeholder relationships.

Self-expression

Alex Korb, a neuroscientist at UCLA, has conducted several experiments to study how the brain benefits when we express ourselves. During the experiments, in an FMRI study, the participants viewed pictures of people with different facial expressions conveying emotional states. Every time the participants viewed the pictures their amygdala reacted to the emotions in the picture. However, one of the most interesting finds in this study was that when a participant named the emotion he was seeing, the amygdala's reactivity decreased and lessened the impact of the emotion. The study even found that when we try to suppress our negative emotions, our inward stress and anxiety get more intense! That is why our dear Sigmund Freud used to say:

Unexpressed emotions will never die. They are buried alive and will come forth later in uglier ways.

What is self-expression?

Emotional self-expression is the ability to express one's own emotions in a safe, clear, effective, and respectful way.

When we express our feelings honestly, we are better equipped to deal with them because we actually know what we are feeling instead of denying it. Expressing feelings in a clear, safe way with accuracy is the only way to properly convey to others what we are feeling and what we want, without being a knee-jerk reaction to hit back at someone. Sometimes wanting to express our feelings can simply be a knee-jerk reaction because you feel hurt, stupid, or rejected. This is being emotional rather than emotionally intelligent.

Core skills of emotional self-expression

Now, that you know that emotional self-expression is the ability to express one's own emotions in a safe, clear, effective, and respectful way, let me ask you something: Do you express your positive and negative emotions in the same way? Do you express them face to face or sometimes do you feel that you can find closure on your own? Most probably you are answering me with a question: So, Emilia, what is the importance of the way I express or don't express my feelings at work? Especially if we cannot bring emotions to the workplace?

Well, if you want to build trust and bonds in your workplace, improve your social skills, have empathy, and be an influence--you need to express both emotions in a skillful way, because emotions run the workplace from bottom to top. So, let's learn how to do it like a master.

Expressing positive emotions

"Congratulations! Job well done!"--How many times, in your workplace, have you said or heard this sentence? I hope your answer is--*"Quite often, Emilia."* Great! Now, you are feeling happy thinking that your boss appreciates your effort and dedication to the work. Well, actually, he or you are just being judgmental about the work. In this short and famous sentence in all the workplaces, there is no acknowledgement and expression of pride, affection, joy, admiration, enthusiasm, satisfaction, or appreciation. Only a judgment. Sad! I know, not everybody masters the art of giving praise or appreciation.

Let me ask you how you express your appreciation for your employees, colleagues, partners, stakeholders, and the board?--*Why is this important, Emilia?* you are asking. The way you express your appreciation is important because if you don't express your appreciation for your workplace family they will feel that you take them for granted, don't value them, ignore them, or use them. Therefore, they don't trust you, they become unproductive, disengaged, disruptive, disobedient, argumentative, and difficult to work with. Is this the outcome you want? Of course not! The good news is that it's very easy to learn and master this skill. Let's learn how to do it.

How to express positive emotions:

- **When and where:** When and where to give praise and show appreciation is so important. Imagine you are a staunch introvert and your team manager during a meeting decides to stand up and say out loud how proud he is of you. Most probably you would be very embarrassed. You would appreciate more if he had done it in a more private way. After all, not everybody is an extrovert. Getting the timing right is also important. Expressing your feelings as the situation arises or when you next see the person involved (if it's soon after) is a far better timing. Of course, if you are furious, it can be good to calm down first. How quickly do you express your feelings at work or at home? Do you take the timing into consideration? By taking in to consideration the right place and time to express your appreciation, you are also taking in to consideration his/her feelings.
- **What to do and say:** You were nominated *Employee of the Month*. A little ceremony takes place in a nice restaurant and your CEO besides giving you the certificate of "Employee of the Month" and your money prize, just says "Congratulations! Job well done!". What is wrong here? Expressing feelings of appreciation and pride, through the giving of gifts is a time-honored tradition. However, what you do and, especially, what you say when you give the gift makes an enormous difference. Simply presenting the certificate of "Employee of the Month" and saying "Congratulations! Job well done!" is not a clear expression of your feelings. When you give the certificate if you add the words: "I appreciate so much your hard work and your commitment to this company. I'm so proud of you and so grateful to have you on my team. Thank you!," you have expressed three emotions--appreciation, pride, and gratitude. In other words, expressing feelings clearly often involves articulating and using a vocabulary of feeling words. When these are used, there can be no misunderstandings.

Expressing negative emotions

There are many ways to express our negative emotions and once we express them, we can calm down quickly, move on, and be in control. I find that expressing my anger and frustration in writing is very therapeutic. If I am at work and I have got angry, by quickly writing down what has happened and my reactions to it, I can calm down and continue with my work. I can re-read what I have written later on at home if I still wish to sort through the issue. Emotional intelligence skills include the ability to defer an emotion so it can be dealt with later. This is not the same as repressing or ignoring it. It's simply being emotionally intelligent. To master the art of expressing negative emotions, such as anger, humiliation, embarrassment, frustration, and sadness, requires a sophisticated self-awareness. Imagine how useful this skill can be when you are having a crazy hectic day, feeling frustrated and stressed, and you still need to interact in meetings, negotiations, or a networking event. By writing down what you are feeling, you have more control over your emotions and can easily change your mood to a more positive one. Let me share with you a little secret that we also use in meditation--smile-- keep smiling for yourself. A smile is the trojan horse to infect us and our environment with a positive vibe.

How to express negative emotions:

- **Separate feelings from judgments**: To express negative emotions properly, you need to be able to distinguish expressions of your own feelings from judgments. For instance, when you say: "You make me feel so angry," "You were so aggressive," or "Your behaviour was wrong," you are just expressing a judgment. You are not owning your own feelings--you are just blaming someone else for how you feel. An emotionally intelligent individual takes responsibility for their emotions; he doesn't blame others for his unpleasant feelings. "I'm feeling angry," "I felt vulnerable," "I'm proud of you for meeting the deadline under such tough circumstances"--this is the right way to own your feelings. Knowing this difference helps you to express your feelings more clearly and wisely, so that you build rather than destroy working relationships.
- **Know your feelings**: To own your negative emotions, it's important that you can properly identify them--just calling it "anger" is not enough. Knowing exactly which feeling it is helps you to understand why it was triggered, how to express it, and how to best manage it and move through it. And because emotions and feelings like to come in bundles, it's important that your emotional vocabulary is good enough so you can be able to select the correct emotional word, such as - "I am feeling humiliated, cheated, thwarted, bitter, and so on." If you want to improve your emotional vocabulary, you can find on the internet several lists with more than 3,000 English words expressing emotional states.

- **Choose the right vehicle of expression:** You don't need to express your negative emotions face to face. In psychotherapy, we use different techniques to express our negative emotions. They are so simple that you can use them anywhere, even in the workplace. You can start by simply naming your feeling--naming is taming. Or, you can write a letter to the person involved but don't send it--tear it into pieces and put it in the trash. Or write down in your journal a free flow of consciousness about how you feel and why. Writing about a recent experience that angered you is very helpful and the best tool to master the art of expressing negative emotions, because practice is key to expressing your anger effectively.

Expressing emotions face to face

I do not recommend the expression of annoyance, rejection, or anger via email or texting. It may be the easy way out, but it doesn't solve the conflict actually, it can escalate it to a point of no return. And no one wants that in a working place. When you are about to hit the send button on that angry email or text--stop:

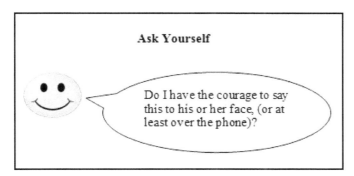

Emotions are usually best expressed when the other person has the opportunity to read your body language and facial micro expressions--whether they are of admiration or annoyance. Emotions are also best expressed when the other person has an equal opportunity to respond face-to-face, so you can talk things through.

Expressing feelings together in a shared situation can help reduce misunderstandings, misinterpretations, and the escalation of conflict (except in situations of abuse, potential violence, or bullying).

How to express negative emotions face-to-face:

- **Assert your needs**: To assert your needs, ask yourself:

- **Write a script**: Talk about what angered you (again in a clear and objective way). Tell the person how you feel, using "I feel" and "I think" statements. State your needs and what you want as clearly and specifically as possible. Finally, mention how the person will benefit from doing what you need. For instance, it might make your relationship stronger or help you reduce conflict. In addition, think about what compromises you are willing to make if the other person cannot or will not give you everything you want. And be sure to practice your script. Anger is a valuable emotion--even though we tend to see it as a problem, anger is actually instructive. What deems it destructive or instructive is what we do with our anger. When we express our needs calmly and without judgment, we show respect to others and to ourselves and maybe we even get our needs met.
- **Use a non-aggressive tone**: People are more likely to listen and respond calmly to you when you approach them calmly and respectfully. Avoid raising your voice or being aggressive. Watching yourself in the mirror or recording yourself as you express your anger also helps you get a better sense of your tone and demeanor.

- **Use non-judgmental language**: Judgmental language includes words such as "bad," "wrong," "jerk," or "selfish." These words are inherently subjective and only fuel arguments. Use facts--people are more likely to respond when being told "When you said I was lazy, I felt hurt," it's very different from telling them "You were a jerk last night." When you are talking to someone, describe what angered you in a neutral way, rather than judging the person as "rude" or "mean". Objectively, describe what that person said or did and how it made you feel.

Consequences of a bad self-expression

When you don't express your emotions clearly, respectfully, and safely, and instead dump your emotions on others or suppress them hoping that they go away, many misunderstandings will arise causing a lot of problems:

- When you don't explain in a clear, respectful, and safe way to others how you feel, they will try to guess how you feel and get it wrong. Being silent about your feelings does not mean that people will ignore them--they will just try to work it out for themselves and they may get it wrong. And in the absence of any declaration from you to the contrary, they will presume that their guess is right, then they may tell others. All this can foster negative gossip, a lack of trust, and grave misunderstandings.

- When you don't express emotions clearly, they may fester and disturb your sleep and drain your energy. How often have you heard of someone being upset by a comment and then stewing on it, only to find themselves lying awake still thinking about it? This means the next day when you face the board you are going to find it harder to think clearly.

- Carrying unexpressed negative emotions for any length of time zaps your energy, leaving you feeling tired, drained, and fatigued, and making it harder for people to relate with you. Who wants that? You will be more stressed and will take it out on staff, partners, or customers.

- If you cannot express feelings of appreciation, pride, and other similar emotions, people may think you are unappreciative or take them for granted. As a consequence, employee engagement drops when employees do not feel valued, appreciated, or supported and turnover increases. For example, I was told recently by a manager that one of his key staff had left him because, she "felt unappreciated." He was so surprised when she told him--he had no idea. He had thought it was obvious that he appreciated her.

Self-regulation

Emotionally speaking, self-regulation is the ability to calm yourself down when you are upset and to cheer yourself up when you are down. Behaviorally speaking, self-regulation is the ability to act according to your core values and beliefs. Several researchers have shown that consistent self-regulation requires focus on your core values rather than feelings. The violation of our own core values invariably produces bad feelings, while fidelity to them in the long-term makes you feel more authentic and empowered. To improve self-regulation, a good place to start is by understanding the biology and function of emotions and feelings, which, at this point, you already know. Self-regulation allows you to experience emotions without being controlled by them. You own your emotions, which helps you to improve your decision-making, overcome setbacks, keep pursuing the things you want, and enhance your social skills, helping you to build strong, lasting, and rewarding relationships.

What is self-regulation?

Self-regulation is the ability of, effectively, managing one's own emotions and how they impact our decisions and behaviours.

Therefore, self-regulation it is the act of taking responsibility for our own emotions. When we take responsibility for the way we feel, it gives us a tool for making decisions that are the most supportive of our mental and emotional health. That in turn, help us to be successful in motivating ourselves to achieve our goals. It helps us to overcome stumbling blocks and remain in action towards the things that we want in life. It let us experience emotions without being controlled by them and, it aids in our ability to build strong, lasting and rewarding relationships—both, in and out of the workplace.

Core skills of self-regulation

Emotional self-regulation comprises the mastery of four different skills listed:

- **Self-control**: The ability to manage disturbing emotions and remain effective, even in stressful situations
- **Adaptability**: The ability to change or be changed to fit changed circumstances
- **Achievement orientation**: The ability to have the drive and passion to accomplish goals, excel, and be successful
- **Initiative**: The ability to take actions without direct managerial influence

Self-control

Emotional self-control is the ability to manage disturbing emotions and remain effective, even in stressful situations. The key is managing, not suppressing emotions--to stop and think before acting. Daniel Goleman in his book, *The Brain and Emotional Intelligence,* talks about the amygdala hijack to refer to the situations when we lose control. During the so-called amygdala hijack, you cannot focus on the work at hand--your brain is highly focused on the threat, and your memory also changes to survival mode, only remembering what is important to keep you safe from the threat. Your old neurological pathways of fight or flight become your default way of acting therefore, you lose the ability to learn new solutions, be innovative, flexible, and change.

How to have self-control:

- **Mindful breathing:** Everybody knows that it helps to breathe. There are many different qualities of the breath, but we only need to learn about two: rhythm and smoothness. If we focus on these two dimensions, even for a few short minutes, the production of cortisol and adrenaline will stop:
    - **Rhythm:** To breath rhythmically means that the in breath and out breath occur repeatedly at the same intervals. Inhale, counting 1, 2, 3, and 4, and then exhale, counting 1, 2, 3, 4, 5, and 6. Inhale again, counting 1, 2, 3, and 4, and then exhale again, counting 1, 2, 3, 4, 5, and 6 this establishes rhythm.
    - **Smoothness:** At the same time, we should invite the breath to be even or smooth, meaning that the volume of the breath stays consistent as it moves in and out, like sipping liquid through a narrow straw. If we manage those two qualities for just a few minutes, the breath assists us in remaining present, making it possible to stay with an intense sensation in the body.

- **Reflection**: To help you identify where your strong reaction is coming from. Take a moment and ask yourself the following questions: Is this situation really a threat? Our knee-jerk reaction may be an over reaction. Take a moment to determine whether or not there is really a threat to something you value. Is the severity of your reaction truly warranted? What action would be best in this situation? Identify the action or behavior that would be best in the situation. It might be taking a break, taking a walk, having a conversation with the other person (or people) involved, apologizing, calming down and then coming back to listen, or it might be just walking away. By identifying what you should do, you are also identifying what you should not do. What do I need in order to be able to take that action? Do you need more time? More information? Do you need to de-stress? You don't want to attempt to take the right action if you aren't in the right mindset or don't have all the tools you need in order to be successful.

- **Reframing**: In order to change your self-talk around the situation. With strong emotional reactions often comes negative self-talk. You can start to practice positive self-talking by using the following positive sentences: "I made an honest mistake. That's frustrating, but I can certainly fix it," "I need to take a break so my frustration doesn't prevent me from doing a good job," "I'm not in a good mood today," "My ideas aren't always the ones chosen. I need to get honest feedback on that last idea," "Let me make sure I have fully understood the goal," "What can I do to help get us there," or "She might be someone who doesn't want a friendly relationship with me, and that's OK."

- **Rehearsal**: Helps you mentally prepare for the action you need to take in order to manage your emotions. A good tool to use is to rehearse your action and behavior in your mind and out loud. Consider how you would like the action to take place in detail. For example, if you are going to have a serious talk with your team manager about a problem you are having with another teammate, what would be the best environment to have the talk? Will you sit or stand? How will you start the conversation? What should your body language look like? What about your facial expression? What are the important points that you need to make, or what are the key pieces of information that you need to get? If it is helpful, you can write an outline or list in order to assist you with your rehearsal.

Adaptability

Adaptability is the ability to change or be changed to fit changed circumstances. The ability to be flexible and agile, and to respond effectively to new challenges. Therefore, it is the most important skill you need to have and use to successfully thrive in your workplace and personal life. Why? As Charles Darwin wrote:

> *It's not the strongest of the species nor the most intelligent that survives. It is the one that is the most adaptable to change.*

To stay competitive, businesses today must change and conform to the latest standards on a nearly real-time basis. This calls for increased focus on developing and establishing the traits of flexibility and adaptability into all levels of the workforce hierarchy. Resistance to change is not a solution. An adaptable mindset is your best tool.

How to be adaptable:

- **Use mental rehearsal**: To think about different ways you could engage. Picture the response. Try to see yourself acting in opposing ways to get to the same outcome. Identify which approach will likely yield the best outcome.

- **Practice holding back your first response long enough**: To think of a second and third solution. Rather than reacting, adapt and thoughtfully respond to the situation instead. Stay in control.

- **Listen more**: When you listen, you are suspending judgment. You are taking in information that will allow you to select the best response to the situation. Use that information to adapt your behavior as needed.

- **Get out of your comfort zone:** Put yourself into very different situations than those you typically encounter. Operating in a variety of situations and roles will help you become more flexible and adaptable.

- **Get feedback:** People who reflect on their performance are more likely to be flexible in adapting to changes in their environment and therefore better able to identify alternative ways of behaving to be more effective in given situations.

- **Laugh at yourself:** Having a sense of humor about yourself only serves to humanize you. When you fail, reflect on what went wrong, adjust course, and don't repeat the same mistake. Learning and improving your adaptability along the way is the goal, not perfection.

- **Get comfortable walking someone else's talk**: Having to support someone else's program or idea when you don't really think that way or agree is a common paradox. Don't let others know that you are not fully on board. Your role is to manage their vision and mission, not your personal one. If you have strong contrary views, be sure to demand a voice next time around.

Achievement orientation

Achievement orientation is the ability to have the drive and passion to accomplish goals, excel, and be successful. A professional with a growth mindset and who is performance-oriented has a strong self-regulation, has high standards, and looks to overcome any circumstance in a positive manner. They have a positive attitude and never give up, and encourage others to do the same. They take ownership for their mistakes therefore, they are always looking to improve. They ask for help when they need it and reward themselves for achieving the goal, keeping their pride from getting in the way of their actions, and delay gratification when necessary.

How to be more goal-oriented:

- **Take personal responsibility for your success**: Initiative, effort, and persistence are key determinants of success at demanding tasks. Failure-avoiding individuals view success as dependent on available resources and situational constraints (for example, the task is too hard, or the marker was biased).
- **See demanding tasks as opportunities**: Anything worthwhile is difficult.
- **Achievement striving is enjoyable**: Associate effort on demanding tasks with dedication, concentration, commitment, and involvement.
- **Achievement striving is valuable**: Value hard work in and of itself.
- **Skills can be improved**: Performance on demanding tasks can be improved with practice, training, coaching, and dedication to learning.
- **Persistence works**: Continued effort and commitment will overcome initial obstacles or failures. Don't assume that you cannot do something until you have tried. And I mean really tried, like tried 3,000 times, not that you tried three times, and ;said "oh I give up."

Initiative

Initiative, under the light of emotional intelligence, is the ability to take actions without direct managerial influence, to begin a process to develop yourself and others. Professionals with initiative recognize that in order to be truly happy, they have to take responsibility for their lives even when that involves making lifestyle changes, learning new skills, or developing new habits. They don't blame others or the universe for their problems, and they look for their own role in their current situation and their path of development. They also take the initiative in problem-solving and conflict resolution. They don't allow disagreements to fester or misunderstandings to linger. They take the necessary actions to clear negative emotions that are stopping or hindering them and they take action to prevent further similar occurrences.

How to have initiative:

- **Never stand still**: Even to stay in the same place, you have to run faster and faster. Hence, for standing out, you need to be creative and constantly search for new solutions and more effective approaches. Ideas are the most expensive matters nowadays and the best contribution you can offer to your organization.

- **Think as a team member, not an employee**: If you decided to take initiative at work, then think about yourself as a team member. This means that each success, and each achievement of the organization is yours as well. Corporate prosperity leads to your personal prosperity too.

- **Speak up and share your ideas**: There is always the need for fresh, powerful concepts. If your suggestions are based on broad research and adequate facts then you have a great chance to see them being realized in the near future.

- **Consider every opportunity**: Opportunities are hidden everywhere, and people who see them are the ones who prosper. Make a habit of constantly asking yourself: "What opportunities for growth can I carve out of this situation?". If needed, think about this same question again and again. Gradually you will find the answer.

- **Challenge yourself**: Tackle new skills and refine your abilities all the time. You learn and grow by challenging yourself. This will give you the knowledge and confidence to show more initiative in current or upcoming projects. It is better to be prepared for an opportunity and not have one than to have an opportunity and not be prepared. That is why you should aim high and constantly grow both as a person and a professional. As soon as you see a chance to use the acquired competence, go ahead and do that.

- **Ask questions**: To take initiative, you should know how things work and how you can improve them. For this purpose, be curious and ask questions. This will give birth to new ideas and ways to contribute to the growth of your organization more and more.

Benefits of good self-regulation

Self-regulation is an essential emotional intelligence skill for anyone. It is even more important for those in customer service, or those face the media or handle hostile meetings. Emotional intelligence enables you to shift emotions such as frustration, irritation, and anger, without dumping them on other people. Then you are unlikely to waste time becoming embroiled in conflicts and are able to prevent conflicts from escalating. Consequently, you successfully avoid interpersonal conflicts at work and at home.

We can see below the major benefits of having a good self-regulation:

- You are able to cultivate pleasant emotions such as feeling calm, appreciation, and enthusiasm and diminish the longevity of unpleasant emotions such as anger, frustration or anxiety, so that you move through them quickly, as you are able to move from one emotion to another as required. You have more choices over the emotions you feel at any given time.

- You are able to reduce the occasions on which unpleasant emotions occur, so that you experience emotions such as irritation, resentment, or helplessness less often. You may be able to shift between emotions so that you are in the best emotion for each task. Tasks require different emotions. For example, if you need to brainstorm innovative solutions to a problem, feeling stressed and tense may counteract this. By being able to shift your emotions into more relaxed and cheerful ones, you may find it far easier to be creative and innovative when you need to.

- You may have less stress and handle stress more easily. Thus, you may be healthier and have less absenteeism from work. You may develop more long-term and productive working relationships with colleagues, direct reports, and stakeholders.

- You may develop greater confidence and thus deal with problems more easily and, consequently, be happier.

- You may be predictable in your behavior so that people come to know what to expect and are not thrown by erratic behavior or unexpected emotional outbursts. This can help build trust between yourself, employees, and senior management, for example. Trust is the foundation for respectful and successful working relationships and collaborative partnerships.

Consequences of lack of self-regulation

Being able to manage your own emotions day-by-day, hour-by-hour, and even minute-by-minute, when you are busy at work and in a highly pressurized environment, takes a high level of emotional self-management, as much stress and misery arise when you lack the ability to self-manage your own emotions. We can see below the major consequences of lacking self-regulation:

- When the levels of stress are significant, you may find it hard to rise above the pressures of your role or job and become tense, hassled, or exasperated. This can lead to health problems so you may be more likely to need to take time away from work. You are also less likely to be an employer or supplier of choice, as your stress can be passed on to others. This may mean you find it harder to attract or retain good staff or you may put off potential clients or customers.

- When you are unable to self-manage your emotions you may get caught up in the negative things that happen in your day at work, and at home, and not be able to see the good things. Thus, you may be negative, critical, and miserable. No one likes working for miserable leaders, employers, or managers. This may lead to an increase in staff turnover, a demoralized workforce, or a reduction in your client base.

- People may avoid you when you lack emotional self-regulation, thus making it harder for you to know what is happening. You may be excluded from invitations to meet people, and then have to work harder to gain the co-operation of people upon whom you depend. These could be stakeholders, colleagues, customers, employees, or suppliers.

- People may not like you or you may not like yourself. Thus, you are more likely to be involved in a conflict, or make a fool of yourself by throwing a tantrum in front of your employees or children, or by being negative to co-workers, clients, or family members. You may be lonely or feel empty inside and seek comfort in drugs, alcohol, or over-eating. You may get sick.

Social awareness

If you have a good social awareness, you can perceive emotional overtones in an organization, team, or interaction, even when these remain unspoken. You are able to read the play in a meeting, negotiation, or discussion and observe the non-verbal signals people give that indicate how they are feeling. These may include voice tone, facial expression, eye movement, head position, postural changes, speech characteristics, and breathing characteristics. You then have the option to respond in a meaningful and influential way.

What is social awareness?

Social awareness the ability to perceive and understand others' emotions and validate them.

Social awareness is being able to recognize relationships and structures in which you and those around you are operating within your organization or your social networks. Therefore, it is also known as awareness of other's emotions.

Core skills of social awareness

Social awareness comprises the mastery of five core skills:

- **Empathy**: The ability to sense other people's emotions and feelings
- **Awareness and acknowledgment**: The ability that enables you to understand and validate the other person's feelings - without agreeing with them
- **Sensitivity**: The ability that allows you to acknowledge how the other person is feeling
- **Organizational awareness**: The ability to recognize and understand how the organizational structures in which you and others operate can influence emotions
- **Service orientation**: The ability to take in to consideration others' needs and help them achieve their goals

Empathy

Empathy is generally defined as the ability to sense other people's emotions and feelings. Contemporary researchers often differentiate between **affective empathy**--our ability to mirror the sensations and feelings we get in response to others' emotions and **cognitive empathy**--our ability to identify and understand other peoples' emotions by perspective taking, to put ourselves in someone else's shoes. When you do that, you gain an understanding of why a person feels or behaves the way they do and what triggered that feeling or behavior. Then and only then can you employ the other emotional intelligence tools in order to influence or manage the emotions and behaviors of others. "Ok, Emilia! But, I don't need empathy to work in the sandbox. Also, I am not a very emphatic person." According to the neuroscientist, Marco Iacoboni, we human beings are, literally, wired to connect. Mirror neurons are always on--meaning we affect one another even when we do not mean to. When we see someone feeling sad, for example, our mirror neurons fire and that allows us to experience the same sadness and to feel empathy. We don't need to think about the other person being sad, we actually experience it firsthand.

How to be empathic:

- **Listen and be vulnerable**: Truly listening can be a challenge. Sometimes we are just waiting to give our own opinion. Increased empathy only comes through interacting with others, so you want your conversations to be as deep and revealing as possible. In order to do that, you need to develop two interrelated skills: emotional listening and making yourself vulnerable. Removing our masks and revealing our feelings to someone is vital for creating a strong empathic bond. Empathy is a two-way street.

- **Be fully present and tune in to non-verbal communication**: Put away your phone, don't constantly check your email, and don't accept calls while you are interacting with someone. The things we say account for only 7% of what we are trying to communicate. The other 93% of the message is in our tone of voice and body language. If while you speak with someone, you scroll through your upcoming appointments, you will miss the bulk of the message.

- **Smile at people**: Smiles are literally contagious. The part of your brain responsible for this facial expression is the cingulate cortex, which is an unconscious automatic response area. A smile releases dopamine and oxytocin, also known as the happiness and bonding hormones.

- **Use people's names and encourage them**: Encouraging people can be as simple as nodding at them while they talk in a meeting. This simple gesture, along with using their name, makes great impact on relationship building.

Awareness and acknowledgment

Awareness and acknowledgment is the ability that enables you to understand and validate the other person's feelings, without agreeing with them. When the person is very expressive through body language, facial expressions, or other non-verbal cues, you can easily be aware of how they are feeling. However, for the less expressive, you need to ask questions, read between the lines of what they are saying and use trial and error until you get to the point where you understand how they are feeling. Once you have a grasp on how someone is feeling, you need to acknowledge their feelings. Acknowledgment does not equal agreement--it means that you are recognizing the other person's position and empathizing with it. By doing so, you show that you are sensitive to how they feel and you value their feelings.

Sensitivity

Sensitivity is the ability that allows you to acknowledge how the other person is feeling. The other person's feelings are information that you need to process--the same way you do with your own emotions. This emotional data is the key to be more self-aware, empathic and, in consequence, improve social awareness. Therefore, don't invalidate someone's feelings only because you don't understand them or disagree with them. Avoid diminishing, belittling, ignoring, judging, or rejecting the other person's feelings by saying things like: "I understand how you're feeling, but I think you just don't understand," "I can understand that you feel that way, but you're wrong," or "I appreciate what you are telling me, but I think you're really off-base." Your goal is to understand why someone is feeling that way and not destroy the working relationship. In a working relationship, your colleague's resistance to a new idea could be indicative of an area of the decision that you have not yet taken into consideration and by invalidating his opinion, you are dismissing important information on your decision-making process.

Organizational awareness

Organizational awareness is the ability to recognize and understand how the organizational structures in which you and others operate can influence emotions. If empathy helps you understand the emotions of an individual, organizational awareness helps you to understand the culture within which those emotions operate. It involves recognizing that there are influences on yourself and others that come from the other people that you are surrounded by. For instance, the corporate culture of your organization is a major influence on how you can or cannot express yourself. In a conservative culture, the display of emotions is looked at as inappropriate. In another organization, you might be admired and encouraged for being expressive. Usually, only by reading the mission, values, goals of an organization or team, can we grasp what is the culture and the emotional intelligence of the organization.

How to have organizational awareness:

- Talk to others and ask them for their thoughts on how to make your department more effective. Find out, in a subtle way, what organizational constraints may prevent certain things from happening in your organization.
- Identify key people inside of your company who influence policies and decisions. Create a chart showing how they and others interrelate and compare it to the formal chart of the organization
- Do basic research on the company itself. What is its mission? What are the values? What are the department's goals? Are there specific goals expected of each team member? What is the culture of the organization?

Service orientation

Service orientation is the ability to take in to consideration others' needs and help them achieve their goals. Therefore, service orientation is built upon empathy for a person's situation. Knowing and understanding the type of environment that dominates your organization prepares you to be ready to help your employees or colleagues achieve their professional goals, be better employees and a happier people. Let's say you have an employee that suddenly started performing poorly. You have a conversation with him about what is going on. You discover that he is no longer feeling challenged in his current position. You use your questioning skills to determine that he is feeling ignored and that the organization does not care about developing him. So with your empathy for his feelings and your awareness of the organization in which you both are operating, you help him identify areas where he could increase his performance level so he feels challenged. Rather than ignoring or belittling his feelings or judging him as a poor employee, you are taking in to consideration his needs and helping him achieve his goals. There you have a win-win situation, because you also win by having a motivated and engaged employee.

How to have service orientation:

- **Start at the top:** If you want your team to care about customers, start by making it a priority at the top. Don't just "say" that you value great service or write it in a memo - live it! Reward it on a regular basis, recognizing those that go over the top publicly and often. Make it clear to everyone that customers have a say at your company.
- **Hire people who fit:** When evaluating potential new hires, consider whether or not they will fit into the culture you have created. Do your best to build a team that's enthusiastic about customer service and is a good personality fit.
- **Get everyone involved:** Everyone should do at least a little bit of customer service, no matter what their job title is. Having your designers, developers, engineers, and everyone else talking with your customers means they all have a good understanding of what the customers want.
- **Trust your team:** Once you have implemented your company values and hired the right people, be sure to let go! Not only will this encourage employees to develop creative ways to serve customers, but your employees will also be happier. Everyone likes to take ownership in their job. Throw away the scripts and free employees to treat customers with their own voice and heart. Let them do whatever it takes to make your customers happy.
- **Establish good lines of communication:** Make sure it is easy for everyone to stay on the same page so that nobody feels like they are facing a difficult problem alone.

Benefits of having great social awareness

When you master the awareness of others' emotions it will be easier to motivate people as you will have high emotional intelligence and a greater understanding of the emotional drivers of their behavior. Therefore:

- You are more likely to be able to show empathy and be regarded as empathic. When you know how someone is feeling, their reactions will come as less of a surprise as you will know when it is the best time to approach someone and when it is best to wait. This could make a large difference to the amount of influence you have and in your ability to persuade others.
- You are able to perceive the impact that you are having on someone else.
- You are able to hear people when they are expressing their emotions without belittling, ridiculing, or dismissing them; for example, not telling them they are "being too emotional." Instead, you are able to ask people how they feel, paying attention to the emotions of others in meetings, negotiations, performance reviews, and other situations in which they emerge at work.

Consequences of lacking social awareness

Many misunderstandings arise when social awareness is lacking. Why? First off, because without social awareness you cannot understand why the others are behaving in a certain way: for instance, gossiping, ignoring you, or trying to manipulate you. You then have fewer options for managing their behavior. We can see below the major consequences of lacking social awareness:

- You take your colleague's or boss's behavior as a personal attack and feel hurt, when no hurt was intended, and it was nothing to do with you.
- You cannot read your audience's feelings about you, your ideas or your organization. Therefore, you pitch your presentation at the wrong level, raising hostility and negation in your audience, which requires considerable relationship repair to recover from it and, because you lack social awareness, you don't know how to repair relationships.
- If you cannot read other people's feelings, you cannot be a successful negotiator. You are not able to persuade or influence them. On the other hand, you also cannot realize when someone is lying to you.

Social skills

Social skills, also known as interpersonal skills or people skills, are the skills that we as sociable creatures developed to communicate and interact with each other. And to convey our messages, thoughts and feelings to each other, we use verbal language and non-verbal language such as gestures, cues, body language, and our personal appearance. Social skills help boost productivity, improve relationships, and increase your general quality of life.

What are social skills?

Social skills mean the ability to ethically manage others' emotions using influence.

A person with great social skills is extremely useful in any workplace, as usually they are the influencers, the leaders, and the ones focused in helping others and the organization. They are easy to talk to and wonderful listeners. Therefore, they are the peace makers, resolving disputes, building bonds, and catalyzing change.

Core of social skills

To master the competence of social skills, you need to master seven skills to manage others' emotions. These are listed as follows:

- **Ethical influence**: The skill to help others help themselves--not to get something out of someone by manipulating them
- **Emotional intelligent leadership**: The skill of having the willingness to be on service, to help others to grow in tandem with themselves
- **Developing others**: The skill of bringing the best out of others to enhance themselves and the organization
- **Building bonds**: The skill of proactively building and developing mutually beneficial, quality relationships
- **Change catalyst**: The skill of recognizing when change is needed, challenging the status quo, championing the need to change, and the role model required for it
- **Conflict management**: The skill of knowing that a conflict is always an opportunity to evolve when the root of the conflict is kindly brought to light
- **Communication**: The skill that enables you to tune in to emotions of others and use that emotional data to influence the other person to choose the best course of action

Ethical influence

Ethical influence is the skill to help others help themselves and not to get something out of someone by manipulating them. In emotional intelligence, we speak of ethical influence to distinguish it from manipulation. You are simply attempting to help your employees or colleagues to achieve their goals and desires. For someone without a personal ethical compass and good social skills, it is very tempting and easy to manipulate others and that is not the aim of enhancing your emotional intelligence competencies and skills. Influence people's emotions by what you say and how you say it. Be genuine and sincere when you compliment your employees or colleagues on their appearance, strengths, patience, thoughtfulness, productivity, for the ideas they have contributed at a meeting or for always brightening up everyone with their kindness and compassion, their smile even when the going is rough. Simple things and genuine words of appreciation go a long way. To be an influencer organization-wide, you don't need to be a leader. But to be a leader, you need to know how to influence.

How to be an ethical influencer:

- **Connect with people emotionally**: If you want to intrigue and influence people, you have to get their dopamine pumping to stimulate the pleasure-reward area in the brain that makes people feel happy. A great way to do that is by having excellent conversation starters. My favorite two are: What personal passion are you currently working on? What was the best part of your day?
- **Be emotionally curious**: Everyone wants to be liked, loved, and accepted. When you make others feel important, your influence goes a long way. Become genuinely interested in them. A great way to do this is to ask them open-ended questions and let them talk about themselves. This helps you build rapport.
- **Use high-powered body language**: The head is held high, the arms are loose, the shoulders are set back, and the chest is out. When you manifest powerful body language, you are seen as more influential. Confident body language not only affects the way others see you but also the way you see yourself.
- **Be vulnerable**: People will perceive you as being real when you admit your weaknesses or flaws. People are able to better relate to you when you open up. Share a vulnerable story from your story toolbox. By doing this, you not only tell a great story but you also are being vulnerable, so it increases your influence in two ways.
- **Ask a favor**: It turns out that asking for help is one of the best things you could do to be perceived as an influential person. This is known as the Benjamin Franklin effect. So freely ask for help in the form of advice, opinions, or guidance.

Emotional intelligence leadership

Emotional intelligence leadership is the skill of having the willingness to be on service, to help others to grow in tandem with themselves. Like influence, leadership is not restricted to hierarchical positions. Leaders can be found anywhere in an organization, especially emotional intelligence leaders. They can be at the bottom rung of the organizational ladder and still be able to perform their job in a way that has their co-workers following along after their example. Because they know how to work with people, keep the peace, use resources wisely, share the credit, support and develop their people. However, as it relates to emotional intelligence, leadership involves appealing to and managing the emotions of others in order to get the job done. That is why you cannot be an emotional intelligence leader if you don't know how to influence others. Leaders can help others become enthusiastic about the vision and mission of the organization. An emotional intelligence leader takes on a leadership role when they see the need, no matter what their position. They guide others' performance, they hold others accountable, and they lead by example.

How to be an emotional intelligence leader:

- **Build optimism**: Your boss does not want to hear what is wrong with a project. He wants to hear your suggestions for solving it or improving it.
- **Show enthusiasm**: Personal energy is contagious, and so is the lack of it. No matter what the job is, complete it with a sense of urgency. When others notice, they will become enthusiastic also.
- **Be flexible**: Show you can handle change by volunteering for a new project or by helping others with change.
- **Stop micromanaging**: Delegate projects to the right employees.
- **Stand by your employees**: Show you trust them, and they will be trustworthy.
- **Ask your peers for advice**: When you are new to a leadership position, you don't know everything. Identify your most respected peers, and ask them how they have succeeded.

Developing others

Developing others is the skill of bringing the best out of others to enhance themselves and the organization. As a leader, how do you assess your leadership ability? Based on your own achievements and development or based on how many of your people got promoted to other divisions or to more responsible positions? What kind of work environment would that be? What would it do to your productivity if every employee knew that you had their future development in mind when assigning work, assessing criticism, or managing projects? Leaders who have the willingness of helping others to grow in tandem with themselves are confident enough in their own abilities. They recognize that helping others to achieve their goals is a win-win situation and it makes them feel connected to and invested in others, which in turn enhances a sense of belonging and teamwork.

How to develop others:

- **Use coaching and mentoring**: Classroom, online, books, coursework. One of the by-products of developing your people is that you gain satisfaction and stature as a result of their success. Who will you help today?
- **Build a learner mentality**: Encourage your people to think of themselves as professional learners as well as (job title). In meetings and one-on-ones, ask: What are you learning that is new or different?
- **Get ongoing feedback from multiple sources**: The key words here are ongoing and multiple. Ongoing: performance improves with the information that is provided as close to an event as possible. That way, the situation is still fresh and the details clear. Multiple sources: when I do 360s for clients, I always insist on feedback from people outside of the person's direct chain of command, even external customers if there is a lot of customer interaction. When someone is working across boundaries on a project, there's a wealth of information available about the ability to build relationships and influence outside of the power sphere.
- **Give first-time tasks that progressively stretch people**: No one grows from doing the same thing more and more.

Building bonds

Building bonds is the skill of proactively building and developing mutually beneficial quality relationships. A natural builder is someone that knows the importance of having a good social network. After all, no man is an island. Even for the professionals working remotely or for virtual teams, the skills of working on building rapport and developing mutually beneficial relationships are the base of their professional success. When you take time and put the effort in to build relationships, you are naturally enhancing your people skills, communication skills, and self-confidence. A bond builder, or social networker sees relationships not just as things that happen, but as bonds that you proactively build aiming for quality relationships.

How to improve building bonds:

- **Ask about their families/pets/significant others**: In your conversations, ask about the people that are close to them. Even a simple "How are your parents/girl/boyfriend?" brings out a human element that creates an opportunity for bonding.
- **Talk about their interests/hobbies/current events**: Find something, an idea or a philosophy, or a hobby that others are passionate about and just ask a question. With the power of social media today it is not hard to find hot buttons to focus on.
- **Give small token gifts**: Small gifts go a long way. A small gift shows that you are thinking of them, that you invested thoughts into them. Small gifts are often more meaningful than bigger gifts on special occasions as they provide reminders of the relationship more often than gifts on special occasions.
- **Ask good questions, and then listen**: When people vent and talk about the problems they are facing, listen and ask questions. If you don't know what to ask, just repeat the last word they said.
- **Always start with a positive introduction**: A strong hello or a smile makes a huge difference in a person's day. And everyone wants that sense of recognition that comes through in your positive greetings.
- **Be comfortable. Be real. Be authentic**: When you are who you are, you share a part of yourself with the other person, creating a stronger bond.

Change catalyst

Change catalyzing is the skill of recognizing when change is needed. It challenges the status quo, champions the change and role models it to others. A change catalyst is a forward-thinker, and is open to change as a way of self-improving, improving the organization, team, co-workers and even customers by change. A change catalyst is the person that understands that change is part of life and part of remaining competitive. And he recognizes that change often brings up fear in people. Yet, a change catalyst does not allow the fear of change to prevent the necessary changes from being made. He removes the barriers to change (old fixed mindset and emotional roadblocks) and influences others to champion the change.

How to be a change catalyst:

- **Clear vision**: A change agent does not have to be the person in authority, but they do have to have a clear vision and be able to communicate that clearly with others. People can be frustrated if they feel that someone is all over the place on what they see as important and tends to change their vision often. A clear vision does not mean that there is one way to do things in fact, it is essential to tap into the strengths of the people you work with and help them see that there are many ways to work toward a common purpose.

- **Patience and persistence**: Change does not happen overnight and most people know that. To have sustainable change that is meaningful to people, they will have to embrace it and see its importance. Many can get frustrated that change does not happen fast enough and they tend to push people further away from the vision, than closer. Change agents just help move people from point A to point B, at their own pace. Every step forward is a step closer to a goal.

- **Ask tough questions**: It is when people feel an emotional connection to something that they will truly move ahead. Asking questions focusing on "What is best for us?" and helping people come to their own conclusions based on their experience is when you will see that people have ownership in what they are doing. Keep asking questions to help people think--don't alleviate that by telling them what to do.

- **Be knowledgeable and lead by example**: Leaders are not just seen as good people but also are knowledgeable about what they are speaking. If you want to create change, you have to not only be able to articulate what that looks like, but show it to others. Change agents need to put themselves in the situation that they are changing. How can you really know how something works if you have never experienced it?

- **Strong relationships built on trust**: All of the preceding points mean nothing if you do not have solid relationships with the people that you serve. The change agents I have seen are extremely approachable and reliable. Trust is also built when you know someone will deal with things and will not be afraid to do what is right, even if it is uncomfortable.

Conflict management

Conflict management is the skill of knowing that a conflict is always an opportunity to evolve when the root of the conflict is kindly brought to light. This is a challenging skill to develop because it requires that you experience conflict in order to learn how to solve it. You may even need to bring conflicts to light that others would rather leave in the dark. However, conflict management will make you a better leader, co-worker, and even parent, spouse, or friend. A skilled conflict manager knows that a conflict is always an opportunity to evolve. It can help individuals or a work group to solve problems, improve processes, heal rifts, strengthen relationships, and learn new skills. Though, to properly manage a conflict you need to discover the root of the conflict and use all the other emotional intelligence competencies.

How to improve conflict management:

- **Build bonds, even with your adversary**: The key to defusing conflict is to form a bond, or to re-bond, with the other party. We do not have to like someone to form a bond, we only need a common goal. Treat the person as a friend, not an enemy, and base the relationship on mutual respect, positive regard, and co-operation. Leaders must learn to separate the person from the problem. Once a bond has been established, we must nurture the relationship as well as pursue our goals. We need to understand each other's point of view, regardless of whether we agree with it or not. The more effectively we communicate our differences and our areas of agreement, the better we will understand each other's concerns and improve our chances of reaching a mutually acceptable agreement. We can all learn to communicate acceptance of the other person while saying no or disagreeing with a specific point or behavior. Feeling accepted, worthy, and valued are basic psychological needs. And, as hostage negotiation demonstrates, it is more productive to persuade than to coerce.
- **Dialogue and negotiate**: Many leaders in conflict situations are hostages to their inner fears and other negative emotions and fail to see the opportunities in resolving them. Talking, dialogue, and negotiation create genuine, engaging, and productive two-way transactions. We need to use energy from the body, emotions, intellect, and the spirit.

- **Raise a difficult issue without being aggressive or hostile:** Once an issue is raised, we can work through the mess of sorting it out and find a mutually beneficial outcome. We should be direct, engaging, and respectful, always helping the other person to save face. In addition, timing is important. Choosing the right time and the right circumstances are part of an effective conflict management strategy.

- **Understand what causes conflict:** To be able to create a dialogue aimed at resolving the conflict, we need to understand the root of the disagreement. Among the common causes of disagreement are differences over goals, interests, or values. There could be different perceptions of the problem, such as "It's a quality control problem" or "It's a production problem," and there may also be different communication styles. Power, status, rivalry, insecurity, resistance to change, and confusion about roles can also create conflicts. It is crucial to determine whether a conflict relates to interests or needs. Interests are more transitory and superficial, such as land, money, or a job. Needs are more basic and not for bargaining, such as identity, security, and respect. Many conflicts appear to be about interests, when they are really about needs. The most conflict provoking losses have to do with needs, and those needs may connect to the deeper wounds people have suffered in their life. Someone passed over for promotion, for example, may seem to be upset about the loss of extra money, when the real pain is caused by a loss of respect or loss of identity.

- **Empathize and reciprocate:** Reciprocity is the foundation of cooperation and collaboration. What you give out is what you get back. Humans have a deeply hardwired pattern of reciprocity. Mutual exchange and internal adaptation allows two individuals to become attuned and empathetic to each other's inner states. Hence a powerful technique to master in any kind of dispute is to empathize with the feelings and views of the other individual by managing what we express, both verbally and non-verbally. This social awareness allows you to make the right concessions at the right time. Once you have made a concession, it is likely that the other party will respond in kind. Moreover, when you recognize a concession has been made, reciprocate with one of your own.

Communication

Every interaction we have involves some form of communication. Under the light of emotional intelligence, communication is the skill that enables you to tune in to the emotions of others and use that emotional data to influence the other person to choose the best course of action. It enables you to build rapport, trust, and long lasting bonds. Other features of this skill include being good at compromising, seeking mutual understanding, dealing with difficult issues head-on, welcoming open and frank discussion, being receptive to good and bad news, and not allowing disagreements to become roadblocks to further communication.

How to improve communication:

- **Don't talk over people**: This demonstrates a real lack of respect.
- **Don't finish other people's sentences**: Research has shown that by doing this you are disempowering the other person because you are taking control of the conversation.
- **Paraphrase**: If you want to show that you have really understood someone, all you have to do is repeat back to someone what they have just said, before you comment yourself.
- **Listen actively**: Focus on active listening instead of passive listening. The difference is that active listening means you engage and respond to the other person based on what they have said; passive listening is simply the act of listening with no response.
- **Maintain eye contact**: By looking the other person in the eye, you are proving that you are interested in what they are saying.

The benefits of having great social skills

The emotional management of others is an essential emotional intelligence skill in the workplace--you cannot lead successfully without it, because peoples' behaviors are driven by their emotions. Your role as a leader is to inspire, motivate, and engage others. Mastering the management of others' emotions means that:

- You are able to develop a supportive atmosphere in meetings so that people feel encouraged to express their opinions and ideas, and as a consequence, you will lessen the ill will of a hostile group (for example, shareholders, ratepayers, or the media), so that they adopt a less antagonistic position by shifting the negative mood of a group to a more positive and productive mood, thus helping your team to have the best emotion for the task.

- If people arrive at a meeting feeling frustrated, dejected, or tense and you need them to creatively brainstorm, you can shift them to a more settled and happier emotion which is more conducive to creativity and innovation. Or, help calm someone down when they are furious, frustrated, or irritated in a meeting, support people suffering from grief, disappointment, or depression so that they feel better, while helping people who are feeling excited, exuberant or ecstatic to stay focused, and inspire and motivate others.

The consequences of having bad social skills

Usually, when one is a leader, manager, CEO, and so on, and lack the skill to managing others' emotions, this influence and shift the mood of the team in the workplace, a tense team and a miserable environment, with gossips, backstabbing, lack of engagement, is the result. We can see below the major consequences of lacking social skills:

- Being able to manage your own emotions day-by-day, hour-by-hour, and even minute-by-minute when you are busy at work and in a highly pressurized environment, takes a high level of skill. You may find your work colleagues are tense and unhappy and stay that way. This can lead to fighting, backstabbing, gossiping, and unproductive working relationships. You may, therefore, end up stressed, tense, and agitated and find yourself having to work longer hours than you wanted.
- You may avoid situations in which strong emotions arise so that when problems first occur you fail to nip them in the bud and just hope they will go away. Instead, they may escalate and cause even larger problems and difficulties in the future. One angry or upset team member can develop into a whole team being angry and upset if it is not dealt with early.
- There may be low levels of employee engagement and productivity. It may be hard to you or your organization to attract or retain good quality staff so that you suffer from a high staff turnover. High staff turnovers waste money and resources.
- You may feel uncomfortable engaging with people in difficult or tense situations because of their emotions and thus avoid completing important tasks, such as performance reviews with your senior managers or staff.

- You may be unsettled or afraid if people are aggressive to you and you can't shift their emotions, which makes tasks such as handling customer complaints extraordinarily hard and stressful.
- People may suck the life out of you so you end up overwhelmed and exhausted. You may be distracted from what you need to do if the people around you are unfocused and very excited.

Summary

In this chapter, we covered the core emotional intelligence competencies and the skills you as an IT professional need to have to master each of the competencies and tips to improve each one.

You have learned the ability of adequately perceiving and understanding your own emotions as they happen (self-awareness), which will help you be more confident, less stressed, less overwhelmed, accept feedback, and stop micromanaging.

You have learned the ability to express your own emotions in a safe, clear, effective, and respectful way (self-expression), which will help you to build quality relationships, better your employee engagement, decrease turnover, be liked, and appreciated.

You have learned the ability of effectively managing your own emotions and the impact they have on your decisions and behaviors (self-regulation), which help you to cultivate pleasant emotions, prevent conflicts, influence others, and build trustful, successful, and collaborative partnerships.

You have learned the ability of adequately perceiving and understanding others' emotions and validating them (social awareness), which will help you be more empathic, have a greater understanding of the emotional drivers of others, be a motivator, and be a successful negotiator.

You have learned the ability to ethically manage others' emotions by influencing their moods and emotions (social skills), which will help you be a great leader, inspire, develop others to achieve their best, increase productivity and employee engagement, and build a healthy and happy workplace.

In the next chapter, we will learn how to use this competencies and skills to build an emotional intelligence corporate culture and, as a consequence, an emotional intelligence workplace for you and your colleagues to thrive in and be happy.

4

How to Build an Emotionally Intelligent IT Organization

In this chapter, we will unravel whether an organization also has its own emotional intelligence. How can we assess the level of emotional intelligence of an organization in the three dimensions in which the organization operates internally and externally? Learn easy but efficient strategies to enhance the level of emotional intelligence in each dimension:

- Does an organization have emotional intelligence?
- The three dimensions in which the organization operates
- Strategies to enhance customer support
- Strategies to enhance your sales team

Does an organization have emotional intelligence?

I know this sounds like a tricky question as an organization is not a sentient being, so how can it have emotions or the need to manage them? Your organization, small or worldwide, is built by human beings:founders, investors, employees, partners, customers, clients, and competitors. Thus, whether you are aware of it or not, their emotions are running your business. Hence, your organization also has emotional intelligence. An emotionally intelligent organization is one that cares and nurtures for its people and forhumankind at large, not only for its profits.

Feeling engaged, feeling excited, feeling motivated, feeling cared for, feeling stressed, feeling overwhelmed, feeling burned out, feeling unappreciated, are all emotions running your organization, from top to bottom. And all these feelings need to be addressed.

Emotional intelligence in an organization needs to be role-modeled by the leaders, whether they are situational leaders or top-of-the-ladder leaders. Also, if you want to build an emotionally intelligent organization, you need to have a vision, mission, values, and purpose that attract emotionally intelligent collaborators. And to keep them on board, engaged, excited, productive, efficient, happy, and proud, you need to build a corporate culture and environment that cares, nurtures, and helps develop your human beings, to bring their best to light if they feel you care about them they will give you their very best and help you grow an outstanding organization.

You need to realize that you are running or building an organization for the future in a volatile, uncertain, complex, and ambiguous world, that the vast majority of your employees, partners, and customers are very young with a very specific set of values, principles, and vision and they want to make a difference in the world and work in an emotionally and physically healthy environment toward a more democratic and humanistic economy.

Around 2020, 46% of the working force will be millennials, and they are known for being driven by purpose. Organizations with a purpose bigger than profit have a growth rate triple that of their competitors who are driven by profit above all. Millennials, your working force of the future, need to be surrounded by people that appreciate and value the work they are doing. They will be on fire if they feel they are working on an organization with a meaningful purpose that wants to make a difference in the world and also cares for the environment, not only for profit. Working in a cool office is awesome, but for your special workforce, a purposeful culture is more important. And a culture of purpose drives exponential sales growth. Put purpose before profit and your team will drive revenue through the roof. People want to make money but they also want to make a difference in the world.

Millennials are also known for having a low-score emotional intelligence, which is not accurate, because when they undergo emotional intelligence training or are coached within an emotional intelligent environment they develop their emotional intelligence competencies and skills very fast and easily. After all, if emotional intelligence is the missing link in the traditional educational system, how could they learn it?

So, how can we assess the level of emotional intelligence in our organization? And, how can we develop and build an emotionally intelligent organization?

First off, many organizations by using Employees Engagement Surveys are already assessing their employees' emotions-feeling engaged, feeling motivated, and so on. However, this is not the same as assessing the level of emotional intelligence of the organizations. As an individual, you have self-awareness and an organization has organizational awareness. Organizational awareness refers to the ability to recognize and understand how structures in which you and others operate can influence the emotions of the people working there. You can gain some level of organizational awareness by doing basic research on the company itself:

- What is the organization's mission?
- What are the organization's values?
- What are the department goals?
- Are there any specific goals expected of each team member?
- What is the culture of the organization?

Imagine that the culture of your organization is very conservative and controlled such that emotional expression is looked upon as inappropriate. In another organization, you might be admired and encouraged for being expressive. Or there might be a very hierarchical structure to your organization so that those you supervise might feel uncomfortable telling you how they feel. Or the organizational structure itself might be driving some feelings in the people you are working with. For example, they may feel frustrated in their current position and feel that there is nowhere else for them to move to or grow, which could be manifesting itself in anger or disappointment. Or a change in organizational structure could have them feeling anxious about the future. These are all areas where you might find clues to how people are feeling.

You can run an **Organization's Emotional Intelligence Assessment,** as shown in the following screenshot, to have a baseline of the level of your organization's emotional intelligence and what you need to improve:

Organization's Emotional Intelligence Assessment

- What emotions, are considered important in your organization - if any?
- What emotions are people encouraged to express?
- Which emotions are people expected to suppress or hide?
- Which emotions are ignored or trivialized?
- Which "positive" emotions are deliberately fostered?
- How comfortable are employees in approaching their team-leader about difficulties they are experiencing?
- What are the written and unwritten emotional rules and norms in your organization?
- To what extent do people feel valued and appreciated?
- How many people enjoy their work?
- How many people feel loyal to the organization?
- In what ways do you ensure there is congruency between the emotions in your organization and the organizational values?
- How are the emotions of conflict handled across the organization?
- What level of emotional intelligence does the CEO display when leading the organization?
- What emotions do your customers experience after being in contact with your organization or business?

Organization's Emotional Intelligence Assessment

The three dimensions in which the organization operates

As you would have noticed, the organization's emotional intelligence assessment covers three dimensions in which the organization operates. They are as follows:

- **The first dimension**: The organization in itself with its vision, mission, values, and principles
- **The second dimension**: The relationships with sentient beings that make the business grow: its people, founders, stakeholders, employees, and so on
- **The third dimension**: The relationships with its customers, clients, partners, competitors, and society at large

These three dimensions work together as a big propeller, creating momentum and bringing your organization to the forefront of success.

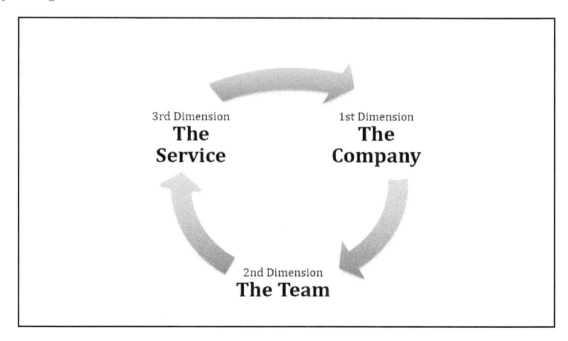

The three dimensions in which the organization operates

The first dimension - the company

I like to call this dimension the soul of the company due to the fact that it is through its mission statement, vision statement, the definition of its mission, and the values, and principles that the organization starts to come to life and establishes its foundations. And if you want to build an emotionally intelligent organization your purpose, vision, mission, values and principles need to incorporate the emotional intelligence concept in order to attract emotionally intelligent collaborators. How can an organization do that? By carefully carving out the vision, mission, values, principles and, most importantly, its purpose to enhance feelings of wellbeing, purpose, meaning, compassion, care, fairness, sustainability, cooperation, dignity, ethics, moral, authenticity, transparency, and openness.

We will address each of them to help you carve out the purpose, vision, mission, values, and principles to have an emotionally intelligent organization from the soul to the roots by referring to the following diagram:

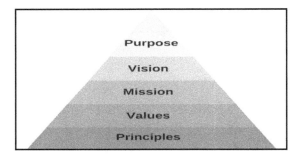

Purpose, vision, mission, values, principles pyramid

Purpose

The corporate purpose of your organization is the company's core raison d`être. It is the underlying objective that unifies investors, partners, employees, and customers at the same time and embodies its role in the broader economic, societal, and environmental context. Your corporate purpose statement needs to inspire your staff, so they can give their very best when working for you. It is through the purpose statement that you can make them feel part of the organization and part of your vision and mission. Belonging is a very powerful emotion. An organization thrives faster when it is able to please its investors, partners, employees, and customers. Often, the corporate purpose is communicated through a company's mission or vision statements, though the purpose of an organization is not its vision, mission, values, or principles. Furthermore, the purpose frequently remains unarticulated and informal.

However, the corporate purpose only resonates with an emotional intelligence concept if it is an authentic purpose. Why? Authenticity is commonly defined as being true to oneself therefore, being authentic in its own actions helps to build, sustain, and increase the feeling of trust in the organization. Yet, corporate actions that are inconsistent with the corporate purpose will lead stakeholders to view the corporate purpose and the company with mistrust and scepticism.

Organizations undeniably need to walk the talk in order to be credible and authentic with regard to their corporate purpose statements. However, talking the walk is also an equally important part of the paradigm, since perception, built on awareness and knowledge gained through experience, learning, and communication, is often reality. Thus, corporate purpose messages must be carefully tuned to indicators that demonstrate that the organization effectively walks its talk. For organizations to build trust with stakeholders, their strategic decisions and actions must be aligned with their corporate purpose, in order for this to be perceived as authentic. How authentic is the corporate purpose of your organization?

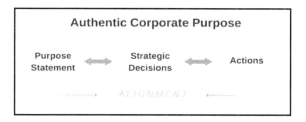

Authentic Corporate Purpose

To ring true, the corporate purpose of an organization needs to resonate internally (for example, employees) or other stakeholders and externally (for example, customers). Thus, we can say that corporate purpose has two dimensions: the internal dimension driven by awareness and the external dimension driven by transparency.

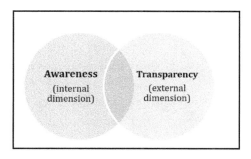

The two dimensions of corporate purpose

Organizations with a good organizational awareness have a deep understanding of their own strengths and weaknesses, what drives or motivates actions taken by its leadership and how this impacts its stakeholders, the community, and the environment. Leaders and stakeholders should pay special attention to whether the organization actively seeks feedback from the stakeholders, whether the organization is aware of the impact the organization has on the stakeholders, or whether the organization understands the drive and motivations behind its actions.

How can organizational awareness be used to assess the authenticity of the corporate purpose?

You can ask the following questions:

- Does the organization seek feedback to improve its interactions?
- Is the organization aware of the impact it has on its stakeholders, community at large, and the environment?
- Is the organization aware of why it does the things it does?
- Is the organization aware of what drives or motivates actions taken by its leadership?
- Is the organization aware of what is truly important for the whole organization, the community, and the environment?

Transparency

An organization that openly shares information with its internal and external stakeholders, and the society at large, is deemed transparent. Open communication and transparency are the bedrock of trust and trustworthy relationships inside and outside the organization. Thus, not only leaders but also stakeholders should be concerned about the level of transparency of the organization. And, in the era of the internet, it is so easy to assess whether an organization is being transparent and how transparent it is. Just ask the following questions:

- Does the organization tell the truth, always? The whole truth or the truth with a spin?
- Does the organization openly share information with its internal and external stakeholders?
- Does the organization own up to its own mistakes, when they are made?
- Does the organization pretend to be something that it is not?

Mission and vision

Mission and vision both relate to an organization's purpose and are typically communicated in written form. Mission and vision are statements from the organization that answer questions about what the organization is, what the organization's values are, and where the organization is going.

A **mission statement** communicates the organization's reason for being, and how it aims to serve its stakeholders, customers, employees, and communities (that is, in the form of social or environmental impact).

A **vision statement** is a future-oriented declaration of the organization's purpose. In many ways, you can say that the mission statement lays out the organization's purpose for being, and the vision statement says, based on that purpose, this is what we want to become.

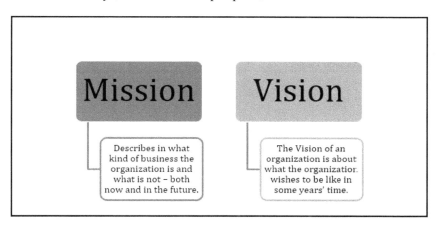

Difference between mission and vision

Mission and vision statements play three critical roles:

- Communicate the purpose of the organization
- Inform strategy development

- Develop the goals and objectives by which you can gauge the success of the organization's strategy

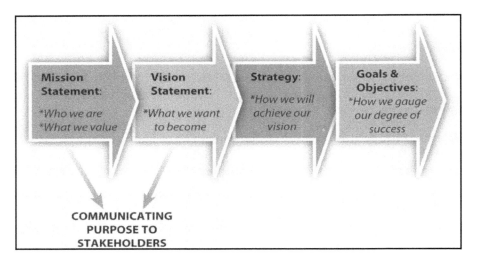

Key roles of mission and vision

Values

Value statement is a belief of an individual or group in which they have emotionally invested. In an organization, it is important that this statement is written and easily available to everyone. Why? Because, these statements become the deeply ingrained principles and fabric that guide employee behavior, company decisions, and actions. Without a statement, the company will lack soul. It is through the value statement that employees and key stakeholders learn what principles they need to embody, what the organization stands for, how its products contribute to the world, and so on. They are true reflections of what the company believes and what management and employees are willing to live by. However these statements don't need to be boring endless pages with the most well-researched values. Use your soul, your heart, and your creativity to write your value statement.

One of my favorite value statements is from a company that builds teddy bears and they truly embodied *bear-ism* throughout the company, as shown in the following figure. Their value statement is creative, simple, and immediately builds trust, brings people together, and unifies the entire organization.

Exemple of Core Values

Reach,

Learn,

Di-bear-sity,

Colla-bear-ate,

Give,

Cele-bear-ate,

Di-bear-sity.

Core value statement from the Build-a-Bear, Inc.

The most important requirement is that your values bring people together and unifies the organization.

Principles

The principles statement gives employees a set of directions. For example, always listen to and build first-class relationships with customers to help us provide excellent standards of service and client satisfaction: for instance, honesty, excellence, accountability, respect, and teamwork.

The second dimension - the team

An emotionally intelligent organization is one that cares for and nurtures their people as a family. Therefore, you need to build an office that is like a home, where your employees feel appreciated, cared for, and protected. You need to build a house that enables personal wellbeing through compassion and kindness.

A place that enables trust, empathy, respect, equality, mutuality, and individuality with a corporate culture that is meaningful, flexible, and empowering.

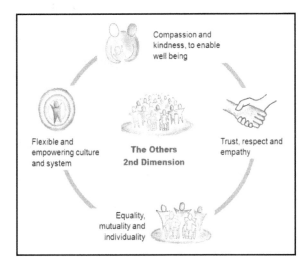

The others- second dimension

How can your organization modify its offices in a way that benefits employees' wellbeing, the environment, and productivity?

From the following figure, in which office would you feel more happy, comfortable, well, and productive: office A or Office B?

Bad office environment versus good office environment

Office A is a worker's worst enemy in terms of wellbeing, productivity, happiness, creativity, and resilience to stress. I know that around the world the tendency is to have open offices like Office A. Nonetheless, open-floor offices with shared working spaces without dividers, instead of fostering collaboration that strengthens relationships between colleagues, lean towards destroying the right environment to enhance creativity, productivity and the wellbeing of the employees. Open offices like the one in Office A are the worst nightmare for introverts to work and shine in. A study from the late 1990s in Canada exposed that after moving to an open office:

- Employee satisfaction, happiness, motivation, and productivity declined
- Attention spans, creativity, and overall output declined
- Stress levels rose
- Co-workers felt distant, dissatisfied, and resentful

Open offices like Office A have high-level noise and interruptions, which makes it very hard to remain focused or regain focus after an interruption. This can affect everything from worker productivity to health.

A very noisy ambiance can damage workers' ability to think and get things done, impairing the ability to recall information and to do basic arithmetic. Multitasking frequently leads to distraction, hence workers who multitask have a much tougher time getting back into their flow after an interruption. Research also shows that the more a worker multitasks, the less he is able to block out distractions, raising his levels of stress and decreasing productivity.

Human beings have the need to feel safe and in a comfortable environment thus, taking away physical divisions is like removing all the boundaries that make humans feel safe and secure when you move all the physical divisions/boundaries from the office the workers feel that they are being attacked and are without any protection. Psychologically, it can be very damaging as the employees feel helpless, unable to control their own environment, not able to decorate their own space, adjust the lighting, have personal objects that are meaningful for them, and so on.

According to a recent study in Denmark, researchers found that people working in open offices, on an average, have 62% more sick days than workers in nonopen offices. That is very compelling evidence that open offices may be one of the worst workplace innovations of the last couple of decades.

Strategies to enhance the office environment

Enhancing your office environment like Office B in the previous image is not impossible and with simple and easy hacks you can make your office more healthy, happy, and productive, where your employees and co-workers feel at home.

- **Building green separators**: Like we saw in Office B, it is easy and cheap to bring some green from the outside to the inside. Depending on where you are located in the world, find out what are the best plants to improve interior environments and build green walls.

- **Adjusting the thermostat temperature**: How many times have you heard, "Is it just me or is it cold in here?" Sometimes when I am in the office with some of my clients, I feel that the temperature is set for the penguins, not for the human beings working there. Low temperatures lead to low productivity and increase the number of sick days. If you give your employees access to control their own thermal comfort, you could see a 3.7% increase in productivity and a 16.2% increase in health benefits.

Examples of open offices with good environment

- **Adjusting the lights and decorating them**: Open offices usually have big, bright lights everywhere. However, all these bright lights have a dark side; they mess with the sleeping patterns of the workers, increase health risks, and lower productivity. If you let your employees control the interior lighting around their workspaces, their productivity can increase by 10.7% because, not everyone feels comfortable with the same levels of light. For instance, I have photophobia, which is an intolerance to strong bright lights. Merely walking under one of these bright lights is painful; imagine if I need to work in one of these offices. Some of your employees may have the same intolerance to light and they cannot adapt their light to a comfortable and healthy level for themselves.

- **Enhancing the views and if possible installing wall-to-wall windows**: Your employees will reward you for it. A 2015 study concluded that just looking at nature can improve focus and productivity. If you increase by 85% the quality of the indoor and outdoor views, productivity will increase by 3.9% and there will be a 20.2% increase in absenteeism benefits with fewer days off. And if your organization wants to see a further increase in productivity, invest in wall-to-wall windows that allow the sunlight to reach 100% of the floor space. Natural daylight not only improves workplace performance, but also increases in more 7.2% productivity.

All the money invested in enhancing the office environment will be recovered with the increase of productivity, fewer sick days, and more happy workers.

 The specific percentages of productivity yielded by these changes may vary for different buildings, depending on the changes that are needed to be done. But the premise behind the recommendations is the same. So, maybe your organization wants to look into how the environment of your office is affecting your productivity.

You might be asking yourself, how all these changes will make my organization more emotionally intelligent? Well, you are taking care of your employees and stakeholders, therefore you are taking care of their emotional wellbeing and enhancing the social awareness of the organization.

- **Creating an office policy of gratitude and kindness**: Yes, I know that it might seem strange to have a policy of gratitude and kindness running the office. However, it stops seeming strange when we realize that our company, our organization, our office are built by human beings, with their idiosyncrasies, their different personality types, different backgrounds, different ways to cope with stress, and sometimes lacking the basic still to live together in harmony. That is why I advise my clients to have a written policy of gratitude and kindness in the office. It is a simple policy with three commitments. Simple practices that I learned when spending three months in a Zen Buddhist Monastery are very helpful when we need to live and work in community. The three commitments are as following:
    - **Practicing togetherness**: Yes, living and working together in peace, harmony, and respect requires the daily practice of cooperation, acceptance, cultivating understanding, open and honest communication, and a willing heart. Practice taking the time to get to know the people around us. Sharing the same office space with others is an opportunity to develop understanding and compassion for ourselves and for those we work with. By being mindful of the people we share the space with, we can identify and appreciate their positive qualities, creating an atmosphere of harmony. We know that when the other person is happy, we are also happy. We can show our respect to our colleagues and the space we share by helping to keep it neat and clean. We try to be considerate of our colleagues. For example, we might like to ask first before we open a window or turn on the light, to make sure it will not bother our colleagues. In this way, we can create a supportive environment for practicing loving kindness through words, thoughts, and actions.

- **Practicing a loving speech and deep listening**: Aware of the suffering caused by unmindful speech and the inability to listen to others, I am committed to cultivating loving speech and compassionate listening in order to relieve suffering and to promote reconciliation and peace in myself and among my colleagues. Knowing that words can create happiness or suffering, I am committed to speaking truthfully using words that inspire confidence, joy, and hope. When anger is manifesting in me, I am determined not to speak. I will practice mindful breathing and walk in order to recognize and to look deeply into my anger. I know that the roots of anger can be found in my wrong perceptions and lack of understanding of the suffering in myself and in the other person. I will speak and listen in a way that can help myself and the other person to transform suffering and see the way out of difficult situations. I am determined not to spread news that I do not know to be true and not to utter words that can cause division or discord. I will practice right diligence to nourish my capacity for understanding, love, joy, and inclusiveness, and gradually transform anger, violence, and fear that lie deep in my consciousness.

- **Practicing gratitude**: People can spend hours in staff rooms bitching and gossiping about everything that has gone wrong and that attitude spreads negativity. This is not emotionally intelligent as it can be very destructive. Gratitude is the opposite. It is noticing, acknowledging, and being thankful for the things that have gone right in our life each day. Gratitude is also a feeling that is contagious like a virus-a good one that increases happiness, wellbeing, lowers stress, and strengthens the relationships in teams and the sense of belonging to a project. I am sure you want to have an office run on gratitude. Yet, it is so easy to include gratitude practices into the office policy, such as the following:

- **Having a gratitude portfolio**: Make a portfolio of things that make you feel grateful. It can include pictures, poems, artefacts, memories, and anything else that elicits the emotion of gratitude. Spend time on it and make it beautiful. Both working on the portfolio and reviewing what you have made will cultivate grateful feelings. Keep the portfolio living and add to it from time to time to keep the experience you have with it fresh. This portfolio could be online, so the other colleagues could see it and participate.

- **Expressing gratitude**: Make a habit of thanking people authentically for the things they do for you and the impact they have on your life. Be aware of the kindness of others and acknowledge it. This practice brings positive emotion to all.
- **Sharing gratitude with a secret partner**: Plan to practice gratitude regularly with a secret partner (maybe a colleague you are not so close to) by sharing good news and discussing things you feel grateful for. Respond actively and constructively when your partner shares, feeling the joy and gratitude with them when they share their blessings.

- **Ritualizing endings**: Take time to acknowledge endings, large and small, and cultivate gratitude for the people and the outcome of that project, before moving forward. Give thanks to your people aloud and share your grateful feelings with them. Little endings happen all the time, and each one can be a cue to give thanks in a new and unique way.

The third dimension - the service

The third dimension of your organization is the involvement of the organization with the community, potential customers, clients, partners, and competitors. Being at service is more than just the corporate social responsibility; it is the relationship building with your customers (through your customer support) and with the new partners and clients (through your sales team).

Corporate social responsibility

In this section, we will not address the corporate social responsibility of your organization. The faces of the organization that in this dimension are important to display emotional intelligence are customer support and the sales team. Therefore, we will only address strategies to enhance the social skills of these two important teams in your organization. It does not matter if you are creating the next big thing in the IT world, if your sales team and customer support do not excel in their social skills.

Strategies to enhance customer support

Customer support is the ultimate example of a tough mind and warm heart they are needed every day to reassure your customers and clients after something goes wrong with your product or service. Though, mindfulness, kindness, empathy, and compassion are the secret skills to endure the tough task of reassure your customers/clients and prevent highly stressful situations. Let's learn how to bring loving, kindness, empathy, and compassion to your customer support team:

- **Use mindful listening**: Good listening means mindful listening, because listening takes a combination of intention and attention. Intention is showing a genuine interest in the other person in their experiences, views, feelings, and needs. Attention is being able to stay present, open, and unbiased as we receive others' complaints. We all love the sweet feeling of being heard with the heart. Though, being a good listener entails the ability to listen to oneself, to be self-aware of your own beliefs, opinions, needs, and fears.

  To improve your self-awareness and enhance your listening skills, necessary to be an excellent customer support member, you need to do the following:

- **Check your emotions**: "How am I feeling now? Is there anything preventing me from being fully present with the customer/client?" If you feel that something is in the way, decide whether it needs to be addressed first or whether it can wait until you are off service. Then return your full attention to the customer/client.
- **Be mindfully present**: Be mindful of your calm and loving presence and extend it to the customer/client with the intention of listening fully and openly, with interest, empathy, and mindfulness. The customer/client will feel it and will be calmer.
- **Mirror the words of the customer/client**: Paraphrasing or summarizing with the words used by the customer/client helps the other person feel heard.

- **Acknowledge the customer's/client's point of view**: Before replying to the customer/client, acknowledge their point of view. Acknowledging is not agreeing with the client, but it involves making the customers/clients feel cared. Use friendly, open-ended questions to clarify your understanding and probe for more. Affirm before you differ.
- **Show the love**: It is useful to find several ways to show your customers/clients how much you value, appreciate, and love them. They will return that love in various ways such as sharing your information, buying more, and ultimately becoming devoted fans and a constant source of referral business. Never miss an opportunity to thank your customers. Thank them on social media, thank them personally, and thank them on your blog. The more thanks you show to your customers, the more they are going to trust you.
- **Call them by their names**: Yes, of course, your customers will know that much of the personalization in emails and so on is automated. Yet, their brains will notice it and appreciate it. Sending personal thank you notes with their names, especially if the note is hand-written, helps build relationships faster and make them much closer. When a customer spends a lot of money buying your products, a nice thank-you phone call is always appreciated. Even if you just leave a voice message, they will know that you thought enough about them to thank them. It is amazing how great a personal phone call can make people feel. And at the same time, you are building a trustworthy relationship.
- **Be easy to contact**: Customers like when they have doubts or problems with your product and can easily contact you. A relationship is a never-ending process, we cannot stop building it. The best way to build a relationship is to have an open communication that is a two-way line. Ask open-ended questions, respond to your customer's questions, and help the communication flow back and forth.
- **Run a satisfaction survey**: Give them some time to use your products or services, then send them a survey that asks about their satisfaction and take another opportunity to thank them.

The more you can surprise and delight your audience, the better. Doing just a little something can make all the difference. Try to think outside the box about the ways that you can please your customers, ways that are inexpensive to you but would mean a lot to them.

Strategies to enhance your sales team

IT sales teams are highly skilled teams with very high skilled people from technical skills to soft and social skills. Great salespeople have the ability to connect on a very human level and create a high-level rapport with their prospects and clients. Pushy salespeople might close the deal, but no one in the team likes working with them. They can get the client to sign on the dotted line, but the customer will not be happy if they find out they have been lied to, or that their needs were not paid attention to.

If you have been having trouble closing deals or getting along well with colleagues, it might be time to consider whether or not you could improve your empathy. Here are a few exercises to enhance it:

- **Caring for your prospects**: Caring comes first because if you don't care how your prospects are feeling and what their needs are, it is impossible to be empathetic.
- **Being empathic**: Empathy is the ability to share another person's emotional experience. For salespeople, understanding their prospects and the client's emotional state helps deepen their understanding. It helps to create the connection that you are sharing their emotional experience. In a lot of people, empathy is a natural skill, though we can always enhance it. How can we enhance empathy? First off, take time to recognize what the prospect is feeling. Body language and verbal cues, especially emotionally charged words, tell you how your prospect is feeling. Once you recognize what emotion(s) your prospect is feeling, feel what they are feeling by putting yourself in their shoes.
- **Putting yourself in their shoes**: Empathy requires that you feel what are they are feeling. It is the ability to say, "Yes I feel what you are feeling." instead of "Yes, I can imagine what you are feeling." For salespeople, this ability helps them create the connection and the foundation of trust. It helps put you on the client's side of the table with them. To develop this skill, literally imagine yourself in the client's position. Imagine how you would feel. Unless you easily cry during movies, this is much more difficult than it sounds. Try working on this during sales calls, but don't limit your practice to sales situations.

- **Listening and acknowledging**: Salespeople spend a lot of their time trying to change people's minds. They move people from taking no action to taking action, from buying from your competitor to buying from you. Yet, too frequently salespeople rush forward trying to change minds without first understanding and respecting the client's views and opinions. Empathy and emotional intelligence allow you to suspend the mind changing until you have built the connection that will allow you to work with their point of view. To develop this skill, imagine yourself as the buyer. Would you want someone to try to change your mind without first taking the time to understand what it is that you believe and need and why you believe it and need it?

- **Listening without judging**: Emotional intelligence and empathy entail the ability to listen to others and to accept that their interpretation of events, facts, or ideas is true for them. To truly exercise your empathy and your emotional intelligence, you have to be willing to listen without immediately passing judgment on the facts or the meaning of what is being said. You have to accept their interpretation as being valid and worthwhile. Listening without being judgmental and without trying to change minds is the most powerful way to create a long-lasting relationship.

- **Working on your self-awareness and self-management**: Changing others' minds means you not only have to exercise these skills with others, you also have to exercise them with yourself. This means being aware of your emotions. Before you can manage the emotions of others, you have to be able to manage your own emotions. One of the most powerful ways to deal with highly emotionally charged events is to simply pause before responding. When an emotionally charged situation occurs, and if what you sell has high stakes for you and your clients they are sure to occur, take the time to pause and collect yourself before you respond. Use that hiatus to decide how your response will help or hurt you in achieving the outcome that you need. Don't focus on the emotions; focus on a response that moves you closer to your needed outcome.

- **Using emotions to drive action**: You have put yourself in your prospect's shoes; now you need to be able to help him to get out of these shoes and move forward. Sales managers and leaders with high emotional intelligence use emotions to drive action. They use negative emotions to create a case for change and to drive their teams to take actions. They use positive emotions to build high-performing cultures that believe that they can succeed. Salespeople have to be able to move people to action, including their clients and their team members. To develop these skills, determine how you can use negative emotions to build the case for change. Start by making a list of the questions that uncover the implications if there is no change. Then, ask questions that help to elicit a vision (or create one) of the implications if a change is made. What would that change look like? What actions would have to be taken to get there? The best salespeople can move though these emotional states and move their clients with them.

Summary

In this chapter, we have learned that an organization also has emotional intelligence. Emotional intelligence in an organization needs to be role-modeled by the leaders, whether they are situational leaders or top-of-the-ladder leaders. Also, if you want to build an emotionally intelligent organization, you need to have a vision, mission, values and purpose that attract emotional intelligent collaborators.

How can we assess the level of emotional intelligence in the organization? And, how can we develop and build an emotionally intelligent organization?

We have learned that an organization operates in three dimensions. The first dimension is where the organization is itself with its Vision, Mission, Values, and Principles. The second dimension is the relationships with sentient beings that make the business grow: its people, founders, stakeholders, employees, and so on. The third dimension is where the relationship is with its customers, clients, partners, competitors, and society at large. These three dimensions work together as a big propeller, creating momentum and bringing your organization to the forefront of success.

We have learned strategies to enhance the level of emotional intelligence in each of the three dimensions, such as how to improve the environment of the office, how to have an office policy of gratitude and kindness, and how to raise the levels of emotional intelligence in the customer support team and also in the sales team.

In the next chapter, we will learn how important it is for a IT Manager to have a good level of emotional intelligence that enables him to know himself and to know and manage their people. Specifically, the emotional intelligence of the five most challenging MBTI (Myers-Briggs Type Indicator) personality types—ESTJ, ENTJ, ISTJ, INFJ, INTP—found with more incidence in positions of management, leadership and in high achievers employees in the IT industry. The strengths and weakness of these five personality types, how they are seen in the workplace as employees, subordinates and managers and how they can improve their emotional intelligence skills to be easier to work with them. And how to manage extroverts and introverts at work, to have a great workplace environment and increase productivity.

5
How to Be an Emotionally Intelligent IT Manager

In this chapter, we will cover how important it is for an IT manager to have a good level of emotional intelligence that enables him to know himself and to know and manage people. Specifically, we will cover the emotional intelligence of the five most challenging **MBTI (Myers-Briggs Type Indicator)** personality types—ESTJ, ENTJ, ISTJ, INFJ, and INTP—found with more frequency in positions of managers, leaders, and high achieving employees in the IT area. We will also cover the strengths and weakness of these five personality types, how they are seen in the workplace as employees, subordinates, and managers, and how they can improve their emotional intelligence skills so that they are easier to work with. We will also cover how to manage extroverts and introverts at work to have a great workplace environment and increase productivity:

- Know yourself and your people
- Emotional intelligence and the Myers-Briggs personality types
- How to manage extroverts and introverts

Know yourself and your people

Knowing yourself is the base of the emotional intelligence build as we have been learning. Thus, by this moment you already have the toll and strategies to improve your emotional intelligence competencies and skills that allow you to know you and what triggers you as well as how to know and manage the other emotions. However, in this chapter, we are not covering these topics again.

Yet, we will cover information about emotional intelligence from the most complex and difficult personality types from the Myers-Briggs types, that are most common to find as managers, leaders, and difficult employees, also known as high achievers. Unfortunately, we have found too often that managers lack basic emotional intelligence skills such as social awareness and social skills and think that the best approach to manage people is to be dictatorial, to set the rules, and then enforce them. Why do managers/bosses behave in this dictatorial way? For the bad bosses/managers out there, it is an act of self-preservation. They think that this old-fashioned mindset makes them look good. They enact grand dictums and punish employees when they don't perform because they think that is how they will survive in the workplace. A bad boss/manager doesn't bother to show empathy. The main goal is to keep the budget in check, for the employees to finish projects on time, and for the main leader to look good in front of everyone else and maybe get a rise. That is the end game for managers, project managers, and team leaders who lack emotional intelligence. However, emotionally intelligent managers know that there are better ways to have a great workplace environment and increase productivity. The secret is to build trust and use empathy—see the world from the eyes of your team. Ask them how they perceive the project. What do they need? The act of showing trust and empathy leads to a better team, which is better for the company.

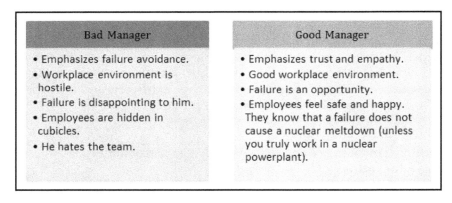

Bad manager versus good manager

Empathy and trust leads to a healthy team dynamic. An emotionally intelligent manager/boss will empower their employees by advocating that it is okay to fail during the process of creating new things that are worthwhile! It is okay to get out of the comfort zone and take risks in trying new processes, new methodologies, new things! It is okay to be who you are and complete tasks in a way that works for you to shine brightly.

Emotional intelligence and the Myers-Briggs personality types

Emotional intelligence and personality are not the same thing, but they work very well in tandem. What I have observed for more than 9 years working with both is that the different MBTI types find some aspects of emotional intelligence easier than others. Each is normal because we all have our own way to deal with our emotions internally (intrapersonal skills) and expressing them openly with others (interpersonal skills). Though, I would love to cover all the 16 personality types here, I cannot. That would be an entire new book. We will cover only the five personality types that find emotional intelligence a challenge, hence, they are more difficult to manage and deal with as they can be very disruptive in the workplace environment and they are ESTJ, ENTJ, ISTJ, INFJ, and INTP. Therefore, we will cover the types in the areas more relevant in the workplace—traits, strengths and weakness, workplace behaviors and how they can improve their intrapersonal and interpersonal skills, for example, emotional intelligence:

- **Intrapersonal skills**: This includes self-awareness, self-regulation, emotional self-control, flexibility, motivation, achievement, resilience, and well-being, and stress management
- **Interpersonal skills**: This includes empathy, energy, social skills, tolerance, persuasiveness, and the ability to lead

I am sure that you will identify some of your colleagues, and even yourself, in the traits of one or more of these personality types. Yet, if you do not know your MBTI type, I advise you to do an online test or hire an expert to profile all your team members. Learning about how your MBTI personality type's emotional intelligence is moulded can help you use your strengths or manage your organization/team to your advantage.

The next chart will give you an overview of the 16 MBTI types:

ISTJ	ISFJ	INFJ	INTJ
factual	detailed	committed	independent
practical	traditional	creative	visionary
organized	service-minded	determined	original
steadfast	devoted	idealistic	global
ISTP	**ISFP**	**INFP**	**INTP**
logical	caring	compassionate	independent
realistic	adaptable	original	theoretical
adventurous	gentle	creative	analytical
self-determined	harmonious	empathetic	reserved
ESTP	**ESFP**	**ENFP**	**ENTP**
activity-oriented	enthusiastic	creative	enterprising
versatile	friendly	versatile	outspoken
pragmatic	cooperative	perceptive	challenging
outgoing	tolerant	imaginative	resourceful
ESTJ	**ESFJ**	**ENFJ**	**ENTJ**
logical	thorough	loyal	logical
systematic	responsible	verbal	strategic
organized	detailed	energetic	fair
conscientious	traditional	congenial	straightforward

The 16 MBTI personality types

Each personality type describes how you mentally process information, depending on sensing, intuition, thinking, and feeling preferences. The combination of these processes and whether or not your type is primarily introverted or extroverted define in the long-term how you receive your energy (Introvert(I) versus Extrovert(E)), how you gather your information (Sensing(S) versus Intuition(N)), how you make your decisions (Thinking(T) versus Feeling(F)) and what kind of lifestyle you feel more comfortable (Judging(J) versus Perceiving(P)).

The following figure helps us to better understand these dichotomies:

THE DIFFERENT PREFERENCES OF EACH TYPE		
EXTROVERTS Active Initiating Expressive Enthusiastic Gregarious	ENERGY	**INTROVERTS** Reflective Receiving Contained Quiet Intimate
SENSING Concrete Realistics Pratical Experimental Traditional	INFORMATION	**INTUITION** Abstract Imaginative Conceptual Theorethical Original
THINKING Logical Reasonable Critical Questioning Though	DECISIONS	**FEELING** Follow intuition Open-minded Accepting Accomodation Tender
JUDGING Systematic Planful Scheduled Early Starting Methodical	LIFESTYLE	**PERCEIVING** Flexivel Open-Ended Adaptable Pressure Prompted Spontaneous

The preferences of the 16 types of personality

Once you have learned about your Myers-Briggs personality types' emotional intelligence and intrapersonal and interpersonal strengths or weaknesses, you will obtain a greater sense of how you process your emotions and the emotions of others, and how you can develop these aspects of your emotional intelligence to further yourself professionally and personally.

The ENTJ personality type

ENTJs are charismatic and self-confident, which makes them natural leaders (though not necessarily good ones). It is true that their charisma and authority draw crowds or followers behind a common goal. Yet, they lack self-management and social awareness, which makes them seem ruthless and very rational. ENTJs do not express their emotions in a positive way, for them emotional displays are displays of weakness, especially in a professional environment. ENTJs will simply crush the sensitivities of those they view as inefficient, incompetent, or lazy and if your team members, colleagues, and so on fear you instead of respecting and trusting you, when you need them they will not guard your back. ENTJs need to remember that they depend on having a functioning team, not just to achieve their goals, but for their validation and feedback as well. They need to remember that their success comes not just from their own actions, but from the actions of the team that props them up, and that it is important to recognize the contributions, talents, and needs, especially from an emotional perspective, of their support network:

| ENTJ | |
Strenghts	Weaknesses
• Efficient	• Stubborn and Dominant
• Energetic	• Intolerant
• Self-Confident	• Impatient
• Strong-Willed	• Arrogant
• Strategic Thinkers	• Poor Handling of Emotions
• Charismatic	• Cold and Ruthless

ENTJ - strengths and weaknesses

In the workplace, ENTJ qualities make them more fit for managerial or executive roles than for subordinate positions. As they are efficient with an open, honest communication style, they get things done in an unmatched way, however, with absolutely no respect for the emotional state of the team members. As subordinates and colleagues, ENTJ personality types are able to adapt themselves to any hierarchical relationship by asserting their opinions, taking the initiative, and accomplishing achievements that others thought were impossible. ENTJs are often known for being high achievers or problem makers, when not properly managed by their manager.

Let's learn, with the help of the following chart, the main traits of the ENTJ at work as an employee, subordinate, and manager:

ENTJ		
Subordinates	**Colleagues**	**Managers**
ENTJ subordinates set out to learn new skills and to seek out new challenges and responsibilities, eager to prove that nothing is impossible with a little hard work. ENTJ slip into periods of absentmindedness when things get slow, but when they feel involved in the projects, they prove well organized and well prioritized. ENTJs hold themselves to very high standards. Objective, rational statements about what is done right and what can be done better are helpful to ENTJs, and far from resenting such criticisms, they appreciate them. Opportunities for growth keep people with ENTJ engaged and productive, and so long as their managers recognize this as their primary responsibility, it will be a fruitful and satisfying relationship.	Among colleagues, ENTJs are sociable and enjoy sharing ideas and critiques in their frequent brainstorming sessions. Natural leaders that they are, ENTJs tend to assert themselves into positions as representatives and project leads, considering their objectivity and charisma the perfect qualities for these roles. ENTJ personalities enjoy working with equals, but people must demonstrate that they are equals. Thus, ENTJs treat with condescension and orragance any colleague they view as being less competent or less driven. ENTJs are strong-willed, dominant, and though they enjoy inspiring and tutoring others, the energy they bring to the process can seem overbearing. When these roles are reversed, ENTJs' mentors should bear in mind that their students are very rational and respect firm confidence – hand-holding, emotional appeals or wavering indecision will likely burn the bridge then and there. In a partnership, what is best is what is most effective, and time wasted sugarcoating reality is just that – time wasted.	ENTJ managers are confident, charismatic communicators, and they get the job done as efficiently as possible, and to the highest standard of quality. All else is subordinate to that objective, but the means by which ENTJs achieve it cause others to adopt this cause as their own. ENTJs are natural leaders, and their ability to formulate a strategy and to identify the strengths of each member of their teams, incorporating those abilities into their plans so that each individual fills a unique and important role, makes them able motivators. Yet, while these efforts boost morale and satisfaction among ENTJs' likeminded subordinates, those seen as inefficient by their ENTJ managers, or who demonstrate themselves to be lazy or to produce shoddy work will know in no uncertain terms of their failure to impress. The only way to recover is to comply, the only alternative is to find a new manager to impress, somewhere else.

ENTJ in the workplace

Emotional intelligence-wise, the ENTJ types lack emotional self-awareness and emotional awareness of others' feelings because they don't read too much into situations, thus they don't fully understand the emotional value of a situation. ENTJ are innovative and creative, and enjoy developing abstract issues and finding solutions for problems, always looking for the next big idea or thing to do. And if others are on a different emotional level, at that time, ENTJ will disregard their emotions; therefore, they are often insensitive. ENTJ lack sympathy and empathy as their ideas of emotions are concrete and predetermined.

And as they lack social awareness, they also lack the meaning of social cues. Although they understand when they occur, they just don't know what to do. Even though very driven and intelligent, the ENTJ needs to take actions to improve their emotional intelligence in the following areas:

- **Emotional self-awareness**: Discovering how your own emotions run your behaviors and actions is awfully important for an ENTJ type's personal emotional growth, as it will allow them to put themselves in another person's shoes.
- **Social awareness and empathy**: Devoting some of your time to the feelings of others and learning to empathize with them will significantly influence your emotional intelligence for the better, allowing you to connect with others on a more personal level. In this way, you should also learn to become more open with your own feelings, so that you can receive sympathy and understanding from your peers as well. If ENTJs are able to put their ambitions aside long enough to connect with others and share in an exchange of emotions and feelings, their emotional intelligence will be seriously improved and they will become more understanding and likeable individuals.

The ESTJ personality type

ESTJs are strong believers in the rule of law and authority. They are the kind of leader that leads by example, demonstrating dedication and purposeful honesty. They reject laziness and cheating, especially in the workplace. ESTJs live in a world of clear, verifiable facts, where the security of their data means that even against hefty resistance, they stick to their principles and push a vision of what is and is not acceptable. ESTJ don't engage in empty talk, they love challenging projects, improving action plans and sorting details, making even the most difficult tasks seem easy and approachable.

Nevertheless, ESTJs don't work alone, and they expect their colleagues or subordinates to reciprocate their work ethics and trustworthiness. ESTJs fulfil their promises, and if partners or subordinates jeopardize them through incompetence or laziness, or are dishonest, they do not hesitate to show their fury. This can earn them a reputation for inflexibility, but it's not because ESTJs are arbitrarily stubborn, but because they truly believe that these values are what makes the society work. The main challenge for ESTJs is to recognize that not everyone follows the same path or contributes in the same way:

	ESTJ	
Strenghts		**Weaknesses**
• Dedicated • Strong-willed • Direct and Honest • Loyal, Patient and Reliable • Enjoy Creating Order • Excellent Organizers		• Inflexible and Stubborn • Uncomfortable with Unconventional Situations • Judgmental • Too Focused on Social Status • Difficult to Relax • Difficulty Expressing Emotion

ESTJ - Strenghts and Weaknesses

In the workplace, ESTJs whether subordinates, colleagues, or managers, generate order, follow the rules, and work to guarantee that their work and the work of those around them is accomplished to the highest standards. Thus, sparing and dodging responsibilities are the quickest ways to lose an ESTJ's respect. Let's learn with the help of the following chart, the main traits of the ENTJ at work as an employee, subordinate, and manager:

ESTJ		
Subordinates	**Colleagues**	**Managers**
ESTJs are hard-working and do things by the book they are unlikely to do much experimenting on their own – adhering to stated responsibilities and fulfilling their duties is their primary concern. Though ESTJs are open to new methods that can be demonstrated to be better yet, when presented with ideas that have not been fully developed, they are stubborn and inflexible. ESTJs are also well-known for their loyalty and dedication, but in some ways this is contingent on their respect. People with this personality type are willing to voice their opinions, especially in deciding what is and is not acceptable if provided with sensible responses that address their concerns, they are often satisfied with that. If ESTJs view their managers as illogical, dishonest or cowardly in their methods, they can be uncomfortably honest, if still calm and level, in voicing their opinions on that as well.	ESTJs enjoy the hustle and bustle of well-organized workplaces. Honest, friendly and down-to-earth, ESTJ personalities are great networkers who enjoy connecting with others to get things done. ESTJ personality type lose respect quickly for those who try to push forward by showing off or promoting bold but risky ideas, making relationships with more inspiration-oriented colleagues a challenge. ESTJs like to feel like they are a part of the team, and a part of the greater organization that they work for. To make sure this happens, ESTJs are nearly always willing to accept criticism that can help to improve their effectiveness, and always keep an eye on their surroundings to make sure they and their team deliver the results that are expected of them.	ESTJs take genuine pleasure in organizing others into effective teams, and as managers they have no better opportunity to do so. While sometimes overbearing, even micromanaging, ESTJs' strong wills also serve to defend their teams and principles against diversions and cutbacks, regardless of who brings them. Laziness and bad work ethic are not tolerated by ESTJs under any circumstances. ESTJs project natural authority, but they sometimes expect this authority to be abided unconditionally, resisting change and demanding that things be done by the book. Whether ESTJs' own book or the existing rules and traditions are used is subject to circumstances, but they do tend to rest on the security of tradition and precedent. Regardless, ESTJs' expectations are clearly expressed, leaving little room or tolerance for deviation from the agenda.

ESTJ at the workplace

Emotional intelligence-wise, ESTJs are confident, realistic in their own abilities and competencies and very disciplined in several areas of their lives, though, ESTJs need to take actions to improve their emotional intelligence in the following areas:

- **Emotional self-awareness and self-management**: For ESTJs, there is no room for emotional interference, either from themselves or from those working with them, only the plan is important and emotions have no place in business. This is a direct consequence of their lack of, or very low emotional self-awareness. To improve this competency, ESTJs should actively assess emotional situations or feelings that are triggered in specific situations, so that they can manage their emotional response accordingly. Being more open and flexible with their own feelings, ideas, and views will also help them improve this emotional intelligence competency.

- **Social awareness and social skills**: The very strict adherence to the organization's plans, goals, and objectives often makes them lack social awareness and social skills causing troubles in a team that does not share the same rigid values and view point. Thus, a great number of ESTJs prefer to work alone, because they feel intimidated by the emotional situations that could arise in the team and the inherent consequences in the outcome of their work. For this reason, ENTJs don't appear to care about making a good first impression (or second or third), focusing only on the outcome of the work. However, ESTJs need the attention of others to provide them with the feedback they need on their accomplishments, otherwise they begin to feel unappreciated. For the sake of the strength of their relationships, ESTJs should start to openly and intentionally show sympathy and empathy toward their colleagues. If ESTJs improve their social awareness and social skills making their peers' emotional wellbeing a priority, they will in turn enhance their own emotional intelligence and become more welcoming, sympathetic, and agreeable to work with.

The ISTJ personality type

People with the ISTJ personality type enjoy taking responsibility for their actions, and take pride in the work. They do not stint on their time and energy and finish each task with accuracy and patience. ISTJs don't make assumptions, preferring instead to analyze their surroundings, check their facts and arrive at practical courses of action. ISTJs have little tolerance for indecisiveness, but lose patience even more quickly if their chosen course is challenged with impractical theories, especially if they ignore key details—if challenges become time-consuming debates. ISTJs can become noticeably angry as deadlines draw nearer.

This sense of personal integrity is core to ISTJs and goes beyond their own minds. ISTJ personalities adhere to established rules and guidelines regardless of cost, reporting their own mistakes, and telling the truth even when the consequences of doing so could be disastrous. To ISTJs, honesty is far more important than emotional considerations, and their blunt approach leaves others with the false impression that ISTJs are cold, or even robotic. People with this type may struggle to express emotion or affection outwardly, but the suggestion that they don't feel, or worse, have no personality at all, is deeply hurtful. ISTJs need to remember to take care of themselves because their stubborn dedication to stability and efficiency can create an emotional stress that can go unexpressed for years, manifesting when it is too late to be treated:

ISTJ	
Strenghts	**Weaknesses**
• Honest and Direct	• Stubborn
• Strong-willed and Dutiful	• Insensitive
• Very Responsible	• Always by the Book
• Calm and Practical	• Judgmental
• Create and Enforce Order	• Often Unreasonably Blame Themselves
• Jacks-of-all-trades	

ISTJ - strengths and weaknesses

When it comes to the workplace, ISTJs are almost a stereotype for the classic, hardworking, and dutiful employee. In all positions, the ISTJ personality type seeks structure, clearly defined rules, and respect for authority and hierarchy. Responsibilities are not burdens to ISTJs, they are the trust that has been placed in them—an opportunity to prove once again that they are the right person for the job. On the other hand, the change that comes with assuming new responsibilities, or in losing old ones, is often a significant struggle for ISTJs. Depending on the position of authority the ISTJ is in—assuming new responsibilities presents as one of the most significant challenges to overcome. However, it is one of ISTJs' most significant challenges to overcome.

Let's learn the main traits of the ENTJ at work as an employee, subordinate and manager with the help of the following chart:

ISTJ		
Subordinates	**Colleagues**	**Managers**
ISTJs crave responsibility, which makes them the go-to subordinates for odds and ends and unpopular projects. Often seen as jacks of all trades, ISTJ personalities can competently tackle any project that comes with a manual. On the other hand, this makes them reluctant to give up responsibilities even when they are overburdened, or when there are better people for the job. The seriousness in ISTJs' approach to their work makes them very sensitive to criticism, leading to some inflexibility. Their stubbornness aside, or perhaps because of it, ISTJs are one of the most productive subordinates because they respect authority and hierarchy, and have no problem following orders and instructions. Punctuality is never a problem, either in terms of showing up to work on time, or in terms of meeting project deadlines. While ISTJs may need clearly set steps and well-defined responsibilities, they are very loyal, dedicated, meticulous and patient in completing their work.	Among colleagues, no one can be trusted more to ensure that projects are finished on time and by the book than ISTJs. Quiet and methodical, the ISTJ keep cool when the going gets tough, but expect their colleagues to share their approach. Significantly different types, especially more emotional ones, baffle ISTJs with their need for emotional support and openness, or capacity for dropping something, half finished. To ISTJs, either something's been done right or it's been done wrong, and sugarcoating it or walking away is not going to fix it. ISTJs value peace and security in the workplace, that is why they love to work alone. Innovations, brainstorming, theories and new ideas all disrupt this comfortable state, and it takes a great deal of respect on ISTJs' part to acknowledge their validity. Once the details have been laid out and a plan of implementation established though, ISTJs are an indispensable part of the team in putting these ideas into practice.	ISTJs love responsibility and the power resulting from it. Pressing themselves hard to meet their obligations, ISTJs regularly go above and beyond their duties, and expect their subordinates to act with the same level of dedication. At the same time, ISTJs' preference for doing things by the book, adherence to hierarchy, and general aversion to innovation makes their subordinates ride a very thin line. It is said that it is better to do first and ask permission later, it is difficult to say whether this applies to ISTJs, as they are very intolerant of their subordinates' failures to meet their obligations, and one of those obligations is to stick to the plan. Believing that truth, at least as far as they see it, is more important than sensitivity. ISTJ personalities are capable of laying down hard criticism, and their willingness to make tough decisions can make perceived insubordination the final trespass.

ISTJ in the workplace

Emotional intelligence-wise, ISTJ's are composed and often internalize their emotions, which every so often can be harmful because when they bottle up their emotions they will overreact when others rub them up the wrong way. Thus, ISTJs need to take actions to improve their emotional intelligence in the following areas:

- **Emotional self-awareness and self-management**: Usually, ISTJs resort to reason to assess their emotions inwardly, and bottle them up, which is not good for their personal wellbeing or to work well in group situations. They should learn how to be more mindful in all areas, how to relax, and how to use more abstract ideas. They should also learn to investigate their emotional triggers at a root level so that they can improve their emotional self-awareness and self-management.

- **Social awareness and social skills**: ISTJ depend so much on their introverted nature, they find it difficult to grasp how others are feeling, so they don't react accordingly, therefore, they can come across as a bit harsh because of their lack of consideration for others, showing their lack of empathy. To improve their social skills, ISTJs need to learn and practice to be more empathetic in the presence of others, by agreeably expressing their feelings, adjusting their reasoning-oriented mind. ISTJs type should open themselves up to the emotions of others while coming to terms with their own emotions, thus helping them to be more receptive to enhancing their emotional intelligence.

The INFJ personality type

INFJs combine a vivid imagination with a strong sense of compassion, and they use their creativity to resolve human challenges. They have the insight to see through dishonesty, disingenuous motives, and how people and events are connected, and they are able to use that insight to get to the heart of the matter. They are inspiring and convincing as they speak in human terms. INFJs have strong beliefs and take actions not because they are trying to advance themselves, but because they are trying to advance an idea that they truly believe will make the world a better place. The INFJ personality type is vulnerable to criticism and conflict, and when someone questions their motives, principles, or values, most probably, their bad side will appear. INFJs are extremely private when it comes to their personal lives, even with close friends. INFJs are perfectionistic, thus they too often drop or ignore healthy and productive situations and relationships, believing that there might be a better option down the road.

INFJs like to know that they are taking concrete steps toward their goals, and if routine tasks feel like they are getting in the way, or worse yet, there is no goal at all, they will feel restless and disappointed. Their passion, poor patience for routine maintenance, tendency to present themselves as an ideal, and extreme privacy tend to leave INFJs with few options for letting off steam.

Thus, they can burnout easily if they don't find a way to balance the reality of the normal daily living with their ideal world.

INFJ	
Strenghts	**Weaknesses**
• Creative	Sensitive
• Insightful	Extremely Private
• Inspiring and Convincing	Perfectionistic
• Decisive	Always Need to Have a Cause
• Determined and Passionate	Can Burn Out Easily
• Altruistic	

INFJ - Strenghts and Weaknesses

In the workplace, INFJs love responsibility and the power resulting from it. Pressing themselves hard to meet their obligations, INFJs regularly go above and beyond their duties, and expect their subordinates to act with the same level of dedication. At the same time, INFJs' preference for doing things by the book, adherence to hierarchy, and general aversion to innovation makes their subordinates negotiate a very thin line—stepping out of bounds must be backed up with just the facts, and results. INFJs are very intolerant of their subordinates' failures to meet their obligations, and one of these obligations is to stick to the plan.

Let's learn the main traits of the ENTJ at work as an employee, subordinate, and manager with the help of the following chart:

INFJ		
Subordinates	**Colleagues**	**Managers**
As subordinates, INFJs are likely to become irritated or annoyed under hardline rules, formal hierarchies and routine tasks. INFJS value diplomacy and sensitivity, and the more democratic and personal their manager's style is, and the more they feel their independence and input are valued, the happier they will be. INFJs act on their convictions, so when they do something, it is something that has meaning to them, if those actions come under criticism, even justified, their morale will rapildy collapse, especially if the feedback was unrequired. A manager's values need to be naturally aligned with their INFJ subordinates for both parties to be most effective. Though usually idealistic, if they feel in conflict, INFJs can lose touch with that sense and end up bitter. But if it is a balance they can handle, with a little encouragement every now and then, INFJs will be hardworking, trustworthy, and more than capable of handling their responsibilities and professional relationships.	As colleagues, INFJs are quite popular, because of their positivity, eloquence their ability to make friends, identify others' motives and defusing conflicts and tension before anyone else even senses a disturbance. INFJs prioritize harmony and cooperation over ruthless efficiency, encouraging a good, hardworking atmosphere and helping others when needed. While this is usually a strength, there is a risk that others will take advantage of INFJs' commitment to their responsibilities by simply shifting their burdens onto their more dedicated INFJ colleagues' desks. Despite their popularity, INFJs are still Introverts (I), and their popularity is not always welcome. They need to step back and act the lone wolf from time to time, pursuing their own goals in their own ways. An unhealthy version of this tendency - withdrawing may pop up when the INFJs sense that their values are being compromised by a ethically relaxed colleague.	As managers, INFJs are often reluctant in exercising their authority, preferring to see their subordinates as equals, coordinating and supervising people, leaving the technical systems and factual details to more capable hands, and working hard to inspire and motivate, not to crack the whip. That's not to say that people with the INFJ personality type have lax standards – far from it – as INFJs' sense of equality means that they expect their subordinates to be as competent, motivated and reliable as the INFJs themselves. Though sensitive, understanding, principled and just, able to appreciate individual styles and to make accurate judgments about others' motivations, if a subordinate's actions or attitude undermines INFJs' ethics or values, they will find little comfort in these qualities. INFJs have no tolerance for lapses in reliability or morality. But, so long as no such lapse occurs, INFJs will work tirelessly to ensure that their subordinates feel valued and happy.

INFJ in the workplace

Emotional intelligence speaking, the INFJs are primarily intrapersonal in their emotional intelligence, understanding complex emotions and moods in others while still keeping their emotions inside, for later self-reflection. Thus, INFJs need to take actions to improve their emotional intelligence in the following areas:

- **Emotional self-expression**: Although the INFJ has a good level of emotional intelligence as they are able to handle their emotions and the emotions of others well, they need to learn how to express their emotions out loud. For instance, when in a group, it would be helpful for INFJ types to try to connect with more people by giving emotional feedback to others. By doing so, they can further their bond with these people. By enhancing these strengths in their emotions and working towards opening up to more people and providing feedback, INFJs can work toward augmenting their emotional intelligence in a positive and effective manner.

- **Social awareness and social skills**: INFJ are very sympathetic and considerate, as well as tolerant of peoples' thoughts, opinions, and beliefs. They make it a point to actively give their confidence to others, and to make others feel confident about themselves, though they could learn how to include themselves more in group situations, especially in the workplace. Even though INFJs are largely skillful at managing their emotions and those of others, they can sometimes become tense or overbearing in big groups, not knowing exactly how to properly manage their emotions and their behavior, especially in a conflict.

The INTP personality type

INTPs see the world as a big and complex machine where everything is interconnected and they love the challenge of analyzing these connections, even if they are a product of their imagination. Their open-mindedness makes them highly receptive to alternative theories as long as they are supported by logic and facts. Regardless of INTPs being very reserved, they can be very enthusiastic when a new idea piques their interest. Though, you can't expect outward fireworks of enthusiasm, a stare into the distance or a silent pacing is more their way of showing enthusiasm. After all, they don't search for emotional validation. They believe that the truth is of the utmost importance thus, most often, they hurt others' feelings with their straightforwardness. Yet, they expect that their honesty is appreciated and reciprocated. INTPs are very shy in any social setting such as parties or networking events, but even close friends might struggle to get into their hearts and minds. INTPs are considered insensitive because they dismiss subjectivity as irrational, failing to show timely sympathy when necessary. They are absent-minded to the extent of forgetting to sleep, rest, eat, and take care of their own health.

If an INTP during a conversation where he is trying to explain one of his brilliant ideas dismisses you with a "never mind," take it as an insult. Their open-mindedness can become a problem when the INTP delays the commitment to a decision with constant revisions and sometimes quitting even before they start.

INTP	
Strenghts	**Weaknesses**
• Great Analysts and Abstract Thinkers • Original and Imaginative • Open-Minded • Enthusiastic • Objective • Honest and Straightforward	• Very Private and Withdrawn • Insensitive • Absent-minded • Condescending • Hates Rules and Guidelines

INTP - strenghts and weaknesses

In the workplace, INTPs, whether they are in the position of colleagues, employees, or managers, love intellectual stimulation, freedom from social obligations, and solitude, though, because they have the tendency to live in their heads and vent inspiration and creativity randomly, they should be paired with a colleague that complements them so that all creativity doesn't get lost. Let's learn with the help of the following chart, the main traits of the INTP at work as an employee, subordinate, and manager:

INTP		
Subordinates	**Colleagues**	**Managers**
Under the right conditions, they are innovative, resourceful, and hard-working, delivering unorthodox but effective solutions. When focused on conceiving new and exciting ideas they ignore the details of execution. A clever manager knows that need to pair the INTP with someone that keep things in order and actually put into practice the often unrefined ideas of the INTP.	For INTPs - colleagues are just a series of obstacles and diversions with occasionally useful knowledge. INTPs love discussing theories with "proven" colleagues, and are available as impromptu consultants. This, however, does not apply to emotional riddles and conflicts in these charged situations, INTP personalities have no clue what to do.	The manager position provides to the INTP the opportunity to direct concepts and theories while others handle the logistics. Their tendency to ignore others' feelings make them very harsh critics as they direct projects according to their perfectionistic standards. They need a delegator who can filter their thoughts and direct their team in more socially productive way.

INTP in the workplace

Emotional intelligence speaking, INTPs are considered emotionally closed off because they choose to ignore their own feelings and the feelings of others in favor of a logical analysis. Frequently, they recognize their emotions, or understand that something emotionally important has happened only after the damage is done. Since they are so fearful about acknowledging and/or sharing their feelings they are very selective about who they choose to associate with on a deeper level than mere acquaintances. Thus, INTPs needs to take action to improve their emotional intelligence in the following areas:

- **Social awareness and social skills**: Regardless of the fact that they are open-minded to others' opinions or thoughts, INTPs often become frustrated, agitated, and even angry when others rely more on their thoughts and feelings to find a solution to a problem, than in logic. In this regard, INTPs need to improve their nonjudgment and acceptance of differences, with kindness, compassion, and mindfulness, even if the INTP finds it illogical or ineffective. The only real way to increase their level of emotional intelligence is to engage more with their emotions and with the emotions of others. Through more exposure and experience dealing with emotions, they will learn how to more accurately navigate them. They surely would significantly benefit from being more open toward the mental and emotional processes of their peers, allowing themselves to open up in response.

Strategies to better manage extroverts and introverts

One of the fundamental differences between extroverts and introverts, in the workplace, is that while introverts think inside their heads, extroverts think out loud. So, while extroverts are talking, they can be working hard to sift through their ideas, to form their opinions and to clarify their thinking. However, the amount of talking involved, and the lack of initial clarity, may annoy other people. What a contrast with introverts who might think quietly to themselves and may leave us feeling frustrated because we don't know what they are thinking. And all the talking that makes the extrovert feel energized, stimulated, and enthusiastic, is draining for introverts. Introverts can also feel that extroverts are wasting their time and feel frustrated, an emotional reaction that may be unhelpful in building a productive working relationship. Extroverts in thinking out loud, may leave people feeling that they cannot be trusted, because they may say things that are only an initial idea that they may quickly be revised.

Guidelines to better managing extroverts

We will now explore guidelines for managing extroverts:

- **Check whether what they said is their final decision**: Extroverts talk things through, thus what they start off saying may not be their ultimate conclusion but only a step in the process toward clarification. Therefore, do not act on what you think is an instruction until you are sure. It could save you a lot of embarrassment if you check in and find out whether what they have said is their final decision or not.

- **Kindly interrupt them**: Extroverts presume you have nothing to say if you are not contributing to the conversation thus, they keep going but wish that you would add your contribution. Meanwhile, if you are an introvert, you may be sitting there wishing they would pause to let you in. Kindly jump in and add your contribution and if they interrupt back, read it as a sign of enthusiasm, not a sign that they are not interested in your input and join back in again! Become more confident at jumping into a conversation.

- **Share more personal things with your extrovert**: Extroverts are often willing to talk about themselves and their lives and can find the introvert secretive in contrast. Thus, share with them things about yourself, they will assume you trust them. Extroverts may think introverts don't trust them or are being deliberately withdrawn or arrogant. Feel at ease talking to them. On the other hand, If you are an introvert, make sure you tell your extrovert when information is not to be discussed or disclosed to others.

- **Kindly ask the introvert to contribute to the conversation**: If you at a meeting or dinner date, invite introverts to contribute, don't wait for them to speak over the top of you because, they will not do it.

Guidelines to better managing introverts

Sadly, work environments do not always support the introvert's style and this can impact on their productivity and effectiveness. When this occurs, it can produce a range of emotional responses, which is why developing more emotional intelligence at work can help introverts. There are so many situations such as noise, the talking, the constant interruptions, and so on that make it difficult for introverts to concentrate and think things through.

Yet introverts are people who are skilled at thinking things through and working steadfastly on tasks and through problems.

- **Time to think**: If one of your colleagues or manager needs an important decision from you, ask them for time to think, for example, you might say, "I need to think this over, can I get back to you in half an hour?" or "This is an important decision, I need to gather all the facts and get back to you tomorrow, if that is ok with you?" This strategy can help you feel less pressurized.
- **Written information**: Introverts like to read things and think them over. So, if you are an introvert, ask for written information before giving your input. If you are the manager of the introvert, provide written information and time before asking for their input. For instance, if you are preparing to brainstorm or preparing for a meeting where the input of your introvert will be required, send them the agenda of the meeting two days in advance.
- **Speak louder**: Introverts tend to speak more quietly than extroverts; thus, they may not be heard or be disregarded during a meeting or a brainstorming session. If you need to get your point across at a meeting, for example, you may need to temporarily raise the volume of your voice. Practice at home in front of a mirror. This is also one of the ways of practicing and improving your emotional intelligence.
- **I don't know**: If you anticipate difficult questions in a presentation and are feeling anxious about thinking on your feet, then you can say, "I don't know the answer right now. I will personally e-mail you the information as soon as I am back in the office and analyze the information." No one loses face and you can feel more confident in handling any question.

We can summarize the preceding points as shown in the following figure:

HOW TO MANAGE EXTROVERTS	HOW TO MANAGE INTROVERTS
• Let them dive right into the project/work • Encourage their enthusiasm • They think out loud - let them speak • Listen to their many ideas • Let them multitask • Respect their independent nature • Let them SHINE	• Let them think to speak • Give them time to make decisions • Respect their private nature • Appreciate their need to work alone • Carefully listen to them • Help them learn at their own pace • Let them SHINE

Basic guidelines in how to manage extroverts and introverts

Summary

In this chapter, we have learned how important it is for an IT manager to have a good level of emotional intelligence that enables him to know himself and to know and manage his people. We have learned the emotional intelligence of the five most challenging MBTI personality types: ESTJ, ENTJ, ISTJ, INFJ, and INTP that are found with more frequency in positions of managers, leaders, and high achieving employees in the IT area. We have learned the strengths and weakness of these five personality types. We have learned how these five personality types are seen in the workplace as employees, subordinates, and managers. We have learned how they can improve their emotional intelligence skills to be easier to work with them. We have learned how to manage extroverts and introverts at work to have a great workplace environment and increase productivity.

In this chapter, we have learned how important it is for an IT manager to have a good level of emotional intelligence that enables him to know himself and to know and manage his people. We have learned the emotional intelligence of the five most challenging MBTI personality types: ESTJ, ENTJ, ISTJ, INFJ, and INTP that are found with more frequency in positions of managers, leaders, and high achieving employees in the IT area. We have learned the strengths and weakness of these five personality types. We have learned how these five personality types are seen in the workplace as employees, subordinates, and managers. We have learned how they can improve their emotional intelligence skills to be easier to work with them. We have learned how to manage extroverts and introverts at work to have a great workplace environment and increase productivity.

6

How to Be an Emotionally Intelligent IT Leader

In this chapter, we will cover the leadership of the future in the IT domain, and the proper mindset that a leader of the future in IT needs to have so he/she can successfully lead their people through a vulnerable, uncertain, complex and ambiguous world. We will also cover the six emotionally intelligent leadership styles, looking at their pros and cons. Finally, we will cover the three dimensions of the 3D model of emotional intelligent leadership of the future.

- What is the leadership of the future?
- The mindset of the emotional intelligent leader of the future
- The six emotional intelligent leadership styles
- The 3D leadership of the future

What is the leadership of the future?

Leadership is about nurturing and enhancing. As Managers manage things, and leaders lead people.

When talking about leadership in the IT domain, we need to bear in mind that we are talking about the leadership of the future, which does not necessarily have anything to do with the concepts and practices of the leaderships of the past. Leadership of the future is not a position, a title, or seniority in the organization. Leadership of the future might even be outside of the organization.

Tech leaders of the future need to think globally. Leaders of the past tended to be domestic, managing people in their own country, in their own region. The local leader didn't have to think about people around the globe. Today, with globalization and the new technologies, where leadership has become global, this is an obsolete vision. Moreover, in the IT area, even if your organization is local, you will have global customers and global suppliers and even global employees, shareholders, and stakeholders. Thus, global thinking has become one of the qualities of the leader of the future. Thus the leader of the future needs to appreciate and nurture multiculturalism as organizations of the future are more and more multicultural. The leader of the future needs to look for the diversity of his followers: cultural diversity, gender diversity, background diversity.

IT leaders of the future need to be technologically savvy--this means that the leader of the future needs to understand technology and understand how the most important technology is going to impact and change our lives, our values, our behaviors, the logistics of the business, marketing, and so on. Thus, the leader of the future needs to be constantly updated with the new technology. And under this umbrella, he/she also needs to follow the new social media presence, not only of the organization, but also the social media presence of the leader.

The IT leader of the future needs to know how to build alliances and partnerships--this means building alliances outside and inside the organization. More and more, in the new world, your direct reports are going to be your partners. Build partnerships with peers across the organization and outside the organization, build partnerships with your customers, with your suppliers, and even with your competitors.

Finally, the IT leadership of the future is a shared leadership. The leader of the past needed to know how to give orders, but the leader of the future needs to learn how to make questions and ask for help. This a very specific leadership quality for an IT leader as you are managing knowledge workers who know more than you about their work. Therefore, you cannot simply tell them what to do. You have to ask, you have to listen, and you have to learn.

The IT leadership of the future needs to be a 3D leadership. What do I mean by 3D leadership? When looking to the most basic traits of success in a leader of the future, we can easily identify three dimensions of leadership. The self (self-development), relationships (social awareness), and service (social skills).

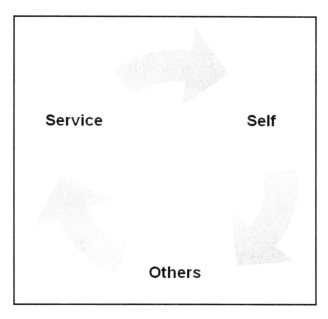

3 dimensions of leadership

A 3D IT leadership of the future is necessarily an emotional intelligent leadership as each of the parts of the triad is a set of the emotional intelligence competencies and skills.

The mindset of the emotionally intelligent leader of the future

The leader of the future, especially in the IT domain, is someone who needs special competencies. His technical knowledge is not enough to help him to success in a volatile, uncertain, complex, and ambiguous world, where the rate of change of the average lifespan of an organization went from the 75 years to 18 years, where the advances in technology, moreover the convergence of several devices in only one with the same utilities, is rampant. This is a world where in the same workplace several generations live and work side by side in constant change--different values, different expectations, and fresh new mindsets brought by the new generations. This is a world where automation is resulting in a heavy disruption of the organizations and society's ways of working and living, as almost everything is increasingly being automated.

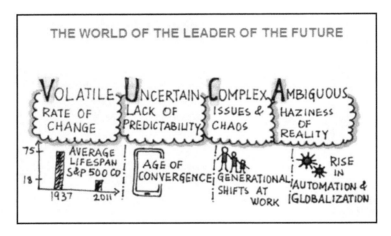

The world of the leader of the future (VUCA) (Source:QAspire.com)

In this world, having a compelling purpose is a mandatory pre-requisite for profits to follow. Traditional hierarchical structures are fading away to give place to purposeful networks and communities of people working together to achieve a shared purpose. Thus there has been an increase of the holacracy systems in organizations due to their flat organizational governance, in which authority and decision-making are distributed throughout a holacracy of self-organizing teams rather than being vested in a management hierarchy. The cumulative impact of these forces demands a new mindset and new competencies, that is, emotional intelligence competencies, for leaders to be able to stay relevant and make a positive difference to people and, hence, business.

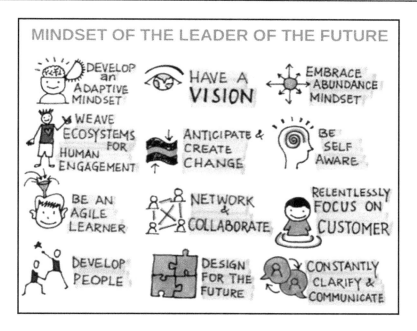

VUCA mindset (Source:QAspire.com)

If you are a leader at any level in a modern organization or aspiring to be one, in tandem with emotional intelligence competencies and skills, you certainly need to have or develop a **VUCA** mindset:

- **Develop an adaptive mindset**: The leader of the future, because of his vision and designing the future, will be in many situations, and the first *man on the moon*. Thus, he needs to be comfortable with change, unexplored paths, and unknown situations.

- **Weave ecosystems for human engagement**: The leader of the future knows that in order to build engaged human communities, he needs to tap into the intrinsic motivation of his people. Because intrinsic motivation taps into the basic drivers of human engagement, such as trust, hope, sense of self-worth, and feeling competent. We need leaders who can build trust through integrity and results, who can mentor and coach others, and who can clarify the meaning of the work people do and build a positive influence.

- **Be an agile learner**: Leaders of the future in a VUCA world need to have a beginner's mind--the curiosity of a child exploring a new world, getting immersed in new experiences as a way to unlearn the familiar approaches and learn new approaches in a more effective and organic way.

- **Develop people**: Having followers is good but if a leader does not empower the followers to be leaders, then he is just a shepherd of a flock of people. Leaders, in this world, have to role-model the behaviors they seek, help people in building their skillset and attitude, create learning forums, design work to tap into potential and, most importantly, lead through their influence and not through their authority.

- **Have a vision**: A compelling vision is the pre-requisite to any community, organization or team to thrive in the future because a compelling vision for the future is the key driver to engage and retain high performing team members.

- **Anticipate and create change**: In a VUCA world, change is fast and constant, and if the leader of the future wants to be in the front row he needs to have a strategic foresight to create change before an external change forces him to react. And, of course, he needs to engage his people in the change process from the beginning.

- **Network and collaborate**: The leader of the future needs to have a social mindset, as he knows that social media and in-person communication are sacred to create collaborative bonds, and a purposeful business.

- **Design for the future**: Organizations are purposeful networks of people; thus, the leader of the future needs to be aware that to design the future we need a compelling purpose that people in the organization share.

- **Embrace an abundance mindset**: An abundance mindset sees possibilities where a constraint mindset sees challenges. In a VUCA world, leaders need to have strategic foresight without losing the sight of the current reality. They need to have a unique ability to see through contradictions towards a future others cannot see.

- **Be self-aware**: It is only when leaders are aware of their preferences, ways of working, and possible blind spots that they can really bring their true authentic selves into the game and bring about a significant difference to the team, organization, and hence the industry.

- **Relentlessly focus on customer**: The leader of the future knows that he needs to be a customer centric leader. This means truly listening to the voice of customers, engaging deeply, and building long-term relationships by adding substantial value to the customers.

- **Constantly clarify and communicate**: Communication and clarity are the currencies of effective leadership when working with a multicultural and multi-disciplinary workforce, where every worker is also a leader and an influence. Thus, the leader of the future needs to have the ability to communicate effectively across cultures, re-iterate and reinforce vision, values and strategies, and help others in clarifying the meaning of their work.

The six emotional intelligent leadership styles

In 2002, Goleman, Boyatzis, and McKee conducted research for 3 years for the Harvard Business Review, with over 3,000 middle-level managers. Their goal was to uncover specific leadership behaviors and determine their effect on the corporate climate and each leadership style's effect on bottom-line profitability. Goleman found that leaders used six styles of leadership interchangeably:

- Commanding style
- Visionary style
- Affiliative style
- Democratic style
- Pace setting style
- Coaching style

Each of the styles comes from the use of emotional intelligence: being acutely aware of the environment, emotional needs, and feelings and adjusting the style to suit the most appropriate setting. These models summarize the techniques, scenarios of when they work best, and the impact on the organization and its goals.

However, critiques of some of these leadership styles need to be addressed. For instance, the commanding and pace setting styles, despite their use, can damage the organization's working environment in the long term. Consequentially, they will affect employee satisfaction and retention and lower profitability. These two types of leadership, though, are useful only in very specific situations and in a very small frame of time. We will learn more about them in case you want to use them when required.

The other four styles of leadership have a proven positive impact on the working environment and also performance, though they also need to be used carefully as they miss the more important traits of an emotional intelligence leadership of the future. Yet, the most effective leader is one who can master at least four of the styles, and who can use the style to suit the situation. Remember, even the commanding and pace setting roles have their uses you just have to use them only when the situation dictates.

Let's learn more about each of the six emotional intelligent leadership styles.

Commanding leadership style

The commanding leadership style demands immediate compliance to its orders--*Do what I tell you, without questioning.* Though the commanding leadership style is the most aggressive, it is also the most effective in times of crisis. It is a style that accomplishes tasks by ordering and dictating, even demeaning followers at times.

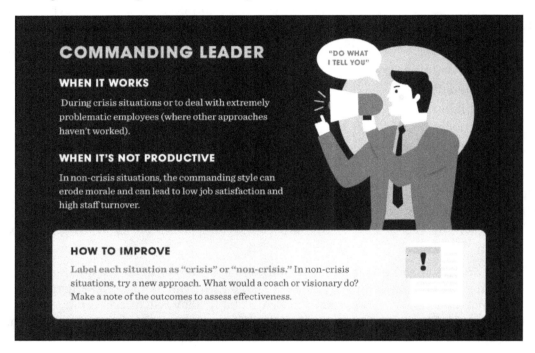

Commanding leadership style

This style is best used in situations where the organization or followers require a complete turnaround attempt which is quite urgent and there is no real time for active group discussions, such as in a crisis, during a disaster, and enforced health and safety compliance improvements under law. The pros and cons are as following:

- **Pros:** Soothes fear by giving clear direction in an emergency
- **Cons:** Drives away talent and contaminates everyone's mood (as emotions are contagious)

This style should only be used for short time frames, just to get the job done, as the long-term impact can be negative.

Visionary leadership style

The visionary leadership style, as seen in the following image, is also known as the authoritative style.

Visionary leadership style

Here, the leader establishes him/herself as being the expert in the company and knows how to inspire and mobilize the team towards a common vision. This is a visionary who sees the way forward, leading the company to success. Following are the pros and cons:

- **Pros**: Moves people towards a common vision
- **Cons**: May lack the ability to help the team members understand how to achieve the vision

This style is particularly effective in times when a new direction is needed. However, use it with caution.

Affiliative leadership style

The affiliate leadership style is renowned for building teams for putting employees first.

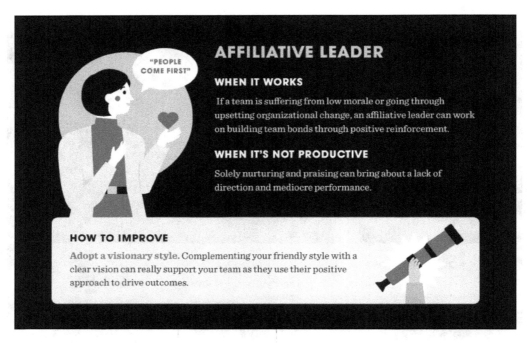

Affiliative leadership style

Employees can expect a great deal of praise and feedback and there is normally a good sense of interconnection with the team. Following are the pros and cons:

- **Pros**: This style is most effective when there are situations of low morale and poor teamwork. Using this method will, in the longer term, create good team bonding and heightened team performance.
- **Cons**: Poor performance will go by without feedback as the leader may feel that conflict will upset the balance.

In this style of leadership, the leader needs to improve feedback and feed-forward skills and adjust their style to suit when necessary.

Democratic leadership style

The democratic leadership style will use the team as decision makers, taking the team vote to make decisions and improvements. Communication is key in this model, as all opinions are listened to as a group.

Democratic leadership style

The democratic leader is merely the chair for effective team decision making. When and only when the workplace is ready for democratic leaders, does this style produce a work environment that employees can feel good about with heightened morale levels. Workers feel that their opinions count, and because of that feeling they are more committed to achieving the goals and objectives of the organization. Following are the pros and cons:

- **Pros**: Values people's inputs and gets commitment through participation
- **Cons**: Sometimes lacks effective action

Pace setting leadership style

The pace setting leadership style its extremely effective only when employees are self-motivated and are highly skilled. These leaders set very high performance standards for themselves and the group and epitomize the behaviors they are seeking from other members of the group.

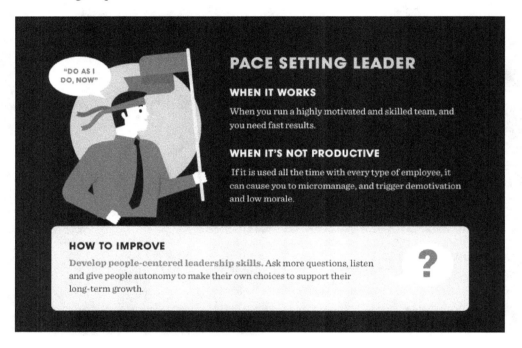

Pace setting leadership style

The pace setting leadership style is useful when a group has been functioning together as an effective team for a while and are now performing in a good team culture. At this point, the leader may wish to step things up and move to a new level of performance for a project or short-term goal.

Following are the pros and cons:

- **Pros:** Gets high-quality results from motivated and competent teams: for example, sales teams.
- **Cons:** Can lack emotional intelligence. Like the commanding leadership style, the pace setting leadership style cannot be sustained for a long time as workers can often burn out due to its demanding pace.

Coaching leadership style

In the coaching leadership style, the leader focuses purely on helping others in their personal development, and in their job-related activities towards a goal.

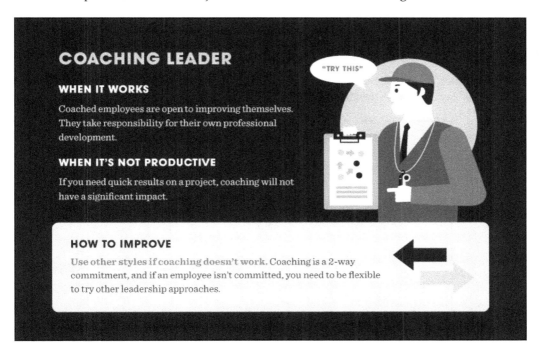

Coaching leadership style

With the use of this style, the leader helps team members upskill and become successful in their development, working closely with coaching, developing, and mentoring them to ensure they have the knowledge and skills to be successful. Following are the pros and cons:

- **Pros**: Helps competent, motivated employees improve performance by building long-term capabilities
- **Cons**: Can come across as micromanaging, when over used

If used well, this is, however, an effective style to develop a learning organization.

A leader with a good score in several emotional intelligent competencies and skills knows that any of these leadership styles are only beneficial when used in a situational leadership context. Therefore, they don't use them as their sample style.

Do you know your type of leadership?

Everyone has their own built-in approach to leading others. Do you know what yours is? Answer the following questions to get to know your leadership style:

Your leadership style scheme

Your leadership style is a part of who you are. The most effective leaders, however, know how to use all these leadership styles and adapt them to the situation. Not every leadership style is effective in every situation, or with every employee. Just as you lead differently, each of your followers responds in their own way. Also, every situation requires its own approach.

Now that you have become familiar with the six styles of emotional intelligence leadership, you can identify your own style and even adapt to the situation at hand. Leadership can and should be situational, depending on the needs of the team. Sometimes a teammate needs a warm hug. Sometimes the team needs a visionary, a new style of coaching. For that reason, great leaders choose their leadership style like a golfer chooses his or her club, with a calculated analysis of the matter at hand, the end goal, and the best tool for the job. Your leadership style is a part of who you are. That is why if you want to be a leader of the future, and build leaders of the future, with vision, and influence, you should be able to be a change catalyst and a guru of your time.

You need to personalize your leadership style and take it to another level. None of the six emotional leadership styles are enough. The leader of the future needs to be a tri-dimensional leader. How? Are you asking me? We will learn it right now!

The 3D leadership of the future

When I mention that the leader of the future needs to be a 3D leader, it is because you need to develop three areas of yourself and, therefore, of your leadership style. You need to start to develop a resilient and balanced **SELF** (self-awareness and self-management), you need to develop your understanding of others and build relationships and partnerships with others, thus you need to develop your social awareness, and finally, you need to develop your social skills as a great successful leader is the one that is always in the service of his organization and the world at large. We will learn about each of these parts and how to enhance each of them and make this triad of development work as a propeller.

Each part is connected to the other and working on the right balance between these three parts of this propeller will propel you higher and higher, creating a rippling effect that makes people follow you and role model you as a leader and human being.

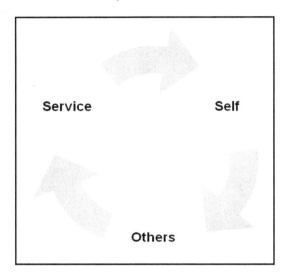

Model of the 3D leadership of the future

Self (first dimension)

We learned in Chapter 3, *Core Emotional Intelligence Skills IT Professionals Need* about the core competencies of emotional intelligence and how to develop them. We also learned that the steps of the base of the EI pyramid are emotional self-awareness and emotional self-management. In Chapter 3, *Core Emotional Intelligence Skills IT Professionals Need* we had a general approach to these core emotional intelligence competencies. Now, as these emotional intelligent competencies are sacred for a balanced leader, we are going to approach them at a more advanced level:

The dual self

Self-awareness

Self-awareness is about understanding ourselves. It is about the realization that we are the source of our own success based on how we think and react to the emotional triggers in our daily life. Knowing our tendencies, actions, and reactions is important, since they hold the key to our outcomes. How we think leads to how we speak, and to how we act and react when triggered by a situation. Therefore, it is so important to learn how to develop this super-power that can turn us into a peak performance professional. To master the emotional intelligence competence of self-awareness, you need to work and develop the three core skills of this power.

Let's learn what these three core skills are and strategies to enhance them:

SELF-AWARENESS SKILLS

Confidence

It's in the top because only when one is
consciously aware of one's emotional triggers
and understand how they manifest one is in
control.

Accurate Self-Assessment

Assess with accuracy how one's emotions are affecting
one's performance, behaviors and relationships.

Accurate Self-Awareness

It's in the base of the pyramid as one needs to be always aware of
one's emotional triggers, thought and behaviour patterns, inner
strenghts & weaknesses

Self-awareness skills pyramid

Strategies to enhance accurate self-awareness

Accurate self-awareness is the base of the self-awareness pyramid because it is the primal need to be aware of one's emotional triggers, thought patterns, behaviours, inner strengths and weaknesses.

Leaders with an accurate self-awareness are able to know at any time, which emotions they are feeling and why they are feeling them, without judgment. An emotional intelligent leader with a high score in accurate self-awareness can easily recognize how their emotions and feelings are affecting their performance and the team work or the environment. They are able to connect the dots and build the links between their feelings and what they think, do and say. On the other hand, leaders who lack emotional self-awareness, often feel stressed and overwhelmed, because they don't know how to establish priorities--health, family, and a balanced work life. They easily get irritated, frustrated or angry and even treat others in an abrasive manner. They are a toxic people and they contaminate others with their toxicity. To build or enhance your accurate self-awareness skills, consistently, practice the following recommendations:

- **Use a self-awareness journal**: Schedule time to practice checking in your emotions regularly, in order to get in the habit of flexing your *identifying* muscles. Bedtime would be a good time to start. Sit quietly, close your eyes and take a deep breath. Ask yourself the following set of questions answer them honestly. There is no right or wrong answer. Just listen to your responses. Self-reflection is a typical activity of leaders with high emotional intelligence. Write your answers in a self-awareness journal. Use a paper one, not a digital journal.
  - How am I feeling now?
  - What am I feeling?
  - Where in my body is the feeling manifesting itself?
  - How long have I been feeling this way?

- **Mindfulness**: Be mindful of the feelings in your body. Be consciously present when your feelings like waves hit the shore. Sense them without judgment. Don't get stuck in an antagonistic relationship with your emotions, thinking of them as bad and something that we should suppress. They only take from 6 to 19 seconds to go away. However, they left you a message, they left you data. They exist to help us. Overcoming this mindset that there are good and bad emotions is one of the hardest parts of practicing emotional intelligence, but it's also extremely liberating. Once you truly make emotions your ally, you are empowered to take control of your life. The first step is acknowledging that emotions are providing you with valuable information.

- **Name your emotion** - Naming is taming. When you feel yourself reacting to a situation, take time to yourself, do some deep breathing to calm down, and name your emotion. Research has proven that naming emotions is an incredibly effective method for reducing the intensity of an emotion. Naming emotions to yourself helps, and naming them out loud helps even more. By bridging the gap between thoughts and feelings, naming emotions helps provide distance between the default, "I am anxious..." to a much less overwhelming "I am feeling anxious". Try to verbalize the emotion - "I am feeling really anxious right now. I can feel it in my stomach and my back. What is the anxiety trying to tell me?". Acknowledging your emotions as they occur gives you more opportunities to learn about yourself by connecting emotions to their causes. The next set of questions will help you to identify your triggers:
    - When did this feeling first start?
    - What was happening when the feeling started?
    - Has its strength changed?
    - How has the strength changed?

- **Explore what the emotion is telling you**: First you identified your emotion with a label, now you are exploring what the emotion is telling you. Make sure that you are dealing with the full emotional story. In a calm state of mind and in a peaceful environment dive deep into your emotions and feelings. Often we feel an emotion that is only the tip of everything that we are feeling. Use the following set of questions to guide you throughout this dive:
    - What's underneath my anxiety?
    - Am I anxious because I feel vulnerable or out of control?
    - Am I anxious because someone has made me look bad and I think others will laugh at me?
    - Am I anxious because I accepted that work assignment even though I really didn't want to?

All of these roots of your anxiety are different, but the resulting emotion is the same. So you need to be willing to look beyond the initial emotion and explore what else you might be feeling, so you can learn how to manage your emotions. Otherwise, you are just addressing a symptom, not the root cause.

Strategies to enhance accurate self-assessment

Accurate self-assessment is the ability to accurately assess how your emotions are affecting your performance, behaviours and relationships.

Leaders with an accurate self-assessment accept their weaknesses and failures as their current state, not their inevitable reality. They are life-learners who are open to new perspectives. Their passion for learning and growth keeps them looking for areas to change and improve. They learn from experiences by reflecting on the situations, hence they know very well what they can and cannot do. They are open to and even proactively seek out feedback from others. They want to ensure that they have all the information possible for their self-assessment. Leaders who cannot admit mistakes, take criticism, or even candid feedback, micromanage others, don't ask for help, and are competitive instead of collaborative. They always want to be *right*, blame others for their mistakes and exaggerate their own value and contribution to the teamwork. These are leaders without self-assessment. To build or enhance your accurate self-assessment skills, consistently, practice the following recommendations:

- **Ask for feedback**: We all have blind spots, thinking patterns, and behaviors. Asking for regular constructive feedback cuts through any self-deceit or one-dimensional views one might hold. Use a 360 assessment or use the following set of questions when asking for constructive feedback:
    - **What suggestions do you have for me to be a better leader?**: What ideas/suggestions do you have for me that can help me be more effective in my work?
    - **Where are we going?**: (As the CEO of the organization, I see where we are going. Where do you think we should be going?) Have this open minded two-way conversation with your direct reports to have the feedback if everyone in the organization is sharing the same vision as you or what you need to change.

Strategies to enhance confidence

Confidence is the top of the self-aware pyramid because only when you are consciously aware of your emotional triggers and understand how they manifest, are you in control.

A self-confident leader knows that he is the only one accountable for the direction and outcomes of his life. Self-confident leaders have an inner conviction about who they are and what they want, that makes them go get the things they want and need in their life. However they also understand what they can control and accept the things that they cannot control. They know their own value and capabilities and don't mind expressing with politeness an unpopular opinion if it is what they truly believe. Leaders who lack self-confidence can never be at the top of the pyramid as they lack confidence in their own judgment. Hence, they avoid challenges and confrontations with people at all costs, even if it will solve a problem, such as speaking the truth to the authority in power. They don't know how to set personal boundaries and demand to be treated with respect from others.

Leaders that are self-confident still consistently work on their strengths and weaknesses. In my coaching programs, I advise delegates to work on personal and social strengths and weaknesses, using the following frame:

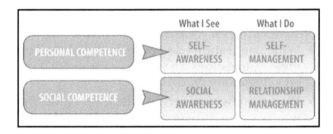

Personal competencies vs. social competencies

- Start a confidence journal and use the frame to make your strengths and weaknesses list:
    - In the strength column, make a list of your significant achievements. These are the areas you excel in already, and you can get additional areas of strengths from your feedback sessions. You can refer to this list when you need to remind yourself of all the things you are good at. Just be sure to keep it updated.
    - In the weaknesses column, make a list of the areas you want to improve.

Attention: Use the weakness list to track the progress of the areas you started to work to improve after receiving the constructive feedback from your peers and direct reports. Eventually, you can move some of these weaknesses over to your strengths list. Seeing that you achieved something boosts your confidence. After finishing your honest listing of strengths and weaknesses, you become more confident and increase your score of self-awareness and self-management, because you become more aware of your emotional triggers. YES! Some of our strengths can be emotional triggers.

- **Practice being assertive**: Saying no is not about being rude, uncaring, or aggressive. Start saying no by first saying, thank you!. Saying no is a skill that helps you to stop becoming overwhelmed by taking on too much, and to gain the respect of other people. Instead of saying "I'm sorry I can't, I'm busy", drop off the reasoning and politely say, "Thank you, no. I won't be able to help you". Sometimes reasons may be needed. Though you need to be able to have the choice as to when you give them and not just to give them automatically. Use a pleasant, warm voice tone throughout. It is easy to sound sarcastic but sarcasm can sour relationships. And stick to what you say and repeat it. Usually, after about three attempts, people stop trying to persuade you otherwise.

- **Start your day with a power pose**: Make it a habit each morning, stand in a high power pose for 2 minutes--this will boost your confidence. While doing your power posture, close your eyes and breathe in deeply for a count of three, hold for one, and then breathe out fully for a count of five. Combining breathing exercises, meditation, and power poses relaxes you and gives you not only a confidence boost but also a powerful boost to start the day. It is scientifically proven that this routine increases testosterone by 20 percent and decreases cortisol (stress hormone) by 25 percent. Hope you are inspired.

Power poses to increase confidence

Self-management

Self-management is the ability of effectively managing one's own emotions and how they impact our decisions and behaviours.

Change is a constant in the world, and the IT world even more. Thus, at all levels, leaders who know how to effectively self-manage their own emotions and how they impact on their own decision-making process and consequent behavior thrive on these changes. When a new database system is announced, for instance, a self-regulating leader will steer clear of a snap judgment, focus on the steps for implementation, and lead the way by example. More positive attitudes at the top mean more positive attitudes throughout the organization.

Self-management skills pyramid

Strategies to enhance self-control

Self-control is the ability to keep disruptive emotions and impulses under control. However, do not over control, ignore or repress the emotions.

Leaders with emotional self-control are able to remove themselves from the situation in which they are experiencing destructive emotions, such as fury and exasperation, until they have returned to a more productive state so that no one gets harmed. In a leadership position, emotional self-control helps the leader to build long-term relationships, gain the respect of the team, colleagues, peers, and so on, and build trust. Leaders who lack emotional self-control are reckless, irresponsible, blame others and the circumstances, and don't know how to take steps to reduce the impact of negative emotions on the team or organization. They hijack meetings with their outbursts of anger. To build or enhance your self-control, consistently, practice the following recommendations:

- **Deep breathing**: If you focus on the rhythm and the smoothness of your breathing, the production of cortisol and adrenaline will stop.
    - Inhale, counting 1, 2, 3, and 4, and then exhale, counting 1, 2, 3, 4, 5, and 6. Inhale again, counting 1, 2, 3, and 4, and then exhale again, counting 1, 2, 3, 4, 5, and 6 this establishes rhythm.
    - At the same time, keep the volume of the breath consistent as it moves in and out, like sipping liquid through a narrow straw. If you manage those two qualities for just a few minutes, the breath assists us in remaining present, making it possible to stay with the intense sensation in the body.
- **Reflection**: To help you identify from where your strong reaction is coming from, take a moment and ask yourself the following set of questions:
    - **Is this situation really a threat?**: Our knee-jerk reaction may be an over-reaction. Take a moment to determine whether or not there is really a threat to something you value. Is the severity of your reaction truly warranted?
    - **What action would be best in this situation?**: Identify the action or behavior that would be best in the situation. For instance, take a break, take a walk, have a conversation with the other person (or people) involved, apologize, calming down and then coming back to listen, or just walking away. By identifying what you should do, you are also identifying what you should not do.
    - **What do I need in order to be able to take that action?**: Do you need more time? Do you need more information? Do you need to de-stress? You don't want to attempt to take the right action if you aren't in the right mindset or don't have all the tools you need in order to be successful.

- **Reframing**: With strong emotional reactions often comes negative self-talk. You can start to practice positive self-talking by using the following positive sentences:

  - I made an honest mistake. That's frustrating, but I can certainly fix it.
  - I need to take a break so my frustration doesn't prevent me from doing a good job I'm not in a good mood today.
  - My ideas aren't always the ones chosen. I need to get honest feedback on that last idea.
  - Let me make sure I have fully understood the goal.

- **Rehearsal**: Consider how you would like the action to take place in detail and then rehearse it in your mind or out loud, so you can build your confidence. For example, suppose you are going to have a serious talk with your team manager about a problem you are having with another teammate: What would be the best environment in which to have the talk? Will you sit or stand? How will you start the conversation? What should your body language look like? What about your facial expression? What are the important points that you need to make, or what are the key pieces of information that you need to get? If it is helpful, you can write an outline or list in order to assist you with your rehearsal.

Strategies to enhance trustworthiness

Trustworthiness is the ability to consistently display honesty and integrity.

Leaders who are trustworthy are leaders who consistently display honesty and integrity. Meaning, that they will make promises and keep them. And when they cannot fulfil their promises they provide an honest and timely explanation. They surround themselves with people of influence, read books, and listen to motivational seminars. Leaders who lack integrity are selfish, they harm their people, they change their opinion to please the public opinion and to be liked. To build or enhance your trustworthiness, consistently practice the following recommendations:

- **Lead by example**: Leading by example is the best strategy to build trust with others, with your team, and to build a culture of trust. Show them that you trust them and they will reciprocate and build a trust culture.
- **Communicate honestly and openly**: By setting an example, stimulate your team, colleagues, peers, and stakeholders to talk with each other in an honest and meaningful way. Encourage them to ask questions, discuss the team expectations, and listen actively.

- **Organize team building**: To encourage the participants to open up and start talking to each other in an open an honest way. *Walk the talk* whenever you have important or relevant information to share, do it openly and immediately. The more you share with your team and the more you prove that you have no hidden agenda, the more comfortable they will feel trusting you and each other.

- **Socialize with your team**: Lunch with them, organize a m*eet and greet*, ask about their families,about their hobbies. Show genuine interest in your people and what is important for them.

- **Prevent groups inside your team**: This kind of group undermines trust in all the team. Have an open conversation with your team about these groups to prevent them.

- **Openly talk about trust**: If you feel that your team is having trust issues, the best way to address it is to run an anonymous survey, and, afterwards, schedule open meet-ups to talk about the issues.

Trust in virtual teams

Managing a group of people that most probably never met face to face or who have never spoken to one another personally is a leadership challenge. However, you can apply the same recommendations as were indicated previously, plus some little changes, that we will cover now:

- Create a webpage or FB group or any other online idea you have only for your team--where every member of the team can have a personal profile.

- Every week or fortnight have a virtual meet and greet to help everyone get to know one another as individuals.

- Have a team charter with the goals and expectations of the team, with an organogram so everyone knows each other's role as well as processes for submitting work digitally.

- Have rules as if the team was working face to face, such as, be on time for conference calls or web meetings, and let the rest of the team know when someone will be absent, or on vacation.

- Lead by example by following through on the promises you make. In a virtual team, keeping your promises is the foundation stone of trust, productivity, efficiency, happiness and pride.

Strategies to enhance conscientiousness

Conscientiousness is the ability to manage your emotions and responsibilities.

Leaders with conscientiousness take ownership of their own emotions and responsibilities. By taking conscientious ownership of your emotions, you have options. You are not at the mercy of others; you are in control. This gives you the power to decide what to do or say next. A leader that lacks conscientiousness does not have ownership of his emotions and responsibilities, blames others, has a poor follow through, and is disorganized in his work and personal life. You can easily spot one as they are chronically late, and are constantly missing appointments, breaking promises, and letting others down. Conscientiousness is a scale and all you need to do is work on moving up the scale until you reach the point at which you are getting the results that you want from life. To build or enhance your conscientiousness skills, consistently, practice the following:

- **Enhance your emotional self-management**: Develop the skill of managing your own emotions and their consequences in your decision-making process.
- **Set goals**: Conscientious leaders are goal oriented--sit down and set some goals that are important to you, and create a plan for achieving those goals.
- **Plan your day**: Take 5 minutes at night and plan your next day. Create a realistic daily schedule, and stick to it.
- **Be punctual**: By being punctual, you show respect for your time and for the people that work and live with you.
- **Always finish your tasks**: Create the habit of sticking to a task, project, or goal, until you cross the finish line.
- **Don't commit to more than you can handle**: When you make a commitment to do something, uphold your commitment.
- **Be perseverant**: Conscientious leaders have grit; they persevere until they get the job done.
- **Bring order to your working space**: Start by decluttering your working space and then create a cleaning schedule that works for you. Take a few minutes to clear your desk before you leave work each evening.
- **Be respectful of others**: Brush up on your etiquette and pay more attention to how your behavior affects others.

- **Meet deadlines**: Stop procrastinating and start handing assignments in on time and meeting project deadlines.
- **Follow a sleep schedule**: Ensure that you get enough sleep, and get up when the alarm goes off.
- **Exercise on a regular basis**: Take up a physical activity that you enjoy and do it on a regular basis make it a routine.

Strategies to enhance adaptability

Adaptability is the ability to adjust to change and overcome obstacles.

To stay competitive, today's leaders must change and conform to the latest standards on a nearly real-time basis. This calls for increased focus on developing and establishing the traits of flexibility and adaptability into all levels of the workforce hierarchy. Resistance to change is not a solution. An adaptive mindset is your best tool. To build or enhance your adaptability, consistently, practice the following:

- **Mental rehearsal**: Picture yourself acting in opposing ways to get to the same outcome. Identify which approach will likely yield the best outcome.
- **Hold back your first response**: Rather than reacting, adapt and thoughtfully respond to the situation. Stay in control--give it a second or third thought.
- **Listen more**: When you listen, you are suspending judgment. Use that information to adapt your behavior as needed.
- **Get out of your comfort zone**: Put yourself into very different situations. Operating in a variety of situations and roles will help you become more flexible and adaptable.
- **Ask for feedback and feed forward**: Leaders who reflect on their performance are more flexible in adapting to changes, and therefore better at identifying alternative and more effective methods.
- **Be supportive**: Having to support someone else's program or idea when you don't agree is a common paradox. Don't let the others know that you are not fully on board. Your role is to manage their vision and mission, not your personal vision. If you have strong contrary views, be sure to demand a voice next time around.

Strategies to enhance your achievement orientation

Achievement orientation is the drive to meet internal standards of excellence.

Achievement orientation is the ability to have the drive and passion to accomplish goals, excel, and be successful. A professional with a growth mindset and performance-oriented mindset has a strong emotional self-regulation, high standards, and looks to overcome any circumstance in a positive manner. They have a positive attitude, never give up, and encourage others to do the same. They take ownership of their mistakes; therefore, they are always looking to improve. They ask for help when they need it and reward themselves for achieving the goal, keeping their pride from getting in the way of their actions, and delaying gratification when necessary. To build or enhance your achievement orientation skills, consistently practice the following:

- **Take personal responsibility for your success**: Failure-avoiding individuals view success as dependent on available resources and situational constraints (for example, the task is too hard, or the marker was biased). Initiative, effort, and persistence are key determinants of success.
- **Enjoy demanding tasks**: Anything worthwhile is difficult. Achievement striving is enjoyable. Associate effort on demanding tasks with dedication, concentration, commitment, and involvement.
- **Value hard work**: Give value to achievement striving, in and of itself.
- **Improve your skills**: Performance on demanding tasks can be improved with practice, training, coaching, and dedication to learning.
- **Be persistent**: Continued effort and commitment will overcome initial obstacles or failures. Don't assume that you cannot do something until you have tried it. Trying it three times and giving up is for losers. Try it 3,000 times if necessary, review your data, ask for help, but keep trying until you make it. If you are going through hell, keep going with a smile.

Strategies to enhance initiative

Initiative is the readiness to sieze opportunities.

Leaders with initiative recognize that in order to be truly happy, they have to take responsibility for their lives even when that involves making lifestyle changes, learning new skills, and developing new habits. They don't blame others or the universe for their problems; they look for their own role in their current situation and their path of development. They also take the initiative in problem-solving and conflict resolution. They don't allow disagreements to fester or misunderstandings to linger. They take the necessary actions to clear negative emotions that are stopping or hindering them and they take action to prevent further similar occurrences. To build or enhance your initiative, consistently practice the following:

- **Be creative**: Even for staying in the same place you have to run faster and faster. Hence, for standing out you need to be creative and constantly search for new solutions, and more effective approaches. Ideas are the most expensive issues nowadays and the best contribution you can offer to your organization.

- **Speak up and share your ideas**: There is always need for fresh, powerful concepts. If your suggestions are based on broad research and adequate facts, then you have a great chance to see them being realized in the near future.

- **Always seek opportunities**: Opportunities are hidden everywhere, and people who see them are the ones who prosper. Make a habit of constantly asking yourself: "What opportunities for growth can I carve out of this situation?" If needed, think about this same question again and again. Gradually you will find the answer.

- **Challenge yourself**: Tackle new skills and refine your abilities all the time. You learn and grow by challenging yourself. This will give you the knowledge and confidence to show more initiative in current or upcoming projects.

- **Ask questions**: To take initiatives, you should know how things work and how you can improve them. For this purpose, be curious and ask questions. This will give birth to new ideas and ways to contribute to the growth of your organization more and more.

Others (second dimension)

The second dimension of the leadership of the future is the others, as in the colleagues, the team members, the employees, the peers, and the stakeholders.

Here in the second dimension is where you need to demonstrate your social awareness so you are able to recognize relationships and structures in which you and those around you are operating within your organization or your social networks. Perceive emotional overtones in the organization, team or interaction, even when these remain unspoken as you are able to read the play in a meeting, negotiation, or discussion.

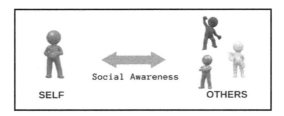

Social awareness

Social awareness

> *Social awareness is the ability to perceive and understand others' emotions and validate them.*

Perceiving emotional overtones in an organization, team or interaction, even when these remain unspoken always gives you the upper hand because you are able to read the play in a meeting, negotiation or discussion. Know how to read the set of non-verbal cues that unconsciously people give away indicating how they are feeling.

This gives you the option to respond in a meaningful and influential way:

SOCIAL AWARENESS SKILLS

Empathy
ability to sense other people's
emotions and feelings

Service Orientation
ability to taking in consideration others
needs and helping them achieve their goals

Organization Awareness
ability to recognize and understand how the organizational
structure can influence emotions

Awareness and Acknowledgemrnt
ability to understand and value the other person's feeling without
agreeing with them

Social awareness skills pyramid

Strategies to enhance empathy

Empathy is the ability to sense other people's emotions and feelings.

Contemporary researchers often differentiate between **affective empathy**--the ability to mirror the sensations and feelings we get in response to others' emotions and **cognitive empathy**--the ability to identify and understand other peoples' emotions by perspective taking--putting ourselves in someone else's shoes. When you do that, you gain an understanding of why a person feels or behaves the way they do and what triggered that feeling or behavior. Then and only then can you employ the other emotional intelligence tools in order to influence or manage the emotions and behaviors of others. We human beings are, literally, wired to connect because of the mirror neurons; hence we affect one another even when we do not mean to. To build or enhance your empathy, consistently practice the following:

- **Emotional listening and vulnerability**: Truly listening can be a challenge. Sometimes we are just waiting to give our own opinion. Increased empathy only comes through interacting with others, so you want your conversations to be as deep and revealing as possible. In order to do that, you need to develop two interrelated skills: emotional listening and making yourself vulnerable. Removing our masks and revealing our feelings to someone is vital for creating a strong empathic bond. Empathy is a two-way street.

- **Be fully present and read non-verbal communication**: Put away your phone. The things we say account for only 7 percent of what we are trying to communicate. The 93 percent of the message is in our tone of voice and body language. If, while you speak with someone, you scroll through your upcoming appointments, you will miss the bulk of the message. Your mirror neurons will a fire lack of interest, lack of empathy, and lack of compassion.

- **Put a smile on your face**: A smile on your face is, literally, contagious. The part of your brain responsible for this facial expression is the cingulate cortex, which is an unconscious automatic response area. A smile releases dopamine and oxytocin, also known as the happiness and bonding hormones. Use them to spread good vibes and boost happiness, productivity, and efficiency.

- **Call people by their name and encourage them**: Encouraging people can be as simple as nodding at them while they talk in a meeting. This simple gesture, along with using their name, makes a great impact on relationship building.

Strategies to enhance service orientation

Service orientation is the ability to take in to consideration others' needs and helping them achieve their goals.

Service orientation is built upon empathy for a person's situation. Knowing and understanding the type of environment that dominates your organization prepares you to be ready to help your employees or colleagues, to achieve their professional goals, and be a better employee and a happier person.

To build or enhance your service orientation, consistently practice the following:

- **Care about your team as you care about your customers**: If you want your team to care about customers, start by making it a priority at the top. Don't just *say* that you value great service or write it in a memo--live it! Reward it on a regular basis, recognizing those that go over the top publicly and often.
- **Hire people who fit the corporate culture**: Do your best to build a team that is enthusiastic about customer service and hire the ones whose personality fits the culture.
- **Get everyone involved**: Everyone should do at least a little bit of customer service, no matter what their job title is. Having your designers, developers, engineers, and everyone else to talk with your customers means they all have a good understanding of what the customers want.
- **Trust your team**: Once you have implemented your company values and hired the right people, be sure to let go! This encourages employees to develop creative ways to serve customers, and they will feel happier. Everyone likes to take ownership in their job. Throw away the scripts and free employees to treat customers with their own voice and heart. Let them do whatever it takes to make your customers happy.
- **Establish good lines of communication**: Make sure it is easy for everyone to stay on the same page so that nobody feels like they are facing a difficult problem alone.

Strategies to enhance organizational awareness

Organizational awareness is the ability to recognize and understand how the organizational structures in which you and others operate can influence emotions.

If empathy helps you understand the emotions of an individual, organizational awareness helps you to understand the culture within which those emotions operate. The corporate culture of your organization is a major influence on how you can or cannot express yourself. In a conservative culture, the display of emotions is viewed as inappropriate. In another organization, you might be admired and encouraged for being expressive. Usually, only by reading the mission, values, and goals of an organization or team, can we grasp the culture and the emotional intelligence of the organization.

To build or enhance your organizational awareness, consistently practice the following:

- **Be curious about your people**: Talk to your employees, colleagues, teammates, peers, direct reports, stakeholders, and so on, and ask their opinion on how to improve your organization, department, service, and so on. Find out, in a subtle way, what organizational constraints are blocking certain things from happening in your organization.
- **Identify the influencers inside your organization**: Who are the key people inside of your company who influence policies and decisions.
- **Research your company**: What is its mission? What are the values? What are the department's goals? Are there specific goals expected of each team member? What is the culture of the organization?

Strategies to enhance awareness and acknowledgement

Awareness and acknowledgment is the ability to understand and validate the other person's feelings without necessarily agreeing with them.

Once you have a sense of how someone is feeling, you need to acknowledge their feelings. Acknowledgment does not equal agreement; it means that you are recognizing the other person's position and empathizing with it. By doing so, you show that you are sensitive to how they feel and you value their feelings.

If you practiced all the other strategies to enhance your emotional intelligence competencies and skills, this one has no strategies to practice, as it is the natural consequence of the enhancement of your emotional intelligence.

Service (third dimension)

The third dimension of the leadership of the future is the Service, as in collaboration, teambuilding, aiding others to develop themselves (customers, non-customers, employees, competition, peers, stakeholders, local communities, global communities, and humankind), being an inspirational influencer, creating solutions, managing conflicts, and leading others in a new direction.

Here in the third dimension is where you need to demonstrate your social skills, also known as emotional management of others' emotions.

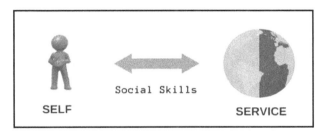

Social skills - the relationship between self and the others

Social Skills

Social skills is the ability to ethically manage others' emotions using influence.

Social skills, also known as interpersonal skills or people skills, are the skills we, as sociable creatures, developed to communicate and interact with each other. And to convey our messages, thoughts, and feelings to each other, we use verbal language and non-verbal language, such as gestures, cues, body language, and our personal appearance. Social skills help boost productivity, improve relationships, and increase our general quality of life.

A leader with great social skills is extremely useful in any workplace, as usually they are the influencers, the leaders, the ones focused on helping the others and the organization. They are easy to talk to and wonderful listeners; therefore, they are the peace makers, resolving disputes, building bonds, and catalyzing change:

SOCIAL SKILLS

Ethical Influence
persuade others to help themselves

Emotional Intelligent Leadership
be on service, help others to grow, have a vision

Developing Others
aid others in development through feedback/guidance

Building Bonds
ability to cultivate/maintain a web of relationships

Change Catalyst
ability to initiate new ideas and lead others in a new direction

Conflict Management
ability to de-escalate disagreements and create solutions

Communication
listen and send clear, convincing messages

Teamwork/Collaboration
ability to promote cooperation and team build

Social skills pyramid

Strategies to enhance ethical influence

Ethical influence is the skill to help others help themselves - not to get something out of someone by manipulating them.

In emotional intelligence, we speak of ethical influence to distinguish it from manipulation. You are simply attempting to help your employees or colleagues to achieve their goals and desires. For someone without a personal ethical compass and good social skills, it is very tempting and easy to manipulate others and that is not the aim of enhancing your emotional intelligence competencies and skills. Be genuine and sincere when you compliment your employees or colleagues on their appearance, strengths, patience, thoughtfulness, productivity, for the ideas they have contributed at a meeting or for always brightening up everyone with their kindness and compassion, and their smile even when the going is rough. Simple things and genuine words of appreciation go a long way. To be an influencer organization-wide you don't need to be a leader. But to be a leader, you need to know how to influence. To build or enhance your ethical influence, consistently practice the following:

- **Connect with people emotionally**: If you want to intrigue and influence people, you have to get their dopamine pumping--to stimulate the pleasure-reward area in the brain that makes people feel happy. A great way to do that is by having excellent conversation starters. My favorite two are: What personal passion are you currently working on? What was the best part of your day?
- **Be emotionally curious**: Everyone wants to be liked, loved, and accepted. When you make others feel important, your influence goes a long way. Become genuinely interested in them. A great way to do this is to ask them open-ended questions and let them talk about themselves. This helps you build rapport.
- **Use high-powered body language**: The head is held high, the arms are loose, the shoulders are set back, and the chest is out. When you manifest powerful body language, you are seen as more influential. Confident body language not only affects the way others see you but also the way you see yourself.
- **Be vulnerable**: People will perceive you as being real when you admit your weaknesses or flaws. People are able to better relate to you when you open up. Share a vulnerable story from your story toolbox. By doing this, you not only tell a great story but you also are being vulnerable, so it increases your influence in two ways.
- **Ask a favor**: It turns out that asking for help is one of the best things you could do to be perceived as an influential person. This is known as the Benjamin Franklin effect. So freely ask for help in the form of advice, opinions, or guidance.

Strategies to enhance emotional intelligent leadership

Emotional intelligent leadership is the skill of having the willingness to be in service, to help others to grow, and take charge and inspire with a vision.

Like influence, leadership is not restricted to hierarchical positions. Leaders can be found anywhere in an organization, especially emotional intelligent leaders. They can be at the bottom rung of the organizational ladder and still be able to perform their job in a way that has their co-workers following along after their example. Because they know how to work with people, keep the peace, use resources wisely, share the credit, and support and develop their people. As it relates to emotional intelligence, leadership involves appealing to and managing the emotions of others, in order to get the job done. That is why you cannot be an emotional intelligent leader if you don't know how to influence others. An emotional intelligent leader takes on a leadership role when they see the need, no matter what their position. They guide others' performance, they hold others accountable, and they lead by example. To build or enhance your emotional intelligence leadership, consistently practice the following:

- **Build optimism**: Your boss does not want to hear what is wrong with a project-- he wants to hear your suggestions for solving it or improving it.
- **Show enthusiasm**: Personal energy is contagious, and so is the lack of it. No matter what the job is, complete it with a sense of urgency. When others notice, they will become enthusiastic also.
- **Be flexible**: Show you can handle change by volunteering for a new project or by helping others with change.
- **Stop micromanaging**: Delegate projects to the right employees.
- **Stand by your employees**: Show you trust them, and they will be trustworthy.
- **Ask your peers for advice**: When you are new to a leadership position, you don't know everything. Identify your most respected peers, and ask them how they have succeeded.

Strategies to enhance developing others

Developing others is the ability to aid others in development through feedback/guidance - bringing the best out of others to enhance themselves and the organization.

As a leader, how do you assess your leadership ability? Is it on your own achievements and development or, based on how many of your people got promoted to other divisions or to more responsible positions? What kind of work environment would that be? What would it do to your productivity if every employee knew that you had their future development in mind when assigning work, assessing criticism, or managing projects? Leaders who have the willingness of helping others to grow in tandem with themselves are confident enough in their own abilities. They recognize that helping others to achieve their goals is a win-win situation: it makes them feel connected to and invested in others, which in turn enhances a sense of belonging and teamwork. To build or enhance your ability to develop others, consistently practice the following:

- **Use coaching and mentoring**: Use the classroom, online, books, and coursework. One of the by-products of developing your people is that you gain satisfaction and stature as a result of their success. Who will you help today?
- **Build a learner mentality**: Encourage your people to think of themselves as professional learners as well as (job title). In meetings and one-on-ones, ask: What are you learning that is new or different?
- **Get ongoing feedback from multiple sources**: The key words here are ongoing and multiple:
    - **Ongoing**: Performance improves with information that is provided as close to an event as possible. That way, the situation is still fresh and the details clear.
    - **Multiple sources**: When I do 360s for clients, I always insist on feedback from people outside of the person's direct chain of command, even external customers if there is a lot of customer interaction. When someone is working across boundaries on a project, there's a wealth of information available about the ability to build relationships and influence outside of the power sphere.
- **Give first-time tasks that progressively stretch people**: No one grows from doing the same thing again and again.

Strategies to enhance building bonds

Building bonds is the ability to proactively cultivate/maintain a web of mutual beneficial quality relationships.

A natural builder is someone that knows the importance of having a good social network. After all, no man is an island. Even for the professionals working remotely or in virtual teams - the skill of working on building rapport and developing mutually beneficial relationships are the base of their professional success. When you take time and put the effort in to build relationships, you are naturally enhancing your people skills, communication skills, and self-confidence. A bond builder or social networker sees relationships not just as things that happen, but as bonds that you proactively build aiming for quality relationships. To build or enhance your ability to build bonds, consistently practice the following:

- **Ask about their families/pets/significant others**: In your conversations, ask about the people that are close to them. Even a simple "How are your parents/girl/boyfriend?" bring out a human element that creates an opportunity for bonding.
- **Talk about their interests/hobbies/current events**: Find something, an idea or a philosophy or a hobby that others are passionate about and just ask a question. With the power of social media today it is not hard to find hot buttons to focus on.
- **Give small token gifts**: Small gifts go a long way; a small gift shows that you are thinking of them, that you invested thoughts into them. Small gifts are often more meaningful than bigger gifts on special occasions as they provide reminders of the relationship more often than gifts on special occasions.
- **Ask good questions, and then listen**: When people vent and talk about the problems they are facing, listen and ask questions. If you don't know what to ask, just repeat the last word they said.
- **Always start with a positive introduction**: A strong hello or a smile makes a huge difference in a person's day. And everyone wants that sense of recognition that comes through in your positive greetings.
- **Be comfortable. Be real. Be authentic:** When you are who you are, you share a part of yourself with the other person, creating a stronger bond.

Strategies to enhance change catalyst

Change catalyst is the ability to initiate new ideas and lead others in a new direction, challenging the status quo, championing the change and role-modeling it to others.

A change catalyst recognizes when change is needed, challenges the status quo, champions the change, and role-models it to others. A change catalyst is a forward-thinker, open to change as a way of self-improving, improving the organization, team, co-workers, and even customers. A change catalyst is the person that understands that change is part of life and part of remaining competitive. A change catalyst recognizes that change often brings up fear in people, yet he does not allow the fear of change to prevent the necessary changes from being made. He removes the barriers to change (old fixed mindset and emotional roadblocks) and influences others to champion the change. To build or enhance your ability to be a change catalyst, consistently practice the following:

- **Clear vision**: A **change agent** does not have to be the person in authority, but they do have to have a clear vision and be able to communicate that clearly with others. People can be frustrated if they feel that someone is all over the place on what they see as important and tend to change their vision often. A clear vision does not mean that there is one way to do things; in fact, it is essential to tap into the strengths of the people you work with and help them see that there are many ways to work toward a common purpose.

- **Patience and persistence**: Change does not happen overnight and most people know that. To have sustainable change that is meaningful to people, they will have to embrace it and see its importance. Many can get frustrated that change does not happen fast enough and they tend to push people further away from the vision, then closer. Change agents just help move people from point A to point B, at their own pace. Every step forward is a step closer to a goal.

- **Ask tough questions**: It is when people feel an emotional connection to something that they will truly move ahead. Asking questions focusing on what is best for us, and helping people come to their own conclusions based on their experience is when you will see people have ownership of what they are doing. Keep asking questions to help people think; don't alleviate that by telling them what to do.

- **Be knowledgeable and lead by example**: Leaders are not just seen as good people but also knowledgeable about what they are saying. If you want to create *change*, you have to not only be able to articulate what that looks like, but show it to others. Change agents need to put themselves in the situation that they are changing. How can you really know how something works if you have never experienced it?

- **Strong relationships built on trust**: All of the preceding points mean nothing if you do not have solid relationships with the people that you serve. The change agents I have seen are extremely approachable and reliable. Trust is also built when you know someone will deal with things and not be afraid to do what is right, even if it is uncomfortable.

Strategies to enhance conflict management

Conflict management is the ability to de-escalate disagreements and create solutions and knowing that a conflict is always an opportunity to evolve when the root of the conflict is kindly brought to light.

This is a challenging skill to develop because it requires that you experience conflict in order to learn how to solve it. You may even need to bring conflicts to light that others would rather leave in the dark. However, conflict management will make you a better leader, co-worker, and even parent, spouse, or friend. A skilled conflict manager knows that a conflict is always an opportunity to evolve. It can help individuals or a work group to solve problems, improve processes, heal rifts, strengthen relationships, and learn new skills. To properly manage a conflict, you need to discover the root of the conflict and use all the other emotional intelligence competencies. To build or enhance your ability to manage conflicts, consistently practice the following:

- **Build bonds, even with your adversary**: The key to defusing conflict is to form a bond, or to re-bond, with the other party. We do not have to like someone to form a bond - we only need a common goal. Treat the person as a friend, not an enemy, and base the relationship on mutual respect, positive regard, and co-operation. Leaders must learn to separate the person from the problem. Once a bond has been established, we must nurture the relationship as well as pursue our goals. We need to understand each other's point of view, regardless of whether we agree with it or not. The more effectively we communicate our differences and our areas of agreement, the better we will understand each other's concerns and improve our chances of reaching a mutually acceptable agreement. We can all learn to communicate acceptance of the other person while saying no or disagreeing with a specific point or behavior. Feeling accepted, worthy, and valued are basic psychological needs. And, as hostage negotiation demonstrates, it is more productive to persuade than to coerce.

- **Dialogue and negotiate**: Many leaders in conflict situations are hostages to their inner fears and other negative emotions, hence, they fail to see the opportunities in resolving the conflict. Talking, dialogue, and negotiation create genuine, engaging, and productive two-way transactions.

- **Raise a difficult issue without being aggressive or hostile**: Once an issue is raised, we can work through the mess of sorting it out and find a mutually beneficial outcome. We should be direct, engaging, and respectful, always helping the other person to save face. In addition, timing is important. Choosing the right time and the right circumstances are part of an effective conflict management strategy.

- **Understand the root of the conflict**: To be able to create a dialogue aimed at resolving the conflict, we need to understand the root of the disagreement. Among the common causes of a disagreement are differences over goals, interests, or values. There could be different perceptions of the problem, such as "It's a quality control problem" or "It's a production problem", and there may also be different communication styles. Power, status, rivalry, insecurity, resistance to change, and confusion about roles can also create conflicts. It is crucial to determine whether a conflict relates to interests or needs. Interests are more transitory and superficial, such as land, money, or a job. Needs are more basic and not for bargaining, such as identity, security, and respect. Many conflicts appear to be about interests, when they are really about needs. The most conflict provoking losses have to do with needs, and those needs may connect to the deeper wounds people have suffered in their life. Someone passed over for promotion, for example, may seem to be upset about the loss of extra money, when the real pain is caused by a loss of respect or loss of identity.

- **Empathize and reciprocate**: Reciprocity is the foundation of cooperation and collaboration. What you give out is what you get back. Humans have a deeply hardwired pattern of reciprocity. Mutual exchange and internal adaptation allows two individuals to become attuned and empathetic to each other's inner states. Hence a powerful technique to master in any kind of dispute is to empathize with the feelings and views of the other individual by managing what we express both verbally and non-verbally. This social awareness allows you to make the right concessions at the right time. Once you have made a concession, it is likely that the other party will respond in the same kind. Moreover, when you recognize a concession has been made, reciprocate with one of your own.

Strategies to enhance empathic communication

Communication is the ability to actively listen and send clear and convincing messages.

Every interaction we have involves some form of communication. Under the light of emotional intelligence, communication is the skill that enables you to tune in to the emotions of others and use that emotional data to influence the other person to choose the best course of action. It enables you to build rapport, trust, and long-lasting bonds. Other features of this skill include being good at compromising, seeking mutual understanding, dealing with difficult issues head-on, welcoming open and frank discussion, being receptive to good and bad news, and not allowing disagreements to become roadblocks to further communication. To build or enhance your communication skills, consistently practice the following:

- **Don't talk over people**: This demonstrates a real lack of respect.
- **Don't finish other people's sentences**: Research has shown by doing this you are disempowering the other person because you are taking control of the conversation.
- **Paraphrase**: If you want to show that you have really understood someone, all you have to do is repeat back to someone what they have just said, before you comment yourself.
- **Listen actively**: Focus on active listening instead of passive listening. The difference is that active listening means you engage and respond to the other person based on what they have said; passive listening is simply the act of listening with no response.
- **Maintain eye contact**: By looking the other person in the eye, you are proving that you are interested in what they are saying.

Summary

In this chapter, you have learned that: the leadership of the future in the IT domain needs to have a global mindset of the business, needs to be technologically savvy, know how to build alliances and partnerships, and that a successful and powerful leadership of the future is a shared leadership.

You have learned the right mindset to lead and thrive in a VUCA world--the vulnerable, uncertain, complex, and ambiguous world of technology of information.

You have learned that the VUCA mindset of the leader of the future is constructed with a developed and adaptive mindset, in a human ecosystem that taps into intrinsic motivation of people, and develops others and influences them into following him, by designing the future, anticipating and creating change, and building the collaborative network to construct the vision of the future.

You have learned about the six emotional intelligent leadership styles: commanding, visionary, affiliative, democratic, pace setting, and coaching along with their pros and cons.

You have learned the 3D model of leadership of the future: Self (first dimension), others (second dimension), and service (third dimension).

In the next chapter, we will cover the best practices to attract the best IT professional to an open position, the best hiring practices for IT talent, and the rules to follow before and during an interview to have the best outcome. We will further see how to prepare for the interview and maintain a legal hiring process and master the behavioral and situational interview processes to screen for emotional intelligence in all the candidates and especially in leadership roles, management roles, as well as roles in the sales teams and customer service.

7
How to Hire Emotionally Intelligent IT Professionals

In this chapter, we will cover:

- The best practices to attract the best IT professionals to an open position
- The best hiring practices for IT talent
- The rules to follow before and during an interview to have the best outcome
- Preparing the interview and maintaining a legal hire process
- Master the behavioral and situational interview process to screen for emotional intelligence in all the candidates and especially in leadership roles, management, sales teams, and customer service

Nowadays, tech companies, when searching for the best fit for their companies, are looking for IT professionals that have not only the best technical skills but also display emotional intelligence skills, as opposed to the school they went to or their grades. Why? Well, because it's proven that emotional intelligence makes the difference when being successful. A candidate with low emotional intelligence lacks the skills to understand and manage their own emotions. They also lack the ability to read other's emotions. They don't know how to handle stress and stressful situations. They become overwhelmed with a high workload. Hence, they lack the ability to solve conflicts, make decisions to overcome sudden obstacles, are negative, and fail to meet the needs of the customers. A candidate with emotional intelligence skills has the ability to work well with others, is a natural leader and motivator, is a team player, a great change catalyzer, and influencer. Emotional intelligence skills, such as self-awareness, social awareness, empathy, motivation, and self-regulation must be taken into consideration at the beginning of the hiring process.

I know that you have limited time when interviewing candidates. Plus, it is not easy to assess emotional intelligence when you don't know how to do it. However, with two interview questions, and the knowledge of what good and bad responses sound like, you can assess by the answers whether the candidate is confident, optimistic, empathic, and can manage anxiety, anger, or doubt. For instance, if you ask your candidate to tell you about a mistake he made in his previous work, depending on the answer, you can assess if he is accountable for his mistakes or if he blames something or someone else. The candidate with emotional intelligence skills knows that making mistakes is part of the working process, as long as the candidate acknowledges the mistake, makes the proper corrections. You can also ask your candidate to tell you about a time he got tough feedback. Emotionally intelligent candidates have self-awareness, self-confidence, and are open-minded, which allows them to receive feedback with a positive attitude. They even use the critical feedback to change and improve. Usually, a person with good emotional intelligence skills sees feedback as a step forward. But candidates with low emotional intelligence, or no emotional intelligence, when receiving feedback get offended, defensive, and give the silent treatment. It is also important to listen to how candidates respond. Do they take time to answer tough questions or say the first thing that comes to mind? Are they comfortable with thorough questions and the silent moment during the time he is thinking? Does the candidate use a vast emotional vocabulary when talking about how he felt during a situation? A person with a good emotional intelligence vocabulary uses specific words such as: "I felt excited", "I felt anxious", "I felt frustrated". If they only use "I felt good" or "bad", it is a sign of low emotional intelligence. Take note if the candidate has a well-developed emotional vocabulary. A candidate's word choice provides a good insight into whether they understand how they were feeling and how the others felt, what caused a situation, and how did this understanding direct them to act?

However, during the interview, if the answer is vague, do follow-up questions. Don't ask the candidates directly about their emotional intelligence skills. The candidate will give you the idealized notion of themselves -- what they would like to be. To overcome this obstacle, you can use behavioral interviewing questions such as the two mentioned previously. Moreover, make sure you get the person to tell you what they actually did and how they behaved. This is where you will hear about the overt demonstration of emotional intelligence. It takes training and practice to get enough details from a candidate, using the behavioral and situational interviewing questions. However, the odds of choosing the best candidate are higher. Preparation is key to a successful, effective interview. Behavioral and situational interviewing questions to assess the technical skills and soft skills (emotional intelligence) of the candidates are crucial to find a good fit. For most organizations, human resources account for 40-60% of expenses and success depends on getting the highest possible return on this outlay. Despite all the complicated rubrics that are often generated, human resource management has only two basic objectives. The first is **productivity/performance**--the more a results-driven team stays emotionally engaged and on the task, the higher the returns. The second objective is **quality of life**--motivation comes from a fair exchange of values between performance and reward sharing. When the quality of both professional and personal life is well addressed, individuals, teams, and the organization are able to produce. What defines the quality of professional life? The values, vision, and environment of the organization. Human resource management begins with the acquisition of talent. Productivity begins with people who have the tools and desire to perform. The team needs to be staffed with engaged people committed to a vision of organizational success. They need to be excited and energized to serve. In this chapter, we will learn about:

- Best practices to attract the best IT fit for a position
- Best hiring practices for IT
- The rules for a better interview outcome
- How to screen for emotional intelligence in a candidate
- How to screen for emotional intelligence in leadership candidates
- How to screen for emotional intelligence in management candidates
- How to screen for emotional intelligence in salespeople
- How to screen for emotional intelligence in customer service candidates

Best practices to attract the best IT professional fit for a position

I cannot think of a case where an IT position is filled with *a just find anybody* mentality. More often the phrase *find the best fit we can afford* is either stated or implied. As in any area of life, there is a lot to be learned from those that do the best job in finding and placing talented individuals. I enjoy working with teams filled with the best fits for that team. Therefore, I want to offer some suggestions for improving the odds at finding that best fit. Better still, suggestions for getting them to accept an offer:

- **Know what you need and make that clear**: People working in IT have many ways to be contacted. Even worse, anyone with a good reputation will be contacted via all those methods on a regular basis. This makes reading or listening to position descriptions an exercise in determining whether it is worth the time. The candidate may review the posting thoroughly, but will often skim it first. A position description that appears to meander around technical buzzwords and role descriptions is an easy one to ignore. The description should never leave the reader wondering what the heck the successful candidate needs to possess regarding skills and experience. A description of a job should also give a feel for a typical day. Detail is important. Thus, avoid generic terms such as *developer with five years of experience or more*. Likewise, avoid specifics when not needed. A description: *Java developer with five years of expertise in an enterprise environment that knows what IT stands for* is going to raise questions. Knowing what IT stands for has no bearing on Java skills. Thus, it is either fluff or someone who has no idea what they are looking for. This may seem obvious in the example. However, requests that include irrelevant details are typical.

- **Assume the job description reader will only scan the description**: Words matter. This axiom applies when someone is actively searching for jobs on a website or flipping through emails and scanning an emailed position. As a potential candidate for a job opening, I always have some key ideas about my skillset in my head. Also, there are some code words I am looking to avoid. This is the same whether a person or a computer is searching the job description. For example, a developer looking for a job that is pure coding might ignore a posting that includes information about testing strategies. Similarly, they will ignore management phrases such as lead, mentor, business strategy, or others that do not focus on the desired coding tasks. Keywords are an important part of a description. However, make sure extraneous keywords that might be considered a negative are avoided.

- **Respect the time of the reader**: If you are looking for someone to do a particular job or fill a specific role, get to the point. Avoid fluff around the description. I have seen developer position postings that include HR boilerplate about lifting heavy objects, repetitive activity, and other similar phrases. This implies the person writing the position has no clue about IT jobs. Instead, they are just slapping technical terms into a template. Your environment may require all that legal boilerplate. In that case, make it easy for the reader to jump to the important parts of the description. The requirements might be valid and an attempt to avoid lawsuits. However, if it makes it look like no thought went into writing up the position, it may deter good candidates. Why would you expect a candidate to spend more time considering the position than was put into writing it up?

- **Understand the position**: When you order a meal at a restaurant, you want to know what sort of ingredients and spices go into the food. Questions asked may include "how big are the portions?" or "how is that typically cooked?". These questions are asked to give you a better sense of what to expect before the meal is ordered or delivered. Likewise, job descriptions should provide the reader with a firm idea of what is required for the position. Thus, the recruiter filling the position should be able to have a feel for what an ideal candidate looks like. Unfortunately, this is often where job descriptions fail. When there is a lack of IT knowledge around the hiring and recruiting process, it leads to detailed and relevant information being lost or never properly created. A recruiter is only as good as the description they receive. A poor job post might cause the author of the job posting to be consulted to clarify the role. However, no amount of clarifying discussion with the recruiter will solve the problem if the author does not understand the position to be filled.

- **Speak IT to fill IT positions--know your audience**: Few things turn off a potential candidate faster than treating them as a commodity. People that choose IT, and stick with it, almost always are looking for more than just better pay or more vacation time. They also tend to know what the going market rate is for their skills. Remember, the best candidates are getting some offers or invitations each week. They also have Google available to find out what a position is likely to pay. Make sure the pay offered is reasonable for the skillset. On the other hand, be ready to play up the career advantages of the position. A position that works with a new, cutting-edge technology is more desirable than one that works with a dying technology. These points are not rocket science, nor are they easy to accomplish without IT knowledge. That being said, how do I recommend that these points get addressed? IT knowledge of the sort needed here can take years to learn. Thus, some of the best recruiters have strong IT backgrounds. They manage to get a head start by bringing that knowledge with them to recruiting.

IT is constantly evolving so even those recruiters with a solid IT background have to keep up with trends and innovations in the world of IT. A driven recruiter can spend hours every week digging into tech journals and blogs, picking the brains of trusted resources, and even take continuing education classes. We want to make it simpler than that.

- **Use the resources available**: IT is constantly evolving, making it so that even those recruiters with a solid IT background have to keep up with trends and innovations. A driven recruiter can spend hours every week digging into tech journals and blogs, picking the brains of trusted resources, and even take continuing education classes. This can be intimidating. There are also podcasts and meetups that can teach IT skills by a sort of osmosis. As always, you get out what you put in.

Best hiring practices for IT

Ever wonder how employers select a perfect match for a job? Their secret lies in these four hiring practices: behavioral interviewing plus situational interviewing, selection assessments, job tryouts, and background screening. We will see more on these topics in the following sections:

Behavioral and situational interviewing

One of the most accurate hiring techniques which is ideal for evaluating skills and competencies necessary for effective job performance is to use behavioral, situational interviewing questions and some standard interview questions.

Behavioral interviewing, as opposed to traditional interviewing, evaluates candidates' past performance by having job candidates describe specific stories, examples, experiences, and results that indicate their ability to perform certain job tasks and responsibilities. Typically, a candidate is asked to provide a description of the situation, task, action, and result in response. Examples of behavioral interview questions include:

- Provide an example of...
- Tell me about an experience when...
- Describe how you did....

Situational interviewing looks at the future. Candidates are presented with a potential problem that they need to think about and come up with a solution to the problem at hand. With the situational interview technique, you are testing the candidates' ability to solve the problems at hand, intelligence, knowledge, and expertise in the field. Situational interviews are reliable indicators about how a candidate will handle situations in the future, because chances are that if a candidate is able to adequately solve the problem, he would also perform that same action if put in that situation.

The only real issues with situational questions are that they do not give the interviewer insight as to your past work history, nor do they show the interviewer how you value your answers. For example, if you are asked a behavioral question about your greatest professional mistake, and you talk about how you mouthed off to a supervisor, that will tell the interviewer that you consider how you treat co-workers as more important than whether or not you made a mistake on a project.

These days, employers do not often use one type of interview question throughout the interview. Most likely, you will experience some behavioral, some situational, and some standard interview questions. That is why it is important that you prepare for all types of interview questions, including both situational and behavioral. Details to take in to consideration when using behavioral and situational interviewing include:

- Give behavior and situational training to the hiring managers, supervisors, and any employee in a hiring role
- Update your job information such as job descriptions, performance objectives, and so on
- Carefully identify the behavior or soft skill you are looking for in a job candidate
- Be tool-prepared for the interview--use note-taking sheets, score-sheets, and forms, and interview guides with the behavior and situational queries
- Be consistent--ask the same core questions to all the candidates, but you can vary the probing
- Be self-aware of your biases as an interviewer, such as having a favorable opinion about the candidates similar to you, or just rely on your intuition

Evaluation tests

The main purpose of using evaluation tests pared with the interview is to help the hiring manager or the person responsible for the selection process. Sometimes, the interview on its own is not enough to assess if the candidate is a good fit to the job position and to the organization.

Depending on the position for which you are hiring, you can choose different types of evaluation tests. For instance, you can use a skill and ability-based test, a personality test, a soft skill test, and so on. Evaluation tests are extremely helpful in providing context on a candidate's interpersonal style, the likelihood of a candidate fit with the values and corporate culture of the organization and, of course, to slim the number of candidates to the open position.

Details to take into consideration when using evaluation tests include:

- Use select assessments only to assess skills or traits that are difficult to measure using the interview technique
- Make sure you are only assessing skills related to the job position you are interviewing for
- Be sure that the assessments you are using during your hiring comply with the standards of reliability and validity
- Make sure you explain to the candidate what kind of test he will take, the reason he needs to take it, when it will be taken, and if, or how, the results of the evaluation test will be provided to the candidate
- Use a trained professional to interpret the results and make the decisions about the cut-off scores
- Never base a hiring decision solely on the results of one assessment
- Before using the evaluation tests, assess them to make sure that by using them you are not discriminating against protected groups

Trials

Job trials are mainly used to assess candidates for technical positions, contact centers, client support lines, sales, manufacturing, and so on. Job trials provide more accurate results of the candidate's competencies for the job position that they are being assessed for. And they are also very effective in showing to the candidates what the job entails. Therefore, they are very effective in reducing turnover in high-turnover positions.

Job trials can have the form of: virtual simulations, replications of the job core duties, sample exercises, work activities, job shadowing experience, realistic job previews, interactive games, role plays, and even video tours. They provide more accurate results of the candidate's competencies for the job position.

Details to take into consideration when using job trials include:

- Use job trials for technical complex work or positions with high turnover due to their level of difficulty
- Make sure that the trial accurately replicates and depicts the core duties of the position that you are trying to fill
- Make the trial engaging and interesting to complete so you have more accurate results
- Use solutions that are reliable to measure the skills you are assessing and that are already validated
- Use with accurate scoring criteria to evaluate the candidate

Background evaluation

Background evaluation is the last step in the hiring process. The chief aim of having a background evaluation into a candidate is to reduce the risk of negligent hiring. Background evaluation includes investigating of references, employment verifications, drug tests, and criminal records.

Details to take into consideration when using background evaluations include:

- Use a third-party provider expert in background screenings
- Don't choose your third-party provider based on cost alone--a higher cost may be a good indicator of a more thorough evaluation
- Since you will be paying good money for a background evaluation, use it only in the final step of the hiring process
- If the background evaluation reveals a criminal record of your candidate, don't eliminate your candidate before you have had a clear conversation with him

These four hiring techniques, when used together, greatly improve your probabilities of hiring the right fit to your organization, since these selection techniques are the best ones to evaluate the candidate's skills, abilities, values, and passion.

The rules for a better interview outcome

Candidates are not the only ones stressed by interviews. The process can be stressful for employers too--especially if you are new to recruiting or conduct interviews infrequently. Good interviewing starts with a clear vision of the role you need to fill. It also requires having an awareness of how to influence the process in a constructive, stress-free way.

Here are the five golden rules to get better interview outcomes:

- **Get clarity about the role and the questions you want to ask**: First develop a job description and candidate profile, then use it to write the interview questions. You can refer back to your candidate and job profiles if you need clarification during the interview.

- **Use a consistent interview process for everyone**: If you're feeling frazzled planning your interview, create a structure where you use the same questions and ratings for every job candidate. Using a consistent interview process turns a nervous interviewer into a confident one. "Ask these 10 questions. Grade each answer. You have 30 minutes, go!" Does this sound familiar to you? Most probably. This is cold and corporate and does not build a rapport with the candidate; therefore, you do not get to know him or her. You can use your emotional intelligence skills, such as empathy, active listening, self-awareness, and awareness of others to build a warm rapport and run an effective interview that way. However, do press candidates by asking follow-up questions about any unclear or open-ended responses. These answers often yield great insights about a candidate's work style or personality, and may create further lines of communication.

- **Relax before the interviews**: Conducting interviews can be nerve wracking, even for seasoned professionals, so take time before each interview to clear your mind and calm your nerves. Do some mindful deep breathing and relax your body. Put a smile on your face to trigger oxytocin and dopamine and enhance your relaxed and happy state. Do some rehearsal out loud if you feel it will help you. Check in with yourself before heading into the interview and return to your plan if you start feeling overwhelmed. As with the candidate, a little self-care goes a long way to clear your mind and build self-awareness.

- **Focus on the candidate rather than your fear/anxiety**: Do not monitor your racing heart or churning stomach. Instead, focus on building a comfort zone for the candidate. Our brains like it when we do good deeds to help others. You receive back what you give. Be the ally of the candidate and start the conversation with positive statements: "I am glad you are here". "I am looking forward to learning more, as your resume is impressive". To put candidates at ease, tells them what to expect: how long the interview will last, the types of interview questions asked and why everyone will take notes or that if they draw a blank, they can skip a question and come back to it. Do your interviews in the coziest place in your office. Avoid overly hot, cold, or dark spaces. Everyone feels less tense when they are comfortable.

- **Be direct without being confrontational**: When you avoid a difficult topic, it is often because it makes you uncomfortable and even tense. But not sharing your concerns with the candidate denies them the chance to respond to them. Share your doubts with the candidates and ask them how they will address challenges. If you are doing a phone interview, share your concerns about a specific situation and ask the candidate to address them in the follow-up interview. If the candidate addresses your concerns in a well-thought-out action plan, then you know what the candidate is able to do and that he is coachable. Be direct and honest with candidates about your concerns. Avoid using negative language or jumping to assumptions. This approach can help you learn something new about the candidate's problem solving skills.

Preparing the interview

Knowing how to *hire smart* is a must for any employer, no matter what the economy looks like. A company that does not think strategically about recruiting could miss out on the best candidates, fail to hire a diverse workforce, or worse, expose itself to liability for discriminatory hiring practices. Hence, annually review and update your hiring process to make sure that you not only comply with the law but that it is still efficient and effective in delivering the best outcomes during the hiring process. Therefore, let's break down the main steps you need to look for, when reviewing and updating your hiring process:

- **Review and update your job description**: Prepare a detailed and thought-out job description that you can use for both hiring and employment purposes. When drafting the new job description comply with the following:
  - Go from general to specific when listing the duties and responsibilities of the job position. For example: As a technical architect you will work as part of a team to deliver innovative, cost-effective and efficient IT solutions to an organization. Your daily duties will include: Identifying an organization's needs; Agreeing plans with the client; Discussing the best products and systems with the client; Explaining plans to designers and developers; Producing progress reports; Dealing with problems as they arise (the path to IT never did run smooth); Advising clients on future developments.
  - State job qualifications and pre-requisites in an objective manner. For example: Must have a degree in maths, computer science, business information systems, or software development. Knowledge in programming, support, and design.
  - Clearly state in the job posting that you are an equal opportunity employer.
  - Clearly, state in the job posting that being chosen to undergo the hiring process is not a guarantee of employment without further requirements.
  - Pay attention to the use of language that might be considered in violation of the law of gender, race, age, or other discriminatory language. If your job post reads like this: Hiring female software developer for a young and energetic team, in most countries in the world, this job post is illegal and is in violation of the laws of gender and age. Something along the following lines would be suitable: Looking for a hard-working software developer that is also a good team player.

- **Have a diversity of sources to recruit**: Recruit at a broad range of colleges and technical schools, attend minority-sponsored job fairs, advertise in relevant community newspapers and, if possible, seek partnerships with organizations that are a source of diverse employees. As well, learn from companies that have a strong commitment to diversity. And keep in mind that unless your workforce is already diverse, relying heavily on recommendations from current employees will only maintain the status quo and will not help you increase diversity.

- **Review the job applications with a lawyer**: To make sure you are not asking for illegal and inappropriate information on your job application forms. For instance, if the country you are working in has laws prohibiting you from asking for the candidate's criminal record, and you have a question about prior arrests on the application form, you are exposing your organization to serious lawsuits and putting at risk the name and reputation of the organization.

- **Regularly train your hiring managers**: Training your hiring managers and all the employees in the hiring process on proper and new interviewing techniques helps to recognize and address recruiting mistakes and keep your organization away from any liability. Make sure that the best practices of the interview are part of the training, such as:
  - **Ask open-ended questions**: Open-ended questions allow the candidate to speak more about himself, helps calm down the levels of anxiety of the candidate, and gives you more information about the candidate's emotional intelligence skills (that is, managing their own emotions, dealing with stressful situations, and communication skills).
  - **Limit the interview topics**: Limit the topics to the issues that are needed to evaluate the candidate's qualifications for the position.
  - **Use your critical thinking to evaluate the answers**: For instance, did the candidate freely disclose all the information asked. Did the candidate fully respond to the queries or was he holding back information?
  - **Take notes during the interview**: Take written notes on a specific form. Don't write your notes on the application form or in the candidate's resume.
  - **Keep your notes about the candidates legal and non-discriminatory**: It could be seen as illegal or discriminatory if your notes are about the gender, race, age, national origin, disability, or other such identifiers of the candidate.

- **Be careful to not make promises or give guarantees of future employment**: Comments such as: *As long as you do a good job, you will always have a position with the company*, or *You are by far the strongest candidate I've interviewed*--can be understood by the candidate as a guarantee of employment.
- **Have at least a panel of two interviewers**: You will have more information about the candidate and make a more accurate decision.

Legal Disclaimer: None of the information provided herein constitutes legal advice on behalf of the author.

Conducting the interview

Conducting a successful interview for both parts can be challenging when the interviewers are not trained and prepared. For a lot of interviewers, building rapport with the candidate doesn't come naturally. This may be because they are shy or because they lack the emotional intelligence skills to cope with the stress of the interview and the social skills to immediately build a rapport with a stranger - the candidate. Plus, in most situations, the person conducting the interview doesn't prepare in advance the batch of questions they need to ask, or the proper follow-up questions to make after any answer. And YES! Many hiring managers or recruiters don't have the emotional intelligence skills to perform their job at the highest level. In fact, many hiring managers dread the interviewing and the hiring--as they are fully aware of the responsibility of hiring the right fit to the job position and add value to the organization and/or client. Hiring is an art, not just a job. There's a lot to learn along the journey. Remember to leave a footprint with every candidate you meet no matter if he was selected or not.

How to identify the right candidate

Identifying the candidate that is the right fit for the position you are hiring, the candidate who is geared for progression in his career, and who can make an immediate contribution to your organization, is a challenge. If you are choosing your candidates based solely on their technical skills, you won't find the right fit. Passion, motivation, and high achievement are tell-tale signs of good emotional intelligence. Therefore, look for the following traits on your candidate during the interview:

- Look for self-awareness and self-assessment--core emotional intelligence skills
- Look for affinity, communication skills, and social skills (good communication skills, good listener, team player, influencer)
- Look for the readiness and willingness of the candidate to come on board of your organization and projects

Evaluating if the candidate has self-assessment

How can you evaluate if a candidate has self-awareness or not and, therefore, self-assessment, when you have no training to assess emotional intelligence?

A few behavioral and situational queries will help you to spot the traits. My strong advice is to start your interview (after building a rapport) with an open-ended question such as:

- As we are interested in knowing your evolution inside your former organization, could you please, walk us through your progression, since you entered in the organization till the current position?

- Follow-up questions:
    - How did you adapt to the organizational changes in your former organization?
    - How did you feel about the changes?
    - What makes you stand out among your peers?
    - If we asked your most fierce critics to tell us about your strengths, what areas you could develop, and your potential in your line of work, what do you thing they would say?
- Follow-up questions for management and leadership positions:
    - How exactly does your former organization make money? What are the two biggest expenses?
    - What is your organization's annual revenue base?

- How many companies does your former organization have?
- How would you describe the hierarchy structure of your former organization?

These are sample queries that allow you, depending on the answers, to evaluate the level of self-awareness and business acumen of the candidate.

;Looking for affinity in the candidate

You know that your candidate is a good fit if he has some affinity with the mission, values, and corporate culture of your organization. Otherwise, you may end up with someone who can do the job technically but who is totally out of sync with the rest of your team and corporate culture.

How do you search for this kind of affinity from your candidate? By asking questions like:

- When working in a team or alone, how much structure, direction, and feedback do you prefer on a daily basis?
- How do you handle constructive criticism from your colleagues and team manager?
- Do you usually need extra time to get your job done, everyday?
- When making decisions, do you generally ask for permission or for forgiveness if the outcome was not as expected?
- Follow-up question:
    - Did you ever, due to being extremely cautious, never make an error when an error was expected to improve the outcome of the work that was being developed?

;Looking for the willingness and readiness of the candidate to come on board

A candidate that is willing to work in your organization, previous to the interview, is going to research you, your mission, your values, your achievements, your competitors, and your present challenges. Also, the candidate will be excited to have the opportunity to talk about his willingness to be part of your organization. Of course, not every candidate will be outspoken. That is why you need to assess the true willingness and readiness of your candidates.

Use questions such as the following to isolate those who are hungriest for the opportunity that you are offering:

- Why do you want to be a part of our organization?
- What do you know about our organization?
- What sets us apart from our competitors in your opinion?
- How do you see your career progression inside our organization, if you were chosen to work with us?

The secret to a successful job interview lies in two key factors: the skills of the interviewer to avoid common hiring mistakes and the skills of the interviewer to assess potential talent in the candidates.

Nevertheless, the high turnover in new hiring is due more to a personality-culture mismatch than a technical skills mismatch and it is here that the soft skills or emotional intelligence of the candidate makes the difference between good hiring or a high turnover.

Finally, use the 80% - 20% technique when job interviewing. Let the candidate speak for 80% of the time at the beginning of the interview. You speak 20% of the time after you have completed your initial round of interview questions. And, always be willing to offer some career advice and direction.

After all, every relationship gives you an opportunity to share your wealth of knowledge and experience with others. If you simply see the interview as an opportunity to give a gift to someone else - whether you hire them or not - you will find that the communication becomes a lot more natural and enjoyable.

Mastering behavioral and situational interview questions

Behavioral and situational interviews favor interview questions that compel candidates to think on their feet and discuss how they have handled specific work-related challenges in the past and how they will problem solve a future situation. The underlying idea is that the best predictor of future behavior is past behavior. Behavior-based interviews are focused on what a person has done in the past and the success they enjoyed as a result. If an individual has a track record of success in their past, the chances are very good that, that individual will carry that success with him or her to the next employer.

It will also help reveal if the candidate is a good potential fit for your organization. In smaller businesses, it is not only the business owners who wear many hats, so you are looking for employees who are flexible and willing to pitch in to get the job done. When it comes to improving your interview skills, it is best to ask questions that will get at their effectiveness in handling tough problems, working with ambiguity, dealing with conflict, and making decisions with limited information.

Today, inherent talents and passion count for much more than a list of past jobs on a resume. Business owners take the preliminary step of identifying the talents required to perform well in the job, rather than merely listing the tasks the employee will have to perform. Just because a candidate has done the job before does not mean the candidate is good or passionate about it.

The behavioral and especially the situational interview questions are very useful to elicit stories that can help assess how the candidate would behave when facing that situation in a real event. Thus, the questions need to be specific and phrased in unexpected ways to avoid standard familiar responses.

Effective behavioral interview questions

Here we will see a sample of the 10 most effective behavioral interview questions:

- Could you tell us about a situation where you needed to work with a very difficult co-worker?
    - A candidate with low emotional intelligence will avoid any accountability in the difficult relationship and put all the blame on the other colleague.
    - A candidate with high emotional intelligence will own his accountability and will not label the other colleague as difficult - he will achieve a workable outcome with the colleague. Conflict resolution, problem solving, empathy, accountability, and communication skills are traits of an emotionally intelligent candidate.

- Could you tell us about a situation where you needed to work with an important and difficult client/customer?
    - Again, a candidate with low emotional intelligence will blame the client/customer and label them difficult.
    - A candidate with a high emotional intelligence will empathize with the client/customer. He will actively listen to the client and use his conflict resolution and problem-solving skills to achieve a satisfactory outcome to the client/customer. An emotional intelligent candidate knows how to manage his own emotions and other's emotions, and has no conflict with authority.
- Could you tell us about a situation where you needed to persuade someone to accept your point of view or convince them to change something?
    - A candidate with low emotional intelligence does not have the skills to be successful in this situation.
    - A candidate with emotional intelligence has empathy, and knows how to listen and how to communicate to influence and change other's opinions. As well, how to build trustworthy relationships? The candidate is able to negotiate, develop, and strengthen relationships with others.
- Could you tell us about a difficult problem you faced and how you approached it? Don't just tell us how you solved it. Describe to us your thought process behind your decisions and actions.
    - With this question, you are looking for how the candidate approaches problems in general. And if he asks for collaboration and feedback from others in understanding the problem, developing possible solutions and implementing a workable solution.
- Could you tell us about a professional mistake/error you have made?
    - With this situational question, you are trying to find out how the candidates takes accountability for his mistakes, if or how the candidates reflects upon mistakes and learns from them.
    - An emotionally intelligent candidate will tick all the boxes here. A candidate with a low emotional intelligence will refuse to admit any past mistakes - which is a sign that the candidate is not willing to or able to learn from past mistakes and errors.

- Tell us about a situation where you had to work under an insane tight deadline? Don't just tell us how you solved it. Describe your thought process behind your decisions and actions.
    - A candidate with good emotional intelligence skills will tell you how he handled the pressure and managed the priorities. He will explain to you his planning process, his communication with his other colleagues, and how they collaborated to achieve the common goal. If he tried to extend the deadline or asked for additional help. And if he fully committed his own time to meet the deadline and asked other colleagues to commit, too.

- Could you tell us a time or a situation where you received a criticism to your work or a not so positive feedback?
    - A candidate with emotional intelligence skills will show in his answer that he is at ease with feedback and criticism as he doesn't take it personally; rather, he sees it as a feed forward moment. He will analyze the critic and the feedback, and make the necessary changes based upon the feedback (that is why he sees it as a feed forward moment). His answer will also show you that the candidate has adaptability, leadership potential, and emotional maturity.

- Could you tell us a situation where you needed to take initiative?
    - This question will help you to assess if the candidate is proactive and has problem solving skills - traits of emotional intelligence. The answer should showcase a situation where the candidate recognized a problem that nobody else was resolving and took initiative to handle it. His actions show a willingness to go above and beyond the call of duty when required.

- Could you describe to us a situation of how you felt when coming into a new team or a new working environment?
    - With this question you are trying to evaluate how a candidate adapts to change, especially in a new working environment/team.
    - Candidates with emotional intelligence will show that they are adaptable and open to change. They are non-judgmental about co-workers, thus they are natural relationship builders and know how to seek help when necessary.

- Could you tell us about a situation where you needed to work with a client or customer who was very different from your personality type?
    - This question allows you to evaluate if the candidate has good people skills, is adaptable to change, and has empathy. A candidate with emotional intelligence will use his empathy and communication skills (active listening) to adapt to the client/customer style.

Behavioral interviewing may require more effort than you would typically invest in an interview. But the advantages are substantial, and will very soon become apparent to your bottom line.

 Behavioral interview--focus on a past experience. *Tell me about a time you had to deal with.*
Situational interview--focus on a hypothetical situation. *How would you handle?*

In a situational interview, the candidates are asked to respond to a specific situation they may face on the job. These types of questions are designed to draw out more of their analytical and problem solving skills, as well as how they handle problems with short notice and minimal preparation.

Effective situational interview questions

Here we will see a sample of eight of the most effective situational interview questions:

- Imagine you are the new Project Manager of your team. But, your team members object to your vision and ideas for the new project. What specifically would you do to address their objections?
    - If your candidate has emotional intelligence, he will ask for feedback about his ideas and take into account everyone's opinion prior to beginning the new project. And he will assure that changes can be made during the execution of the project if the team members are not satisfied with the outcomes. He will have meetings with the team to discuss his plans and show how the company will benefit with the changes and the final project.

- Imagine that you are responsible for an important project and that near the completion phase, you are assigned to another important project that needs to be completed immediately. How do you prioritize and handle the multi-tasking situation?
    - A candidate with emotional intelligence will: first, before beginning the new project, assess what needs to be completed; second, estimate how long it will take; third, assess what resources are needed to successfully complete the project; and, fourth, if after the assessment, he concludes that the new project cannot be completed by the deadline, he will request that the project be assigned to someone else.

- Imagine one of your subordinates is performing below average. What specific actions could you take to help him?
    - A candidate with emotional intelligence would talk with the subordinate, with empathy and an open mind. His priority would to be identify if the factors contributing to the poor productivity are work related or personal. If the candidate does not have coaching or counseling training, he should advise his subordinate to look for the coach or counselor of the organization to help him overcome his problems and get back to being a good performance worker.

- Imagine that you responsible for ensuring that a very important project is finished before Christmas. You need all your workers giving their best to make sure the project is completed by the deadline Meanwhile, a co-worker decides to take an entire week of work off to enjoy vacation time. How do you address the problem.
    - A good candidate would: first, find out how much vacation time the worker used during the year and, second, ask the worker to postpone his vacations to after the project is finished as all the workers are needed to meet the deadline.

- Imagine that you finished one of your projects before the deadline. And now the client is claiming that the project is not meeting all the project specifications. What would you do?

- A candidate with emotional intelligence would: first, before handling the project, review his project planning to make sure that all the project specifications - time, requirements, deadlines, budget - met the approved specifications. If he found something went wrong, he would bring the issue to the attention of his superiors and ask for a realistic extension of time to make sure the project met all the specifications. Or, if he spotted that actually something went wrong, he would review his project planning process to see what went wrong, and why the project was not done on time according to specs. He would take the necessary actions to assure it never happened again.

- Imagine that you don't agree with the viewpoint of your supervisor on how to deal with a problem. How would you handle the situation?
  - An emotional intelligent candidate would have used his empathy to view the problem with his supervisor's perspective. Even if after seeing the problem with his supervisor's perspective he could not agree with the solution proposed, he would suggest new solutions, until they find one that would be a good win-win situation for both.

- Imagine that you are hired, and that you need to take important job-related decisions? What actions would you take?
  - An emotional intelligent candidate would take in consideration three perspectives, before making the decisions: first, he would assess if the decision has a negative impact in the company (bottom line, name, reputation); second, he would assess how the decision fits within the scope of the company's core values; and third, he would determine how the decision would benefit the company.

- Imagine that your boss is absolutely wrong about an important work-related issue. What would you do?
  - An emotional intelligent candidate would assess the personality of the boss.
  - If the boss doesn't like to have his authority challenged, is narrow-minded, doesn't like to receive criticism or others opinions, just be polite, and try to understand the situation from his perspective.
  - If the boss is open-minded, likes to receive outside opinions and suggestions and constructive criticism, first validate his perspective. Then make suggestions that would be better, more efficient, and more effective to accomplish what he wants.

Assessing emotional intelligence traits in candidates

Looking for emotional intelligence traits in job candidates during the interview process is not difficult--especially if you have the right questions to ask. In this section, we will start with general questions that you can use with all candidates. Then we will cover specific questions to specific job positions, where emotional intelligence is of the utmost importance.

The most effective questions to spot emotional intelligence in a candidate are:

- If you had the chance to have dinner with one of your role models or someone that inspires you, who would that be and why?
    - The answers give you a sneak peek into what are the candidate's passions and inspirations. And even the behavioral patterns the candidate respects.

- Imagine you have the chance to start tomorrow your own company. What would be the three core values?
    - The candidate's answer gives you the insight into his core values and priorities.

- As the team leader of your team, how would you help your teammates to cope with organizational changes in your company?
    - When facing organizational changes, you want to have a team leader who has self-awareness, social awareness, empathy, leadership qualities, is a change catalyst, and knows how to cope with change.

- From all the lasting friendships that you built in your former job, who are you going to miss the most?
    - Building relationships/lasting friendships is a major sign of emotional intelligence. It means that your candidate cares for others.

- Do you feel that you are still missing an important skill or expertise? What is it?
    - You want a candidate to be hungry to learn more, improve, evolve, be better than yesterday, and add value to his work and to the world. People who struggle to answers this question are the ones who think they already know it all.

- Can you teach me anything, as if it was the first time I am learning about it. It can be anything: a game, a lesson, a skill, and so on?
  - If the candidate has emotional intelligence, his answer will reveal several qualities, such as: technical ability to explain something to a person who is less knowledgeable in the subject; empathy to ask empathic questions to the person being taught (Is this making sense to you? Am I explaining myself properly?); and if the candidate takes time to think before speaking.

- We know that you had great success in your former organization. Could you tell us three factors you would attribute to your success?
  - The answer to this question will reveal if the candidate is a selfless person or a selfish "me-me-me" person. Look for the team player that brings something positive to the organization.

Assessing emotional intelligence in leadership candidates

Nowadays, as emotional intelligence skills are so important in a leadership position, we can find several reliable emotional intelligence tests to assess the level of emotional intelligence of your leader.

However, during the interview process, there is a batch of specific questions that you can ask your candidate with the aim of spotting the traits that are more important for your organization. Even if your organization provides you with the results of a previous emotional intelligence test from the candidate, you should make your own evaluation during the interview. Adding your own evaluation to the data received from your industrial psychologist can help you further interpret their reports. To identify candidates with high emotional intelligence and eliminate those who could leave collateral damage in their wake, my advice is that you spend at least 30 percent of your interview time focusing on questioning to identify four competencies: self-awareness, self-management, social awareness, and relationship management.

Please note that you don't need to ask all of these suggested questions. One question per competency may be more than enough. Here we are just providing you with a sample of the most effective questions to evaluate each of the competencies.

Sample questions - self-awareness

The answers to the following questions will give you an insight into the level of self-awareness of the candidate:

- Could you tell us about a situation where someone (colleague, stakeholder, client/customer, and so on) interpreted in a negative way something you did or said--even though, your intention was good? Could you explain to us why they gave a negative interpretation to your words/actions?
- Have you ever found yourself in a situation where you felt uneasy and uncomfortable to the point you needed to adjust your behavior to fit in with the environment? How did you know that you needed to adjust your behavior to adapt? And what action did you take to adjust?
- When you know in advance that you will be facing a stressful and negative situation, do you purposely prepare in advance to deal with it? What do you do to prepare yourself? And how does it work out?
- Do you feel that you still miss a professional expertise or a skill?
- We all have had times when we had to reach out to others for help Could you tell us when was the last time you asked for help in your work?

Sample questions - self-management

The answer to the following questions will give you insight into how the candidate manages his emotions and how emotionally resilient he is when facing troublesome and stressful situations.

Please note: the answers to the first two questions will reveal if the candidate is accountable for his own actions and emotions or if he just puts the blame on others.

The answers to the remaining questions will give you insight into the emotional resilience of the candidate.

- Imagine that you don't agree with the viewpoint of your supervisor on how to deal with a problem. How would you handle the situation?
- Could you tell us about a decision you made without addressing the problem first with your executive team members? Why did you decide not to address the issue with your teammates?

- Could you tell us about a time when you thought that things could not get worse for your business, but they did? How did you handle the situation?
- Could you give us an example of a time when you made a professional error or mistake? What happened? What was the outcome? What did you learn from the situation?

Sample questions - social-awareness

The answers to the following sample questions will give you insight into the candidate's natural propensity toward empathy, humility, and willingness to take responsibility for his actions:

- Could you tell us about someone you work with on a regular basis that you find difficult to get along with? Were you able to build a peaceful relationship with that colleague?
- Could you tell us about a situation when one of your co-workers felt you were unfair in your decision making? What did you do?
- What traits do you have that could match with our corporate culture?
- What makes you stand out from the competition and add value to our organization and help us to achieve our goals?

Sample questions - relationship management

The answers to these questions will give you insight into the candidate's interpersonal relationship skills, the ability to inspire and influence others, create resonance to a company's mission or vision, challenge the status quo, and bring out differing perspectives in a collaborative fashion:

- Could you tell us about a time or situation where you have lost your optimism? And how did you recover it?
- Could you tell us about a time or situation where you, as a leader, felt it was necessary to bend the rules. What were your actions? Why did you do it? How did you feel about it?
- Could you tell us how do you know that you created a positive work environment and great corporate culture in your former organization?

- Tell us about the most difficult boss you have had? Could you find a common ground with him? How did you find that common ground? Did you learn something from that boss? How did that knowledge further your career?
- Could you tell us about a time or situation where you failed to establish or maintain a relationship with a peer?

As always, watch for cues to how the candidate is feeling through their body language and tone of voice used when answering the questions.

Many companies try to ensure their selection decision by extending the interview process. I don't recommend this, as it can cause candidate fatigue and may result in emotional intelligence mismatches due to a lack of focus. Chances are that including questions designed to uncover the emotional intelligence factor in your hiring process will ultimately save your organization time and money. One note of caution, do not load all these questions into your interview. You will overwhelm and maybe even scare away the candidate.

A good balance is to spend 20 percent to 30 percent of the interview on questions designed to highlight emotional intelligence competencies and the other 70 percent to 80 percent on questions that focus on expertise and past experience, with an emphasis on asking the candidate to provide metrics about the outcomes or results. As you work your way through these traditional expertise-related interview questions, remember to watch for how the candidate reads and responds to cultural situations and works with others. No doubt, emotional intelligence is rarer than book smarts, but my experience says it is actually more important in the making of a leader. You just cannot ignore it.

How to look for leadership potential in a candidate

The right interview questions can help you identify a candidate's leadership potential. During the interview, you will want to go beyond a candidate's surface qualities and discern traits such as personal confidence to spotlight traits that your organization values.

The following interview questions are sourced from professionals in companies of all sizes to help reveal a candidate's management and leadership skills.

Pay attention to whether people talk about themselves (*I did this*) or their teammates (*we did this*) when answering general interview questions or direct leadership questions.

Sample questions include:

- What led to your last two promotions?
- Tell me about a subordinate you helped develop.
- Tell me about the leadership training you have received.
- What is the most difficult decision you have had to make in your career?

If the answers to these questions all point to a person who develops a team, we have a potential leader. If the candidate's answers are focused on that person rather than on others, the person is not deemed to be a potential leader.

Good managers find better ways to get the job done. Job candidates who don't have previous leadership positions can answer hypothetical questions about how they'd improve processes and products.

Sample questions include:

- If you returned to your previous job as the boss, what would you do to create a better workplace?
- What things were done well there?

If they tell us how bad the boss was and how bad the place was, that could indicate that they are negative. In each question, we are looking for winners and complainers. Will they bring to us the ability to make a difference, to be able to see areas for improvement?

Consider how long you have to develop leadership. Match the time frame of your questions to the length of time people typically stay with your firm, and determine if the job seeker would be willing to put in the extra time to eventually take on a managerial role.

Sample questions include:

- Where do you see yourself in 2 years?
- Tell me about a time you had to get yourself quickly up to speed in a new role in the past, either at work or outside work? What did you do and how did that work out?
- If they have had a past leadership role: How long did it take you to get to that position? What did you do to get there?

In the past, many organizations would ask, *Where do you see yourself in 5 or 10 years?* but that leaves things open-ended. We won't pretend that 5 years or 10 years is a benchmark for employment we will start celebrating as early as 2 years.

Quantify a candidate's past management experience by asking for details:

- Did you train or mentor (formally or informally) subordinates or peers? How many people and in what ways? Did you develop the training yourself?
- Where and how did you save money for your employer or client(s)? How much money in total or how did you accomplish unique jobs/tasks to save money for your employer or client(s)?
- What new processes did you install and what were the results? What was saved (time or money) or what did the processes increase (productivity)? How did you personally have a hand in accomplishing those savings or improving processes?

If the resume has the answers to these questions, then you know the candidate has the potential for becoming a good leader and manager, or perhaps a team lead, then supervisor. Look for objective, provable and documentable information, such as *I supervised a team of two, and we worked together to do this project*, and the results were (metrics showcasing how many, how often, and the total of something), rather than subjective language, such as *I am good with people*.

For job candidates with prior leadership experience, including students who have led extracurricular activities, ask interview questions that qualify their leadership experiences:

- Tell me about a past leadership role.
- What was your goal or objective?
- What did you accomplish it?
- What was the feedback you received from peers on the outcome?

When an individual gets into telling the story, you'll be able to pick up on the nuances on how they lead. Do they say, *I did this*, or *I sought out these skill sets in my peers*? Find those individuals who really have the diversity of those experiences, that can articulate what was done, how they made decisions for the team, and areas where the team's diverse viewpoint was critical.

Assessing emotionally intelligent management candidates

There is been a lot of talk lately about a lack of management skills brought on by the exodus of the Baby Boomers from the workplace, coupled with many Millennial's lack of experience and soft skills. To help close the leadership gap, experts in the human resources and hiring areas were asked to share how they discern a job candidate's willingness and potential to develop management and leadership skills in the interview process.

Here are insights from the experts to identify a job candidate's leadership and management potential:

- **Before you start your search, know what leadership and management look like in the organization**: To spot potential leaders and managers, first define what skills and capabilities good leaders have. Without those standards, each individual making hiring decisions will apply their own beliefs. Have a framework to evaluate internal and external talent for effective leadership. Your organization needs to agree about what are indicators of potential leaders and managers. What leadership capabilities are critical.

- **Ask people straight up**: Do you want to be a manager? Not everyone enjoys being in charge. During the interview process, hiring managers should directly ask job candidates if they are interested in managing others. Being straightforward, rather than navigating the intricate results of a comprehensive personality test, can yield positive results.

- **What to do when a job seeker lacks management experience**: Managing a project requires task-related and people-related skills. Use a person's preferences for those responsibilities to evaluate leadership potential. Make a list of task-related items (creating a work breakdown structure, managing a project budget) and people-related items (meeting with team members to get input, reviewing and giving feedback on project team members' deliverables). During interviews, ask job candidates to rate how much they like doing each task on a 1-to-10 scale. If the candidate's responses suggest a strong preference for tasks over people, he or she is unlikely to find job satisfaction as a people manager. You can adjust the question to fit experienced managers by asking, "What are your favorite aspects of project management?" Observe if they mention people-related or task-related items.

- **We did this versus I did this**: The key interview question to evaluate this skill is: "Tell me about the project you are proudest of in your career." If the candidate describes situations that could have easily been attributed to a single person, but he came across explaining how he let "his team" take credit for the accomplishments, it is the best sign of a leader. The lesson: leaders talk about team building, rather than focusing on individual accomplishments.
- **Ask interview questions that reveal character**: It is hard to mentor character, morals, and values. It's something that's innate in that person.
- **Seek out those who try hard and embrace management tasks**: I like to ask them What do you want to do in 3 to 5 years? How do you see yourself accomplishing that? What can we do to help you get there? Check for those candidates who have a vision for the future that includes management or leadership.
- **Entrepreneurs often have leadership and management skills**: People who have started businesses have a wealth of connections and are quite resourceful. Even failed entrepreneurs can make solid leaders. In hiring, it is not whether the business did well or not, but what the applicants learned from their successes and failures. Everyone succeeds and fails in some manner. We want to know if the applicants understand how to replicate their success and avoid similar failures.
- **How do you handle a disgruntled employee in your department who has made a habit of arriving late to work and causing minor disruptions during the day as well as a declining morale among the rest of the staff?**: Uncovering skills and character traits beyond surface attributes is the key take away when scouting for strong leadership. Use the interview process to evaluate the candidate's character, ambitions, and personal successes before choosing your next front runner. The results might surprise you.

Assessing emotionally intelligent sales people

There comes a point where your business cannot grow without a team of great salespeople. A solid sales team serves as cheerleaders for your product or service and keeps your client pipeline moving. Great sales teams are collaborators who see opportunities to improve the business - not just land another deal. The best salespeople at fast-growing organizations are doing a lot of internal collaboration with marketing or finance. They are being asked to contribute to R&D and product development. The best salespeople are collaborators.

Here is how to hire a sales team that rocks:

- **Screen for skills that your stars demonstrate**: If you already have top sales performers at your organization, use an assessment tool to identify what makes them successful and then hire for those traits. Most organizations have some type of profile or assessment that creates a standard relative to what's needed to succeed. A lot of good sales organizations are trying to validate their selection decisions with assessments that go beyond subjective interviews. Using an assessment tool can help you create a behavioral and situational interviewing process that screens for the traits and competencies that ensure success at your organization. Because innate traits are difficult, if not impossible to change, you can help ensure your new salespeople are a good fit from the start. For instance, either you are ethical or you are not.

- **Look for natural helpers**: The best salespeople are the ones that genuinely empathize with customers and care for their needs. Therefore, when hiring a salesman/woman look for natural helpers. Customer needs are different and expectations higher in this era of informatics, where customers don't even need to leave the couch to buy whatever they want. Thus, the new salesperson needs to know in advance what each customer likes and needs. They have more information and alternative choices, so they have elevated expectations when it comes to personalization and customization. That puts a new kind of pressure on both the sales organization and the individual contributors. When hiring salespeople, look for people who think of themselves as helpers and teachers. They will be helping customers think, execute, solve problems, and approach business differently. They are almost more like consultants. The **helper approach** also works internally as well. You will see that the best salespeople and fast-growing organizations are doing a lot of internal collaboration with marketing or finance. Salespeople are being asked to contribute to R&D and product development. They are the best collaborators as they know the customers' needs better than anyone in the organization.

- **Ask about data skills**: The line between being a sales rep and a product analyst, nowadays is very thin, as data is increasingly important in sales tools to evaluate prospects, customers, deals, and even technique. As the use of data and data analytics grows throughout organizations, look for sales candidates who can evaluate and mine data for insights and also use emotional data for insights to the needs and expectations of the customers. Sales professionals who are excited to work with technology and data are a huge asset to your entire company, not just to your sales team.

- **Look for micro marketers:** Micro marketers are the forward-thinking salespeople who are using social media and other tech tools to gain online social presence and influence of the company. As you hire salespeople who understand social selling, look for sales candidates who have a robust and professional presence on social media. They have the digital mindset to be brand ambassadors and thought online leaders and influencers. They share insights from others as well as original ideas and information on how companies can use those insights for themselves. Understanding the value of social media and promoting ideas through social media is a vital skill for salespeople.

- **Compensate based on performance**: Research has found that salespeople are more committed when they have some kind of incentive or variable-based compensation. Thus, compensate your sales team based on performance through incentives and bonuses and they will be more engaged.

- **How would you handle an angry customer who was promised the delivery of the product on a certain date but because of manufacturing delays the company was not able to deliver on a timely basis?** The answers to this question will give you the insights to assess if the sales candidate has the emotional intelligence traits of empathy, self-management, conflict-resolution, adaptability, and social skills to handle the situation.

Assess emotional intelligent customer service candidates

Providing excellent customer service is critical to business survival in today's competitive marketplaces. Mediocre customer service can quickly torpedo your company's reputation.

Research says 42 percent of people encounter poor customer service at least monthly and that can hurt a growing business's reputation. And in today's connected online world, great customer service, regardless of the industry, is essential. Good customer service skills are valuable for employees in all positions and industries, even those who don't work directly with customers.

Let's look at what are the most important emotional intelligence skills to look for in a customer service candidate:

- **Communication skills**: This one is easy to spot. The best salespeople have great communication skills. They use active emotional listening to try to understand the customers' personality and needs--to hear the intent behind what is being said. They share useful information with the customer and with their colleagues. They like to receive feedback and use it to feed forward when some mistake was made or a skill needs to be improved.

- **Body language**: As you conduct the interview, pay attention to the tone of voice the candidate is talking, if he is listening and thinking before making a statement, or asking more in-depth questions. Look for the non-verbal cues through his posture, hand gestures, and micro-facial expression.

- **Problem-solving skills**: Being nice and a good communicator is not enough to be a successful customer service expert. Your customers expect that your customer service representative also has the knowledge and ability to solve his problem when the customer is complaining. To assess if your candidate has this skill ask him to tell you about problems he has faced with customers and how he handled it. You are looking for evidence that he knows how to work through issues in a logical way.

- **Conflict resolution skills:** Conflict resolution skills require the ability to stay calm under pressure and not take personally the criticism towards the service/product or anger of the client. In an interview, we look for candidates who are comfortable answering questions because this usually translates into someone who can naturally converse with customers. To assess if the candidate has a good conflict resolution skill use one of the behavioral and situational questions learned in this chapter.

- **Positive and friendly attitude**: Managing customer relationships with a positive and friendly attitude is paramount to ensuring that customers do not churn due to poor support. In the interview, ask how candidates have dealt with difficult customers and listen for attitude. Extroverted people who tend to be friendly and engaging with strong communication skills and empathetic listening skills are generally well suited for this role. Look for answers that honor a customer's needs and offers information about how issues were resolved.

Summary

In this chapter, we covered the best practices to attract the best IT fit to an open position, the best hiring practices for IT talent, and the rules to follow before and during an interview to have the best outcome. We also covered how to prepare for the interview and maintain a legal hire process, and how to master the behavioral and situational interview process to screen for emotional intelligence in all the candidates, especially in leadership roles, management, sales teams, and customer service.

You have learned that the best practices to attract the a good fit of a candidate to IT are: know what you need and make that clear to your candidate in the job description, use all the resources, speak IT to IT people, know your people, and understand the position's requirements.

You have learned that the best four practices to hire the best IT professional, with a lower turnover, are behavioral interviewing and situational interviewing, selection assessments, job tryouts, and background screening.

You have learned that to have the best outcome of an interview, you need to follow five simple rules: get clarity about the role and the questions you want to ask; use a consistent interview process for everyone; relax before the interviews; focus on the candidate rather your fear/anxiety; and be direct without being confrontational.

You have learned that when creating a job description, you need to follow the law and keep all your hiring processes legal.

You have learned to ask the right questions in order to master the behavioral and situational interview processes and to screen for emotional intelligence in a star candidate or in leadership, management, salespeople, and customer service candidates. In the next chapter, you will learn how a sales team uses self-awareness to debrief sales meetings, uses assertiveness to enhance opportunities, uses empathy to enhance trust and a rapport with prospects and customers, and uses mindfulness to be present and focused, and will deal with a potential problem and practice active listening.

8

Preventing Stressful Situations with Emotional Resilience

In this chapter, we will cover how to build emotional resilience to better cope with stress, anxiety, shame, guilt, depression, lack of support from family, friends, employers, the feeling of being overwhelmed, stressed out, depressed, and burnout. Emotional resilience, in the context of emotional intelligence, can help build and enhance new skills and abilities that help you to cope and even prevent some of these situations. It does not mean you will be free of anxiety, stress, or anger as these emotions can be useful. However, they can be frightening and overwhelming at times. Therefore, it is important to build good emotional resilience to help you in the moments you need it the most, to manage your emotional states. Therefore, we will learn about the five pillars of emotional resilience, listed as follows:

- First pillar: Stay calm, cool, and collected
- Second pillar: Control your emotions
- Third pillar: Create positive emotions daily
- Fourth pillar: Develop self-compassion
- Fifth pillar: Be grateful and forgive

What is emotional resilience?

Emotional resilience is the skill to adjust to change and move on, from negative or traumatic experiences, in a positive way. To keep a healthy balance between a tough head and a warm heart. As you build your emotional intelligence competencies and skills you are also building your emotional resilience, though a person with a high level of emotional intelligence still gets frustrated, angered, stressed, or anxious. The main difference is that a person with emotional resilience knows how to prevent and bounce back from those situations. Emotional resilience does not mean pushing your emotions down or away, or ignoring them altogether. It means acknowledging and managing them well. Your heart needs to stay open for you, so you can care for yourself in even the worst times. Before you delve into the five pillars of emotional resilience, I would like to share with you the best advice to be resilient:

- Being resilient is not blocking out your feelings with drugs, pretending that everything is OK when it is not, or being too tough to tell someone you are proud of them, love them, or appreciate them, not crying when someone you love dies, ignoring everyone else and always putting yourself first, being aggressive, verbally violent, or looking for a fight.

- Being resilient is staying calm and clear headed when pressure and stress around you are high, so you can bounce back quickly from upsets, set-backs and bad moods or emotions. In other words, you don't get stuck in bitterness, anger, or resentment as you have the mental toughness to guard against being sucked in. Keep a sense of humor: losing your sense of humor and no longer laughing at issues you would normally laugh at, are one of the early warning signs of too much stress. Keep things in perspective, rather than letting emotions such as anger, exasperation, or anxiety distort your worldview, so you can judge situations fairly. Do not take personally comments or actions, that are not meant for you, don't waste time and energy with gossips, retaliating, sulking, or being upset. Don't take on board other people's problems, stupidity, or emotions, but stay compassionate and caring for others. This requires mental toughness and a warm heart. Look after yourself psychologically, spiritually, and emotionally, too often when people are no longer resilient and they become overwhelmed, tense, or stressed, and stop looking after themselves and indulge in self-defeating behavior. Feel and express your emotions in ways that are safe, clear, and healthy. Emotional denial or suppression of what you feel may be needed at specific times in order to survive but not on a daily basis. If emotional denial and emotional suppression are your daily basis, normal depression and burnout will be the sure outcomes and no one wants that. So, let's learn how to build the strong pillars of our emotional household.

The five pillars of emotional resilience

We are going to learn how to build our emotional resilience upon five emotional pillars so that we can endure the setbacks of life and work. The five pillars of emotional resilience are:

- **First pillar**: Stay calm, cool, and collected because when you apply your emotional intelligence skills to develop a sense of calm like this at work, emotional intelligence can enhance and increase your life and work satisfaction. You will no longer be buffeted by your environment and what happens to you. Instead, you will be able to take responsibility for your emotional reactions. Bliss!
- **Second pillar**: Control your emotions; emotional intelligence is about feeling your emotions, knowing they are there and why. Express them and move through them in a healthy way.
- **Third pillar**: Create positive emotions daily because happy workplaces benefit productivity, and boosts the sales, it is a great branding strategy, supplies lower staff turnover, boast creativity, lower the costs, stop gossips, prevents stress, depression and burnout.
- **Fourth pillar**: Develop self-compassion because, without self-compassion people become miserable, stressed, overworked, develop self-hate, are self-critical, have unrealistic expectations and even expect perfection.
- **Fifth pillar:** Be grateful and forgive because when you don't forgive you release and flood your body with all the chemicals of the stress response and spend the rest of your life in being the victim of your own thoughts and behaviours.

First pillar - stay calm, cool, and collected

Here we are only citing some examples to help you reflect on the areas in which you could keep your own cool at work. For instance, a colleague says something potentially hurtful but you don't respond with a snide comment in fact, you just assume the other person is having a bad hair day.

Don't take things personally, as everybody is fighting a battle that you know nothing about. Something goes wrong, but you don't swear at your computer or kick the photocopier when they don't work, or take it out on the help desk or the administration personnel. Sometimes it is the small situations that irritate and annoy people the most, and yet they can be the easiest to fix, from a calming point of view.

Staying calm in these situations is a healthy level of emotional intelligence as emotions such as anger can be a health hazard. Someone makes a snide remark--you don't go over and over it, in your mind, and fester on it, you let it go and stay content. Imagine that the snide remark is floating on the air and now settles in the dark cloud above the head of the author of the snide remark, and heavy rain starts to pour on him/her. Use your imagination to create a positive mindset and change the mood. This means no waking up at three o'clock in the morning plotting revenge!

Having the emotional intelligence skills to avoid sulking, clamming up, and festering can bring sleep benefits. If you have to give a presentation to an executive you don't go into fear and anxiety. Instead, you do your best and shine, and get a nod from the CEO at the end to indicate he or she is impressed! Use your imagination and rehearsal, as practice makes perfect and eases the anxiety. When you apply your emotional intelligence skills to develop a sense of calm like this at work, emotional intelligence can enhance and increase your life and work satisfaction. You will no longer be buffeted by your environment and what happens to you. Instead, you will be able to take responsibility for your emotional reactions. Bliss! This is an example of high emotional intelligence worth developing.

Keeping calm and cool with annoying co-workers

Why get upset with others or react to their every action? Does it actually help you? In most cases, probably not. Do you get angry, irritated, or frustrated with people or about situations over which you have no control? If you can stop your irritation and replace it with calm, then no matter how frustrating, silly, or upsetting people are, you can keep your cool. If you don't get irritated by people at work, you will be happier and less stressed no matter what your working environment. Keeping your levels of irritation, frustration, and anger to a healthy, low level is a display of a great emotional self-management. If you are always firing up and getting agitated, frustrated, or exasperated, you are burning yourself out. Those emotions add stress to your body, and stress causes inflammation in the body, which in turn can lead to disease. Yes, feeding yourself a frequent and regular dose of anger, irritation, and frustration is a health hazard. So, let's learn how to keep cool with irritating people:

- **Be realistic**: Getting annoyed does not stop the other's behaviours. Do they change their behaviors to make you happy? Are you expecting people to follow your rules and be perfect? People don't change their behaviors to please you. Understand that everyone is different, accept it and move on with your life. But you have the power to change from being annoyed to a more pleasant mood. Do something that makes you laugh--a funny song, a joke, and so on.

- **Enquiry**: Ask yourself if your getting annoyed by someone else's behavior helps you in any way? If getting annoyed by people only makes things worse for you, why get irritated? Annoying people is not worth it. Use your power to change how you feel. Focus on something else. Use a deep breathing technique. One of my tricks to deal with annoying people is play in my head the Muppet Show music. Maybe it works with you. Give it a try.

- **Predict and have fun**: Can you predict what people will do and don't do that will frustrate you? If so, you could have fun with this so that your irritation lessens. For instance, a client I worked with used to get irritated by what she called *stupid questions*. When I asked her if she knew in advance what stupid questions she would be asked, she said, "Yes, I hear the same ones every day." Why get irritated when you know in advance what will happen? Most annoyed people are often predictable. Enjoy your predictions and laugh about them. Applying emotional intelligence with annoying people can be fun.

- **Change your reaction**: A different response can diminish the escalating cycle of irritation. If you have always responded in the same way, and the problem continues, then change the way you respond. You have the power to change the way you react to others. You don't have the power to change the others. Do you realize that others can see you as the annoying one if you always react in some way to some trigger?

- **Talk to people in advance**: Don't just fester and complain inside your head. For example, simply saying something along the lines of, "Hi John, I noticed that in the last couple of meetings when I am presenting my projects to the Board you always interrupt me. Can we work out a strategy to overcome this as I sometimes miss what you say and think you miss what I say? What do you think?" Voice your concerns with consideration and kindness. But be careful to not patronize, be sarcastic or mean, and avoid implying that the other person is stupid. Managing your emotions and keeping your cool can involve many different strategies.

Don't take things personally

Every organization has people in it who can be critical, angry, or snide. However, if you want to keep your cool with these types of people and communicate effectively with them, you need to ensure you do not take personally the things that they do or say. Or don't do or don't say.

When you take things personally you become awash with unhelpful emotions and end up saying and doing the wrong thing, or escalating a conflict. Being able to keep your cool at work is important for your career success and for the relationships that you build with colleagues, co-workers, stakeholders, and customers.

Let's learn how not to take things personally:

- **Laugh**: Laughter can be a wonderful way to stop yourself from feeling hurt or upset. If you can keep light about a potential snide comment, then the comment has no power. This doesn't mean that you leave yourself open to abuse. Though you can easily brush off potential hurtful comments and not take them to heart. Then you don't get hurt.

- **Delay your response**: Delaying is like ducking when someone throws something at you. Pause before you respond. Then you give yourself time to think of a good response. And to make sure your reply is polite and kind, so as to not hurt the other person.

- **Don't take it personally**: Work out what is specifically about you and, what is a general complaint that you happen to get because you were in the same place as the other person. When it's not specific to you, don't take it as if it was.

- **Monitor for early signs of irritation**: Monitor for early signs of tension, irritation, or hurt and let them go, before they develop. Each of us will have physiological changes that occur early on, in the process of becoming hurt or frustrated. If you can catch your stomach tightening, your neck tightening, or your hands grasping, early on, you have more chance of letting go and not hooking into the other person's comments or emotions. Monitor them, and then let them go immediately before they take hold.

- **Breath deeply**: Breathe deeply so your breathing remains calm, regular, and deep. If your breathing speeds up and becomes shallow it could be a sign that you are getting hooked in. Keep breathing in and out. No, I'm not joking! You are more likely to take something personally if you aren't breathing! Your emotions are in your body. Even in a meeting, it is possible to put your hand on your midriff to give yourself a physical reminder to keep your breathing deep and regular.

Handling a high workload without being overwhelmed

Handling a high workload can be a very emotionally charged experience requiring emotional resilience.

Staying content, productive, and emotionally healthy while busy and handling all your many responsibilities without feeling overwhelmed is a sign of a great emotional self-management.

Let's learn how to stop the feeling of being overwhelmed by a heavy workload:

- **Be active and healthy**: Being healthy is so important in managing a busy life and responsibilities. It is harder if you have a headache or flu or backache to avoid becoming stressed. So take care of yourself: your children deserve it, your colleagues need it, and you will be happier because of it. The busier you are the more important it is that you eat healthy food--no junk, all good food so that you take care of your mental and physical health. Desiring a work-life balance requires you to take care of your body, mind, and spirit. Just because you feel tired and cannot be bothered to exercise does not mean you shouldn't do it.
- **Be positive**: Ditch negativity, complaining, and anger. These negative emotions don't make you happy and increase the stress load. Instead, on a daily basis train yourself to incline towards positivity and gratitude. Negative emotions, such as resentment, frustration, and anger only add to stress. Do not feed your feelings of being overwhelmed by more negative feelings. It is typical of low emotional intelligence people.
- **Sort demands into areas**: Separating demands into different areas reduces the feeling of being overwhelmed by work. I find this stops me from getting overwhelmed by how much there is to do. As I can move from one section to another instead of seeing it all in one overwhelming mass. In contrast, if I don't have these groups, I end up looking at one big, incredibly long to-do list and freak out. Separating out demands helps to manage emotions. It is an essential emotional intelligence skill.
- **Do the priorities**: Your next step is to identify the priority tasks in each area. And do only the priorities. Each day I identify the number-1 priority in each area and do that. I try to do the priorities first before any unimportant nice-to-do things. Knowing your priorities is being emotionally intelligent. Are you doing your priorities? Do you even stop to ask yourself what they are?

- **Change priorities at any moment**: Be flexible, your priorities are not set in stone. Be prepared to change priorities at any moment. It is impossible to always know in advance what the priorities are. I, therefore, decide what my priorities are, each day, (or even each hour):
  - **First**: Decide which of the areas of the work are the key priority that day
  - **Second**: Prioritize the chores in that area
  - **Third**: Do it

Once done I check out and move on to other sections. Be prepared to change priorities at any moment. Being willing to re-evaluate very often is vital. Rigidity only builds stress. This is emotional intelligence in action. How flexible are you? Are you clinging to your plan? Be prepared to change priorities at any moment.

Second pillar - control your emotions

Emotional intelligence is not about damping down, escaping from, or suppressing your emotions. Emotional intelligence is about feeling your emotions, knowing they are there and why. Expressing them and moving through them in a healthy way. There will be times when you will get upset, sad, or frustrated. It is only natural. If someone close to you dies I would expect you to feel sadness, loss, and grief. You may miss this person and feel there is an emptiness in your life, you may be angry because they have left you, you may feel bleak and lonely without them. These are all normal reactions. The speed with which you move through your emotions will depend on the severity of your initial reaction and the nature of the event, as well as on your level of emotional intelligence. Naturally, you wouldn't be expected to stop grieving a day after your loved one died. This also applies to everyday events and emotions. When you get angry because your team failed to meet a deadline at work. Or furious when you were ignored at a meeting. Or hurt and insulted when someone said you were slack, fat, or incompetent. Can you move through these emotions and let them go quickly?

Let's learn how to calm down our strong emotions:

Be mindful during a conflict

As human beings, we are groomed by evolution to protect ourselves whenever we sense a threat. In our modern context, we do not fight like a badger with a coyote or, run away like a rabbit from a fox. But our basic impulse to protect ourselves is automatic and unconscious. We have two amygdalae; they are responsible for detecting fear and preparing our body for an emergency response. When we perceive a threat, the amygdala sounds an alarm, releasing a cascade of stress hormones. Adrenaline and cortisol immediately flood our system preparing us for fight or flight. When this deeply instinctive function takes over, we have been triggered. The flood of stress hormones creates body sensations like a quivering in our solar plexus, limbs, or our voice, increased heart rate or sweaty palms, rapid and shallow breathing, heat flush, throat constrict, or the back of our neck tighten and jaw set. The active amygdala immediately shuts down the neural pathway to our prefrontal cortex (the rational brain), so we become disoriented in a heated conversation. Complex decision-making disappears, as does our access to multiple perspectives. As our attention narrows, we find ourselves trapped in the one perspective that makes us feel safest: *I am right and you are wrong*--even though we ordinarily see more perspectives and our memory becomes untrustworthy. The brain drops the memory function, altogether, in an effort to survive the threat. When our memory is compromised like this, we cannot recall something from the past that might help us calm down. In fact, we cannot remember much of anything. We are filled with the flashing red light of the amygdala indicating *Danger, react! Danger, protect! Danger, attack!* In the throes of an amygdala hijack, we cannot choose how we want to react because, the old protective mechanism in the nervous system, does it for us even before we glimpse that there could be a choice. That is why when during a fight with your partner or friend, you literally cannot remember a positive thing about them. *Ok Emilia! All that amygdala hijack sounds terrible, so what can we do to stop it or prevent it?* You can learn and practice Mindfulness.

Mindfulness is the perfect awareness technique to employ when a conflict arises. Practicing mindfulness in the middle of a conflict demands a willingness to stay present, to feel intense, to override our negative thoughts, and to engage our breath to maintain a presence with the body. Like any skill, it takes practice.

Let's learn the steps to use mindfulness during a conflict:

1. **Stay present**: By default, our mind is running in auto-pilot so that it becomes more difficult to be mindful. But with daily practice we can turn our default mode to be mindful, be present. In the beginning when you are being emotionally triggered, you may notice a change in your tone of voice, griping sensations in the belly, or a sudden desire to withdraw. In the moment that you feel you are being triggered, breathe deeply and bring to your mind an image that gives you inner peace. Stay put and present, to be curious and explore our experience. My visual cue to help me calm down is a mental image of my Reiki students during the practicing classes--as it is an image of pure love, serenity, kindness, and compassion. It helps me to immediately relax.

2. **Stop the judging mind**: You need to completely let go of the judging mind. When we feel threatened, the mind immediately fills with all kinds of difficult thoughts and stories about what is happening. To stop the feedback loop between your thoughts and your body you need to forget the story just for a minute. If the negative thoughts persist, so do the stressful hormones.

3. **Focus on your body**: **Body Scan Meditation** is a great tool to practice focusing on feeling and exploring whatever sensations arise in the body. We allow the mind to be as open as possible, noticing the different places in the body where sensations occur, what is tight, shaky, rushing, or hurts. We pay attention to the different qualities and textures of the sensations, and the way things change and shift. We can also notice how biased we are against unpleasant or more intense sensations. Feel your sensation naturally, just as they are, don't try to control or change them.

4. **Breath**: Rhythm and Smoothness. If we focus on these two dimensions of breathing, even for a few short minutes, the production of the cortisol and adrenaline will stop. Rhythm--inhale, counting 1, 2, 3, and 4, and then exhale, counting 1, 2, 3, 4, 5, and 6, then inhale again, counting 1, 2, 3, and 4, and then exhale again, counting 1, 2, 3, 4, 5, and 6; this establishes rhythm. Smoothness at the same time, the volume of the breath stays consistent as it moves in and out, like sipping liquid through a narrow straw. If you manage those two qualities for just a few minutes, the breath assists you in staying present with intense sensations in the body. Paying attention to our body re-establishes equilibrium faster, restoring our ability to think, to listen, and relate. Each time we succeed in being mindful of our body in moments of distress, we develop our capacity. Before we know it, our old habit of fight or flight is changing, and the world is a safer place.

Self-calm your anger

We may compare our anger to a small child, crying out to his mother. When the child cries the mother takes him, gently, in her arms and listens and, observes carefully, to find out what is wrong. The loving action of holding her child with tenderness already soothes the baby's suffering. Likewise, we can take our anger in our loving arms and right away we will feel a relief. We don't need to reject our anger. It is a part of us that needs our love and deep listening just as a baby does. When we feel calm and cool, we too can look deeply at our anger and see clearly the conditions allowing our anger to rise. When we feel angry it is best to refrain from saying or doing anything. We may like to withdraw our attention from the person or situation, which is watering the seed of anger in us. I am not talking about pathological rage here, I am talking about the normal types of frustration and anger that everyone can experience.

Let's learn four techniques to help you self-calm and ease your anger:

- **Kindness and generosity**: It is so easy to become frustrated by someone when you label them selfish, mean, bossy, difficult, stupid, a loser, or something else equally harsh. Realize, you may be completely wrong in your interpretation of what is going on. Be kind to others and your frustration will ease. If in doubt, judge people kindly. For example, when someone is yelling at you, or doing something frustrating that you don't like, if you think, "How dare you yell at me, who do you think you are, I don't get paid enough to put up with this," you are likely to get and stay angry. In contrast, if you feel kindness towards them, such as this woman is having a lousy day, I will help her. It may be easier to calm down your own anger.
- **Laugh**: The old saying that laughter is the best medicine, still rings true in these days of emotional intelligence. Laughter is a good antidote to frustration, anger, and irritation. When you can make up a funny story about what has happened and laugh at the situation you are angry about, then your anger may calm.
- **Write down the anger**: If you are at work and have got angry, by writing down what has happened and your reactions to it, you can calm down and keep going with your work. You are not repressing or ignoring your anger you are just deferring it to a later moment, when you can deal with it in a safer and calm way.
- **Know why you are angry**: Understanding the causes of your anger and reflecting on them, helps you to calm down. Emotional intelligence considers all emotional causes, not just the ones in the present moment that seem to trigger your anger. Are you angry because of something that has happened in your history? Or are you adding your history to the present moment and, therefore, adding fuel to something small and making it appear bigger?

Managing your anxiety

Feeling anxious in a stressful world is common. But if you don't learn how to cope with your anxiety your reasoning and decision-making process will be badly affected. And also, your body. I am not talking here about pathological anxiety disorders. I am talking about the normal types of anxiety that everyone can experience. If you feel that your anxiety is severe or debilitating please seek appropriate professional help.

Let's learn five techniques that can help you manage your anxiety:

- **Catch it early**: If you can notice the early signs of your anxiety it gives you the choice to reduce it almost immediately before it develops and becomes overwhelming. Be aware of your emotions, not just when they are so strong that they hit you in the face. But when they are just there as small signs, flickering in the background. Meanwhile, take deep breaths, with rhythm and smoothness.

- **Accept it**: How you react to your emotions is an aspect of emotional intelligence and makes a huge difference to your ability to manage them. If you notice an early sign of anxiety you have the option to remain neutral about it, just to accept it, or even to reverse it. After all, it is only an emotion, and emotions are like waves on the beach, they come and go. Keep breathing!

- **Observe it**: Become a detached observer. It is simply anxiety building and fading away. Like the waves on the beach. When you feel anxiety and panic about it, and try to run away from it, and hate it, and live in dread of it, and become sure you are going to die from it, you are more likely to make it worse. Panic about panic doubles the panic! Emotional intelligence is not about avoiding emotions, nor is it about getting lost in them and overwhelmed by them. Patience is more likely to help you than getting impatient and irritated. Keep breathing!

- **Focus on something else**: By focusing on something serene and calming, you get moments of rest from the anxiety and find it calms down. Believe it or not, it is impossible for the mind to concentrate on more than one thing at a time. It can *kid* you that it is possible as it can jump from one thing to another and back again, very quickly, but it cannot hold serenity and anxiety at the same time.

- **Meditate**: Meditation is not like taking a happy pill and suddenly your mind is free from anxious thoughts and you bliss out! It is training the mind to tame anxious thoughts. What meditation also does, in terms of anxiety, is return the control to you. People become aware of their anxious thoughts arising and know how to soothe and calm them. Start with five minutes, 3x a day. Progressively increase the time.

Third pillar - create positive emotions daily

There is an old saying--*Don't take your emotions to work with you*, but it's nonsense and not at all emotionally intelligent. In fact, it denies the whole process upon which emotional intelligence is built, that is, that emotions matter and are valuable.

Happiness at work can be of enormous benefit, not only to an individual, but to a team and a whole organization. In fact, if you want to have an emotionally intelligent team or organization, you need to be able to promote happiness as one of the ingredients of your culture. A happy workplace benefits productivity, boasts the sales, it is a great branding strategy, lower staff turnover, boost creativity, lowers costs, stops gossips, and prevents stress, depression, and burnout.

Let's learn five simple techniques that help to build a happier workplace:

- **Stop negativity**: When you have a stressful job, and especially, one that you don't like, your negativity gets the better of you. Why? Because, you keep talking to yourself about what is bad about it, and talking to other people about what is bad about it. You are making your own misery. Having miserable people at work makes a workplace toxic and can lower employee engagement, buy-in, and productivity. Instead of being miserable at work transform how you feel into something more productive. My work is very stressful and tiresome, but pays my bills and let me help others: friends, family, and so on. I am grateful. This is emotional intelligence in action.
- **List 10 good things about your work**: Practice recognizing, acknowledging, and saying good things about your work. This is one way to transform your emotions. At first, if you are not used to noticing the good things about your work it can take some discipline. OK! You can argue with me that you cannot find one good thing to say about your work, never mind 10! But you can do it! Start with basic things like, your income every month and the things you can do or buy with the money. The good things that your work enables you to do for your co-workers, or for your clients, customers or stakeholders, your family, and society. We are all cogs in the machine, so whether you empty dustbins, put data onto computers, you are helping others. How does your job help you serve? Be grateful for that.
- **Make your workplace nicer**: If you are not happy at work, then make your workplace a happier place for you to be in. Listen to gentle music through headphones, getting a plant for your desk, bring cookies to your colleagues, whatever will bring you some cheer. And cheer is contagious.

- **Praise yourself**: Happiness comes as a result of our actions, not from suffering in silence hoping that it will arrive. Being emotionally intelligent is not about waiting for others to help us feel happy. It is about taking responsibility for our own emotions. One of the reasons you may not be getting the praise you deserve is that everyone else is busy and is not noticing what you do. What you can do is: let them know about your good work. Jot down in a success journal, the things that worked well. Tell your family and friends of your success.

- **Take a break**: Break up your working day by doing something that boosts your mood. Find something that is easy to do at work and helps you refresh. Some people simply wear themselves out at work and deplete their energy so badly that it is hard to stay happy simply because fatigue is so strong.

- **Have a bank account of positive emotions**: Imagine you have just dropped and broken your mobile phone, and find it's going to cost you $200 to repair it. The unexpected bill will cause distress and other negative consequences for weeks if your bank account is depleted. It is the same thing with emotional situations. If your emotional bank balance is full of positive emotions and you have to draw on some of them to counter a negative emotion, there are still plenty of positive emotions left. If the emotional bank balance is depleted and there have been no recent deposits of positive emotions upon which to draw, then the negative emotions will make a bigger dent on your emotional wellbeing. Increasing your balance of positive emotion builds your resilience, creativity, and ability to be solution-focused.

Fourth pillar - develop self-compassion

And if I asked you to name all the things that you love, how long would it take for you to name yourself? Being able to feel compassion for yourself and others, when applied wisely, is all part of being emotionally intelligent.

Why does developing self-compassion matter? It matters because, without self-compassion people become miserable, stressed, overworked, develop self-hate, are self-critical, have unrealistic expectations, and even expect perfection. When you are self-critical you are also negative, hard, and judgmental towards others' problems, errors, and behaviors. This makes no one happy. Of course, knowing all the theory about self-compassion is only part of the story. Applying it, on a daily basis, to yourself is what will really make the difference to your emotional intelligence in this area. Are you willing to work on this aspect of your emotional intelligence?

Let's learn five ways to help you develop self-compassion:

- **Have a success journal**: At the end of each day write down all the good things you have done. It can be as little as smiling at a colleague, picking up a piece of litter in the street, or opening the door for someone. The size is irrelevant. Keep adding to this list so that each day you focus your mind on the good things you do. At the end of each week read your list.

- **Reward yourself**: Write down an agreement with yourself as to the reward you will get when you have achieved your goals. Choose whatever is a good reward for you. And enjoy it. Be nice to yourself. Fostering positive emotions is all part of developing your emotional intelligence and emotional resilience.

- **Spread the love**: Emotions are contagious. Be compassionate towards yourself, treat yourself well, look after yourself so that you can also help and care for your employees, your stakeholders, your customers, your clients, your team members, your suppliers, family, children, parents, friends, neighbors, and anyone with whom you come into contact. For example, all your team will benefit far more from you being their manager if you are kind towards yourself and them, as well as being competent, rather than you being mean or critical or off work sick and thus increasing their workload. Care for yourself so you may care for others.

- **Set aside time for yourself**: Compassion towards yourself can be trained as a habit. Each day, decide in advance when you will rest and relax. Each day, get into the habit of reviewing your day. It can be a time before going to work, a lunch break, an evening bath, yoga, practicing loving-kindness meditation, and so on. Everyone needs rest and relaxation. It is a basic human need. Plan your rest in advance. Developing and having compassion for ourselves is all part of developing our emotional intelligence and emotional resilience.

- **Ask for help**: Helping yourself by asking for help is a way of showing compassion for yourself and a good way of using your emotional intelligence. You do not have to journey through this life on your own. Do not moan that no-one is helping you if did not ask for help. Even when the work has been assigned to you and you are in trouble, ask for help. Do not worry that people will think bad of you because you want help. By asking for help you remove the tension and agony in what you are, you move more quickly through a task you may spare yourself of making mistakes, develop better relationships with your colleagues, learn new ideas, information and skills, free up time to do more rewarding activities, and at the end, you are more productive and happier.

Fifth pillar - be grateful and forgive

Gratitude is a feeling, an appreciation of what you do have, an acknowledgment of what has gone right, an appreciation for the things that others do for us, an appreciation that our lives are better than others.

- **Feel grateful**: Gratitude is a positive emotion and not just a thought or an acknowledgment. Feeling gratitude is an important emotion, and being able to express gratitude is part of having emotional intelligence. When I was a child my parents instilled in my brother and me the need to write -Thank You letters for any presents we received. I still write thank you letters. However, now I have the feeling of gratitude to go with the thank you. There is more to gratitude than just the words "Thank you" there is also a sense of appreciation, a feeling of gratefulness.

- **Be grateful for what you have**: Gratitude involves focusing on what we do have and being thankful for it. We appreciate things that belong to us, the parts of our body that work, the food in our fridge, the money we receive, our car and the garage to keep it in, the clothes in our wardrobe, the partner whom we love, the father who lives nearby, the ring we inherited, the ergonomic chair we sit on, the office desk we work at, the internet connection we have, and so on. That is what gratitude is, and it can help us develop our emotional intelligence by increasing our positive emotions, and thus, our emotional resilience and emotional self-management. Gratitude means we notice and express appreciation for what goes right in our life. It is so easy to gloss over these things and take them for granted. Imagine a staff room that ran on gratitude. Now, that would be emotionally intelligent! How much gratitude and emotional intelligence are displayed in your staff room?

- **Be grateful for help**: No man is an island. You may think you can be autonomous and live without the support of others, but in fact, it's not possible and none of us do it. We just take for granted what others do for us. Gratitude means that we notice and we are grateful for the things that people do for us, not just the acts of personal kindness that people deliberately do for us, but the day-to-day things that happen with us barely noticing. Be grateful for the water in your kitchen tap is only made possible by a group of people who build dams, lay water pipes, and monitor the flow and provision of water. Without them, you would not get water. Giving thanks and feeling appreciative of this kind of service is part of developing gratitude. Be grateful for the garbage collectors--imagine how difficult your life would be if this didn't happen? Gratitude is acknowledging the value of such a service. Appreciating the things that others do helps you build more positive emotions in your life, and thus, develop increased emotional resilience and higher levels of emotional intelligence.

- **Be grateful that you are better off than others**: How easy it is to feel sorry for ourselves, to feel that our lives are not good enough and that we are really hard done by. Stop for a moment! This is not gratitude, this is misery. Gratitude, by contrast, is noticing how much worse off others are and appreciating and being thankful for our own lives, in comparison. Imagine that you are feeling a little bit sick. You go to your doctor. Your doctor asks for a series of tests to find out what is wrong with you. You don't like doctors, or exams, and dread hospitals. Stop for a minute and compare your situation to the situation of a mother in a very poor region, who has no food, water, doctors, or medical supplies, to treat her sick baby. You could find much to be grateful for and appreciate. What would that mother give to actually have a doctor to go to? To have access to medical tests to find out what is wrong? And to have treatment available to herself and her family? When you stop and compare your life with those of others who are less well off than you are, and you express appreciation, then you have gratitude.

Thankfulness awakens our brain's pleasure centers, and our bodies produce bio-chemicals that activate a strong and powerful sense of our potential, well-being and connection. Our bodies respond with vitality and a stronger immune system. We may be inspired to serve others, to contribute to the greater good. So, why not give thanks. Something that also is very important to increase our vitality and immune system is the act of forgiving the wrongdoer of our life and ourselves. Because, when you don't forgive your body releases all the chemicals of the stress response as if you were in danger. Each time you react, adrenaline, cortisol, and norepinephrine enter the body. When you hold a chronic grudge, you could think about it 20 times a day, and every time all those chemicals flood your body and brain and those chemicals limit creativity, and limit problem-solving. Cortisol and norepinephrine cause your brain to enter what we call "the no- thinking zone," and over time, they lead you to feel helpless and like a victim. When you forgive, you wipe all of that clean. Forgiveness is an emotional intelligence choice.

Forgive

Forgiveness means that we have decided that we will leave the hatred and the suffering behind, so as to give ourselves the chance to become friends with our past and move towards a more fulfilling future. But how can you forgive the person who treated you in such an awful, selfish, and destructive way? How can you overcome the shock, the terror, and ultimately this strong desire for revenge? Going through grief and anger are prerequisites to the decision to forgive.

Let's learn five ways that help you to be more forgiving:

- **Do not push yourself to forgive others immediately**: Use the time at your disposal to process the loss to experience sorrow, to live with your wound. And this has nothing to do with revenge. It is simply the acceptance you need, not the oppression, a truly emotional and painful process.

- **Stop wearing the mask i**ts *OK for me as long as you are OK*: ;By acting like this, you skip the healthy process of recovery from your trauma. You pass all stages of your emotional reactions that you are allowed to have and you never express your anger. You prefer to lock it somewhere deep inside you. And one day, without further notice it will come to disturb your sleep.

- **Move on with your life**: What we do to ourselves by not moving on with our lives may have even worse consequences than the wrong-doings that we suffered. The decision to forgive has nothing to do with the other, but with ourselves. Yet, it is normal to be angry, to hate, to be disappointed by someone, and allow yourself to express all these feelings in a healthy way.

- **Separate the person from the behavior**: We all react in different ways according to the situation. For instance, if someone threatens one of your loved ones you are able to beat them. Even if you are a peaceful person. We are not our behaviors, so don't confuse the person with the behavior that hurt you.

- **Protect yourself and your dignity**: Forgive doesn't mean forget. If we allow someone to come to our house and rob us, we will forgive him. But we will not forget. If we forget, then probably we will be robbed again!

There is no time limit within which one must pass through all the stages of grief, anger and result in forgiveness. Friends, relatives, or even a counselor can support us throughout this process. If someone is rushed to "close the case" by going directly to forgiveness, then that person is suppressing their feelings or even denying them and their importance. The fact that these feelings are skipped doesn't mean that they disappear. They are there, they live and breathe and they wait for the next opportunity to come up to the surface. And then, either they take the form of some psychosomatic symptoms, or they appear as anxiety, depression or panic attacks, or as aggressive behavior. Compassion, tolerance, forgiveness and a sense of self-discipline are qualities that help us lead our daily lives with a calm mind.

After learning how to build emotional resilience to stress based in the emotional intelligence competencies and skills, I could not end this book for IT professionals that work in highly stressful conditions without a special word in how to prevent burnout using the new emotional skills learnt and also by knowing a little better the differences between stress and emotional burnout so you can prevent or identify them in the early beginning and ask for the proper help. Let's learn about burnout.

A special word to prevent burnout

Burnout is a state of emotional, mental, and physical exhaustion caused by excessive and prolonged stress. Burnout is the outcome when you feel overwhelmed by work, emotionally drained, and unable to meet constant demands. You begin to lose motivation, interests as stress piles up. Most people are not aware that a burnout situation is more destructive to them that being overstressed. And a burnout is the outcome of being over-stressed for too long. Of course, to prevent a burnout situation first you need to know the symptoms of a burnout. But first let's learn the difference between stress and burnout:

Stress vs. Burnout	
Stress	**Burnout**
Characterized by overengagement	Characterized by disengagement
Emotions are overreactive	Emotions are blunted
Produces urgency and hyperactivity	Produces helplessness and hopelessness
Loss of energy	Loss of motivation, ideals, and hope
Leads to anxiety disorders	Leads to detachment and depression
Primary damage is physical	Primary damage is emotional
May kill you prematurely	May make life seem not worth living

First and foremost, burnout and stress are not the same thing, though burnout could be the outcome of a very stressful situation for too long time, without you taking care of yourself, like we have learnt in the five pillars of emotional resilience.

Stress, in general, denotes a sense of too much. Too many pressures, which demand too much of you physically, intellectually, psychologically, and emotionally. You are drowning in responsibilities, but still you can feel better when everything is under control.

Burnout, on the other hand, is the sense of being drained. You feel empty of energy, empty of motivation, empty of emotions, empty of caring and love. Alone, helpless, hopeless. People experiencing burnout often don't see any hope of positive change in their situations and they fail to notice that burnout is happening to them.

The main causes of burnout

In workplaces where people are undervalued, overworked, and unappreciated the risks of having a burnout increase exponentially. And high-achievers' are more at risk. The main causes of burnout can be broken into three main areas: lifestyle, personality, and workplace:

- Personality
    - High-achieving
    - Type A personality
    - Perfectionists
    - Pessimists
    - A control freak
    - Staunch Introverts

- Lifestyle
    - Assuming too many responsibilities
    - Poor or not enough sleep
    - No time to relax and socialize
    - No supportive network - family, friends, and so on

- Workplace
    - Chaotic and high-pressure workplace environment
    - Monotonous and repetitive chores
    - Lack of challenges and opportunities to grow
    - Lack of praise and recognition for good work
    - Being micromanaged
    - Overly demanding job expectations

The red flags of burnout

The red flags or signs of a burnout at first are subtle, but when we have a good emotional awareness we can immediately know that something is wrong with us and that we need to address the problems. If you pay attention and act to reduce your stress, you can prevent a major breakdown. If you ignore them, you will eventually burn out. The main symptoms of burnout can be spotted in three areas: emotional, behaviors, and in our body:

- Emotional red flags of burnout:
  - Feeling alone in the world
  - Feeling hopeless, helpless, trapped, defeated
  - Becoming cynical with a negative outlook
  - Lack of motivation, satisfaction, and purpose
  - Sense of failure and self-doubt

- Behavior red flags of burnout:
  - Choosing to be isolated from other people
  - Resorting to addictive substances, such as alcohol, drugs, and excessive food
  - Withdrawing from responsibilities, coming late to work and leaving early
  - Procrastination
  - Blaming others for your frustrations

- Physical red flags of burnout:
  - Constant headaches
  - Feeling drained all the time
  - Lack of appetite or uncontrollable appetite
  - Poor sleep, despite constant fatigue
  - Being sick frequently, due to lower immunity
  - Muscle pain due to stress, especially in the back

How to prevent burnout

There are plenty of things you can do to regain your balance and start to feel positive and hopeful again. The following advice on how to prevent a burnout situation and regain your emotional balance is nothing new to you, if you read the other chapters. However, let's learn some positive steps you need to do to regain your life.

Build or expand your social network

Reaching out to others and building relationships is the most basic technique of human survival. Humans beings are hard wired to connect a simple smile releases natural antidepressants that make us feel happy, cared, and loved. It is scientifically proven that a hug stimulates the release of oxytocin, serotonin, and dopamine, significantly reducing worry, and lowering the heart rate:

- **Build close relationships with your partner, children, or friends**: Try to put aside what is burning you out and make the time you spend with loved ones positive and enjoyable.
- **Build relationships with your co-workers**: When you take a break, instead of paying attention to your smart phone, engage with your colleagues. Have happy hours after work with your colleagues. But avoid the negative-minded who that spend all the time complaining.
- **Do some volunteering or join a support group**: Joining a support group can give you a place to talk to like-minded people about how to deal with daily stress and to make new friends. It is never too late to build new friendships and expand your social network if you feel that you have no one to turn to.

Changing your life's outlook

Burnout is an undeniable sign that something important in your life is not working. Take time to think about your hopes, goals, and dreams. Are you neglecting something that is truly important to you? Burnout can be an opportunity to rediscover what really makes you happy and to slow down and give yourself time to rest, reflect, and heal. Of course, for many of us changing jobs or careers is far from being a practical solution. Whatever your situation, though, there are still things you can do to improve your state of mind:

- **Re-evaluate your priorities**: If you hate your job, look for meaning and satisfaction in your family, friends, or hobbies. Focus on the things that bring you joy.
- **Get plenty of sleep**: Feeling tired can exacerbate burnout by causing you to think irrationally.
- **Focus on aspects of the job that you do enjoy**: Even if it is just chatting with your co-workers at lunch, changing your attitude towards your job can help you regain a sense of purpose and control.

- **Make friends at work**: Having strong ties in the workplace help reduce monotony and counter the effects of burnout.
- **Set boundaries**: Say *no* to requests on your time. You already learnt how to say *Thank You! No*.
- **Unplug a couple of minutes daily**: Put away your laptop, turn off your phone, and stop checking email, when you are off duty.
- **Have creative outlets**: Burnout interferes with your ability to perform well, increases rigid thinking, and decreases your ability to think accurately, flexibly, and creatively. Having some type of creative outlet will keep you engaged and motivated. Choose activities that have nothing to do with your line of work.
- **Practice relaxation techniques**: Yoga, meditation, and deep breathing activate the body's relaxation response, a state of restfulness that is the opposite of the stress response.
- **Take time off**: If burnout has already set in, use up your sick days, ask for a temporary leave-of-absence, go on vacation do anything to remove yourself from the situation. Use the time away to recharge your batteries and pursue other burnout recovery steps. Look for professional help.

Have a healthy lifestyle

A healthy lifestyle includes having a healthy diet and doing exercise, even when you don't feel like it. What you put in your body has a huge impact on your mood and energy levels throughout the day:

- **Don't drink alcohol**: Alcohol can temporarily produce a sense of relaxation, but the flip side is that alcohol causes anxiety.
- Reduce or eliminate your intake of sugar, caffeine, trans-fats, refined carbs and foods with chemical preservatives or hormones. This is not even food! Does your car work on caffeine?! Neither does your body, especially your brain. The artificial food and beverages quickly lead to a crash in mood and energy.
- **Boost your brain and your mood**: Eat more Omega-3 fatty acids in salmon, herring, mackerel, anchovies, sardines, seaweed, flaxseed, and walnuts. Your brain will love it!
- **Stop smoking**: Like the alcohol, nicotine may first give you a sense of relaxation when you are stressed, but both are very powerful stimulants, making you even more anxious.

- **Exercise daily**: I know that when one is going through a burnout, exercise is the last thing you want to do or even think about. Even though exercise is a powerful antidote to stress and burnout. I am talking here about low-impact but simple physical exercise; it will boost your mood and increase your energy levels. 15-20 minutes in the morning, 15-20-minutes at the end of day. Plus, some deep breathing and five minutes of meditation. These little bursts of activity will boost your mood and energy for two hours. And if you do it with a smile on your face or laughing of yourself it will double the boost. Walk, dance, train with weights, swim, whatever pleases you most. This not only boosts your mood, but also increases your energy levels, sharpens your focus, and relaxes both the mind and body. Do mindfulness walking - instead of focusing on your thoughts, focus on your body and how it feels as you move - the sensation of your feet hitting the ground, the cool or the warmth, the wind on your skin, and so on. During your walk try to identify five different things: sounds, scents, colors, forms, whatever. By shifting your focus from your thoughts to your body you are maximizing the stress relief and well-being.

Summary

In this chapter, we have covered the five pillars of emotional resilience: stay calm, cool and collect (first pillar), calm down when strong emotions arise (second pillar), create positive emotions daily (third pillar), develop self-compassion (fourth pillar), be grateful (fifth pillar) to know how to build emotional resilience and cope with the stress, anxiety, shame, guilt, depression, lack of support from family, friends, employers, the feeling of being overwhelmed, stressed out, depressed and burnout.

You have learnt that emotional resilience is the skill to adjust to change and move on, from negative or traumatic experiences, in a positive way. To keep a healthy balance between a tough head and a warm heart. As you build your emotional intelligence competencies and skills you are also building your emotional resilience.

You have learnt that being emotionally resilient is not blocking out your feelings with drugs, pretending that everything is okay, when it is not or being too tough to tell someone you are proud of them, love them or appreciate them, not crying, when someone you love dies, ignoring everyone else and always putting yourself first, being aggressive, verbally violent or looking for a fight.

You have learnt that to keep your cool with irritating people you need to be realistic, understand and accept that you are always to come across irritating people. And that we all are different as we are all brought up differently. Therefore, getting annoyed by people because you expect them to behave in the way you would like them to behave is not very emotional smart.

You have learnt how not to take things personally, by laughing, delaying your response, monitoring your first signs of irritation, separate what is personal and what is not, breathe deeply so your breathing remains calm, regular, and deep.

You learnt how to stay content, productive and emotionally healthy while busy and handle all your many responsibilities without feeling overwhelmed.

You have learnt emotional intelligence is not about dumping down, escaping from or suppressing your emotions. Emotional intelligence is about feeling your emotions, knowing they are there and why. Expressing them and moving through them in a healthy way.

You learnt how to be mindful during a conflict and that mindfulness is the perfect awareness technique to employ when a conflict arises. As it allows you to override the conditioned nervous system with conscious awareness. Instead of attacking or recoiling, and later justifying your reactions, stay present, participate in regulating our own nervous system, and eventually, develop new, more free and helpful ways of interacting.

You have learnt how to manage your anger. And that you don't need to reject your anger as it is a part of you that needs your love and deep listening. And that the four best techniques to self-calm your anger are: kindness and generosity, laugh, enquiry why are you angry with that situation, and write down your anger as a therapy.

You have learnt that feeling anxious in a stressful world is common. But if you don't learn how to cope with your anxiety your reasoning and decision-making process will be badly affected. Hence, you have learnt that the best way to manage your anxiety is catch it early, accept it, focus in something else and meditate.

You have learnt that happiness at work can be of enormous benefit, not only to an individual but to a team and a whole organization. And if you want to have an emotionally intelligent team or organization, you need to be able to promote happiness as one of the ingredients of your culture. A happy workplace benefits productivity, boasts the sales, it is a great branding strategy, lower staff turnover, boast creativity, lower the costs, stop gossips, prevents stress, depression and burnout.

You have learnt that being able to feel compassion for yourself and others, when applied wisely, is all part of being emotionally intelligent. And that developing self-compassion matters, because, without self-compassion people become miserable, stressed, overworked, develop self-hate, are self-critical, have unrealistic expectations and even expect perfection. And when you are self-critical you are also negative, hard and judgmental towards others' problems, errors and behaviors. This makes no one happy.

You have learnt that burnout is a state of emotional, mental, and physical exhaustion caused by excessive and prolonged stress. What is the different between being stressed and being burnout? The emotional, behavior, and work causes of burnout, the red flags when we are undergoing a burnout situation and how to prevent it.

You have learnt the importance of gratitude in our life and well-being and that gratitude is a feeling, an appreciation of what you do have, an acknowledgment of what is gone right, an appreciation for the things that others do for us, an appreciation that our lives are better than others. That thankfulness awakens our brain's pleasure centers, and our bodies produce bio-chemicals that activate a strong and powerful sense of our potential, well-being and connection and our bodies respond with vitality and a stronger immune system.

You have learnt that forgiveness begins with the decision to forgive, but it does not end there. It is a process that takes time and requires our commitment to a life full of experiences, but without repressed emotions. Forgiveness means that we have decided that we will leave the hatred and the suffering behind. So as to give a chance to ourselves to become friends with our past and move towards a more fulfilling future.

You have learnt that compassion, tolerance, forgiveness, and a sense of self-discipline are qualities that help us lead our daily lives with a calm mind.

Bibliography

Boyatzis, R. The Competent Manager: A Model of Effective Performance. New York: Wiley. 1982.

Boyatzis, R. E., Cowan, S. S., and Kolb, D. A. Innovations in Professional Education: Steps on a Journey to Learning. San Francisco: Jossey-Bass. 1995.

Cherniss, C. Emotional Intelligence and Organizational Effectiveness. In C. 2001.

Cherniss, C., Goleman, D., Emmerling, R., Cowan, K., and Adler, M. Bringing Emotional Intelligence to the Workplace. New Brunswick, NJ: *Consortium for Research on Emotional Intelligence in Organizations,* Rutgers University. 1998.

Cherniss, C. and Goleman, D. The Emotionally Intelligent Workplace. San Francisco: Jossey-Bass. 2001.

Cherniss, C., and Adler, M. Promoting Emotional Intelligence in Organizations. 2000.

Alexandria, VA: *American Society for Training and Development.*

Damasio, A. Descartes 'Error: Body and Emotion in the Making of Consciousness. New York: Putnam. 1994.

Davis, M., and Kraus, L. Personality and Empathic Empathy, in H. Ickes (ed.). 1997.

Empathic Accuracy. NY: *Guilford Press.*

Fernandez-Araoz, C. The Challenge of Hiring Senior Executives. In C. *Cherniss & D. Goleman* (Eds.), *The Emotionally Intelligent Workplace* (pp. 182-206). San Francisco: Jossey-Bass. 2001.

Goleman, D. Working with Emotional Intelligence. New York: *Bantam Books. 1998.*

Goleman, D. Emotional Intelligence: Issues in paradigm building. In C. *Cherniss & D. Goleman* (Eds.), *The Emotionally Intelligent Workplace,* (pp. 13-26), Jossey-Bass: San Francisco. 2001.

Mayer, J. D., Salovey, P., and *Caruso, D. R. Emotional intelligence as Zeitgeist, as Personality, and as a Mental Ability.* In *R. Bar-On* and *J.D.A. Parker* (Eds.), *Handbook of Emotional Intelligence* (pp. 92-117). San Francisco: Jossey-Bass. 2000.

Mayer, J. D., and *Salovey, P. What is Emotional Intelligence?* In *P. Salovey* and *D. Sluyter* (Eds.), *Emotional Development and Emotional Intelligence: Implications for Educators* (pp. 3-34). New York, NY: Basic Books. 1997.

Mayer, J. D., Caruso, D., and *Salovey, P. Emotional Intelligence Meets Traditional Standards for an Intelligence.* Intelligence, 27, 267-298. 1999.

Thornton, G. C. III, and *Byham, W. C. Assessment Centers and Managerial Performance.* New York: *Academic Press.* 1982.

Index

P

pace setting leadership style
  about 160
  advantages 160
  disadvantages 160
parietal lobes 48
primitive brain
  about 43
  brain stem 44
  cerebellum 44
purpose
  about 109
  transparency 110

R

rational brain 43
reptilian brain 43

S

sadness
  actions 31
  states 29
  triggers 32
self (first dimension)
  about 164
  others (second dimension) 180
  self-awareness 165, 166
  self-management 172
  service (third dimension) 185
  social awareness 180
  social skills 185, 186
self-awareness
  about 63, 64, 165, 166
  accurate self-assessment 64, 68
  accurate self-awareness 64, 65, 66, 67
  benefits 70
  confidence, strategies enhancing 170, 171
  core skills 64
  low self-awareness, consequences 71
  self-assessment, strategies enhancing 169
  self-confidence 64, 68, 69
  strategies, enhancing 167, 168
self-expression
  about 71, 72

consequences 77
core skills 72
emotions face to face, expressing 75, 76, 77
negative emotions, expressing 74, 75
positive emotions, expressing 72, 73
self-management
  about 172
  achievement orientation, strategies enhancing 178
  adaptability, strategies enhancing 177
  conscientiousness, strategies enhancing 176
  initiative, strategies enhancing 179
  self-control, strategies enhancing 173, 174
  trustworthiness, strategies enhancing 174, 175
  virtual teams, trusting 175
self-regulation
  about 78
  achievement orientation 82
  adaptability 81
  benefits 84
  consequences 85
  core skills 78
  initiative 82, 83
  self-control 79
service (third dimension) 185
service, organization operates
  customer support strategies, enhancing 121
  sales team strategies, enhancing 123
situational interviewing 203
social awareness
  about 85, 86, 180
  acknowledge, strategies enhancing 184
  awareness 87
  benefits 90
  consequences 90
  core skills 86
  empathy 86, 87
  organizational awareness 88
  organizational awareness, strategies enhancing 184
  sensitivity 88
  service orientation 89
  service orientation, strategies enhancing 183
social skills
  about 91, 185, 186